# THE NIGHT
# IS A
# JUNGLE

by

## KIRPAL SINGH

*Sawan Singh Ji Maharaj*
*(1858-1948)*

*Dedicated*

*to the Almighty God*

*working through all Masters who have come*

*and Baba Sawan Singh Ji Maharaj*

*at whose lotus feet*

*the writer imbibed sweet elixir of*

*Holy Naam — the Word*

Originally published in 1975

This Edition published in 2007 by:

RUHANI SATSANG
Divine Science of the Soul
250 "H" Street, #50
Blaine, WA 98230-4018 USA

www.RuhaniSatsangUSA.org
Tel: 1 (888) 530-1555

ISBN 978-0-942735-18-5
SAN 854-1906

Printed in the United States of America
by Print Graphics Pros • (949) 859-3845

*The night is a jungle — do your work (worldly duties) in the daytime and then benefit from the night. The true purpose of having the human form is to make daily progress toward the great Goal, so sit down each day and see where you are. As the renunciate leaves everything and goes to the woods, you can sit down nightly in your home, forgetting the world and freeing yourself from all entanglements.*

*It is only through a living Master that we can contact the Almighty God within us. In Sant Mat, contemplation of objects or images is not advised, as this is harmful to progress. Photographs of the Masters are for remembrance and recognition only, and on no account should we become attached to such external practices.*

*****

*Spirituality cannot be bought or taught, but it can be caught by contact with spiritual people. Moreover, Nature's gifts such as air, water, light, etc., are free. Spirituality is also Nature's gift and is also given free by the Masters. Likewise, Spirituality cannot be acquired from books, which is a fact all sacred scriptures uphold. Books are a valuable record of the inner experiences of others in Spirituality. They fill gaps in history and contain messages from past Masters, which help us to verify the facts revealed by a living Master, thus confirming our faith in the Science.*

—from the booklet, *"Man! Know Thy-Self"* (pages 9 and 20), by Kirpal Singh.

**When they gave me a medal — the Order of St. John of Jerusalem — I (Kirpal Singh) was called to Pandit Nehru who was Prime Minister of India at the time, and he told me, "It is an honor to my country." When you (Initiates) progress (within), it is an honor to me, you see. To do something worthwhile is an honor to your Master.**

— from page 12 of the talk, "Your Life Should Show Criteria", by Master Kirpal Singh, published in the May 1974 issue of *Sat Sandesh* magazine.

# THE NIGHT
# IS A
# JUNGLE

by

## KIRPAL SINGH

*Sant Kirpal Singh Ji*
*(1894-1974)*

# TABLE OF CONTENTS

*Sant Kirpal Singh Ji*
*(1894-1974)*

# Introduction

THE AUTHOR of these discourses, Param Sant Kirpal Singh Ji, the great prophet-mystic of the present age, left the physical plane on August 21, 1974, in his eighty-first year, after a lifetime of service to the universe. It is our hope that this book will, in some small measure, serve as a memorial to him; although the only memorial that can possibly do his life and mission justice will be the full growth and development of the seeds that he planted in the hearts of his 120,000 disciples.

Kirpal Singh was born in Sayyad Kasran, a little village in the Punjab (now part of Pakistan) on February 6, 1894. A lifelong search for God led him to investigate the claims of many Sufis, yogis and mystics; but he remained skeptical and refused to take anyone as his Guru unless he had some direct proof of his competence. He prayed to God to manifest to him directly, without going through any human; his prayers were answered, and he began seeing the form of a bearded man, made of light, in his meditations. He did not recognize the form, and thinking that it was Guru Nanak, the founder of the Sikh religion, continued his meditation practices and abandoned his search, content that God had spoken to him. Seven years later, in 1924, he visited the town of Beas in the Punjab order to spend some time on the banks of the Beas River. Someone asked him if he had come to see the

Master. "No, is there any Master?" So, after enjoying the riverside (he dearly loved water, especially rivers) he went to the ashram nearby, and there, in the person of Baba Sawan Singh Ji, he met the same form on the physical plane that he had been seeing in his meditations for seven years. He was initiated the following day, and devoted the rest of his life to the practice of Surat Shabd Yoga, the spiritual discipline taught by Baba Sawan Singh.

He was never a monk or renunciate, however. Married at an early age, he had three children (one of whom died in infancy), and supported himself and his family by working for the Indian Government. Beginning as a clerk at a pittance wage, and with no college education, he worked his way up to as high a post as was available to a native Indian in those colonial days, with hundreds of employees under him. When he retired in 1947, he had won the love and respect of his Indian subordinates and British superiors alike; and for the rest of his days, he met all his personal needs from his pension, never taking a penny for himself from his disciples.

He sat at the feet of his Guru for 24 years, and very quickly penetrated deep within. By the early thirties, Baba Sawan Singh was mentioning his name to those who asked if he had any advanced disciples; by the late thirties, he had been assigned the job of writing *Gurmat Siddhant,* a two-volume spiritual classic in the Punjabi language which was, at Kirpal Singh's request, published under Sawan Singh's name. In the year 1939, he was asked by his Master to initiate 250 persons at the regular monthly initiation—an unprecedented honor for any of Sawan Singh's disciples, and one of the traditional ways by which a Master indicates his successor. All through the thirties and forties, he held Satsang regularly at Lahore and Amritsar, and often gave discourses with his Master sitting by his side; as he used to say, "I talked to my Master and the people enjoyed!" In fact, he was holding Satsang on April 2, 1948, at the Dera Baba Jaimal Singh—his Guru's ashram at Beas—when the news came that Baba Sawan Singh had died. Just the day before he had received the transfer of spiritual power through the eyes, which verifies and makes possible the continuance of the power from one human pole to another; he had previously, on October 12, 1947, been told by his Master that he would succeed him. At that time, he had begged him to stay on in the physical form and just give orders as he willed; but that prayer was not answered and now he was gone. Heavy of heart, he left for Rishikesh in the Himalaya Mountains with three close disciples (one of whom was Bibi Hardevi) and spent the next five months in almost continuous *samadhi* or absorption in God.

During this period, he adopted the traditional way of life of a sadhu or renunciate, removing his turban and letting his hair (uncut since birth, as is the Sikh custom) hang loose, and wearing a simple white dhoti. It was at this time that he met the Maharishi Raghuvacharya, then in his early nineties, who became his close friend and disciple. The Maharishi, who had penetrated into the astral plane by means of strenuous Ashtang Yoga practices involving *pranayam,* etc., at once recognized that here was a great soul indeed, and got up from the circle of disciples where he was sitting and bowed down before Kirpal Singh—thus demonstrating the greatness of both of them. Kirpal Singh in his turn always treated Raghuvacharya with respect and deference, even though the latter freely told everyone that Kirpal Singh was his Guru. Raghuvacharya died in 1971 at the age of 115; he was a *pundit* or Sanskrit scholar as well as a great yogi, and to see those two giants together was the sight of a lifetime.

Finally, having drained the cup of spiritual ecstasy and become one with his Father, he received the orders from within: "Go back into the world and bring My children back to Me." Returning to a newly independent India, still reeling from the shock of the secession of Pakistan and the unbelievable suffering that that entailed, he went straight to Delhi, the center to which the Punjabi refugees were pouring, and began his work there. By 1951, he had established Sawan Ashram on the outskirts of the city, and the satsangs were being attended by five thousand or more souls. His work continued to grow, with one expansion after another: in 1955, he made his first foreign tour, spending several months in the United States and Europe. This was the first time that a Saint of his stature had visited the West, and the first time that the Surat Shabd Yoga had been explained there by an authentic Master of the system. Four of the talks given by him during this tour are included in this volume, and they show the complete simplicity and clarity with which he presented these very profound concepts to an audience almost totally unfamiliar with Eastern thought; for in 1955, the recognition of the depth and relevance of Oriental ideas and spiritual practices that is now so all-pervading over here had barely begun. As a result of this tour, hundreds of Westerners took the initiation and began the practice of Surat Shabd Yoga; representatives were authorized to give the initiation instructions while the Master was physically absent (after prior sanction from him) so that the work could continue and grow; and small centers of disciples sprang up in most of the major cities of America and Europe. These disciples in turn influenced others, and the number of initiates began to grow steadily.

In India the work continued to grow at a headlong pace as the Master's reputation as a holy man who actually lived up to what he preached, and to what the scriptures said, grew more and more widespread. In 1957 he was elected President of the infant World Fellowship of Religions, an office he was to keep for fifteen years and four World Religions Conferences; finally resigning in 1971 after it became evident that nothing more could be accomplished in that direction. In 1962 he was awarded the Order of St. John of Jerusalem, Knights of Malta, for his spiritual and humanitarian work; the first non-Christian in history to receive this honor. On this occasion, Prime Minister Nehru sent for him to offer his personal congratulations; they had a long talk, and the Master's unofficial but intimate connection with the Prime Ministers of India began. (He advised both Prime Ministers Shastri and Indira Gandhi on several occasions, and they reciprocated by addressing the various Conferences presided over by him.)

In 1963, he made his second world tour, this time, as President of the World Fellowship of Religions, meeting national and religious leaders on their own terms and applying the healing gospel of love to the very thorny world of practical politics. He met Pope Paul VI, the Patriarch of the Eastern Orthodox Churches, and many European royalty and government figures on all levels; and to them all he presented the idea of the unity of man. Side by side with his work on this level, he continued initiating seekers into the Surat Shabd Yoga and showing them the way Home.

As the work increased in the West and more and more seekers after truth were led to Kirpal Singh, many of them developed a strong yearning to study with him in India over an extended period of time, and to get to know him in a personal way. The first Western disciple to stay at Sawan Ashram was Rusel Jaque, an American writer, who spent six months with him in 1959. His poetic, sensitive report of his stay (*Gurudev: The Lord of Compassion*, published in 1960, now out of print) did a great deal to encourage others to come and see for themselves what was there. And they did— a trickle at first, then more, until by the early '70's there were almost always forty or fifty Westerners in residence at the Ashram for periods ranging from three weeks to six months.

During his last year, this number skyrocketed upward, as he, knowing he was leaving, threw open the gates and issued a general invitation to all his non-Indian disciples. Throughout the winter and spring of 1974 there were from two-to four-hundred disciples from countries outside of India consistently at his feet, in addition to the thousands of Indian followers who flocked to his door.

The final facet of his many-sided mission was born on February 6, 1970, when the concept of "Manav Kendra" was presented to the public. Manav Kendra means "Man Center" and as Kirpal Singh often explained, it was an ashram but more than an ashram. Dedicated to man-making, man service, and land service, the plan was to establish five of these centers throughout India—one each in the north, south, east, west, and center. Each center was to be eventually self-supporting and would serve as an agricultural example for the farmers in the area—combining traditional Indian methods with scientific know-how. Each center was also to include a free hospital, a free elementary school, a home for the aged, facilities for studying languages, and a library of comparative religion and mysticism, in addition to the esoteric instruction and "man-making" program that was to be the core. Two of the five centers were set up and functioning when Kirpal Singh left the physical body; the original Manav Kendra at Dehra Dun in the Himalayas where, during the years 1970 and 1971, he personally labored twelve hours a day to get it off the ground, was joined in 1973 by the second center at Baroda, near Bombay. Whether or not the other centers are established, and how well the existing centers function, is now up to his disciples.

On August 26, 1972, the Master left on his third and final world tour. This time he was greeted by huge crowds and followed everywhere he went by approximately a thousand disciples, most of them young people who had been initiated in the last few years. Although his body was finally showing signs of deterioration and his extraordinary vigor and staying power was at last diminishing, he nevertheless put in fourteen- or fifteen-hour days throughout the tour, gave countless talks, saw thousands of people in private interviews, and initiated more than two thousand new disciples before the tour ended on December 31 in Rome.

The outward climax of his mission was the calling of the great World Conference on Unity of Man in February 1974, seven months before his death. With invitations to spiritual and government leaders in India and throughout the world, the Conference was attended by two thousand delegates and approximately fifty thousand non-delegates; among the distinguished visitors who responded to the Master's call were the Venerable Nichidatsu Fuji of Japan, Pir Vilayat Inayat Khan of the International Sufi Order, Yogi Bhajan, Acharya Sri Tulsi Ji, Archbishop Angelo Fernandes of Delhi, and the Prime Minister (Mrs. Indira Gandhi), Vice President, Defense Minister, and Foreign Minister of India, along with many others. This great Conference, an extension of the idea of Manav Kendra, had an electrifying effect on all those who took part in it; again, it is up to his disciples and those in whom he planted the basic idea of unity to carry on this work.

His last major effort on behalf of unity took place at the Kumbha Mela in Hardwar, where, on April 12, 1974, he organized a large number of sadhus and holy men into the National Unity Conference, pledged to work together for the elimination of religious strife and the economic uplift of the poor people of India. This was the first time in the known religious history of India that anyone had been able to persuade the traditionally independent sadhus to join together for a common good; as he later said, "It was very difficult to bring them to sit together."

At the great Bhandara in honor of his Master, at the end of July, he gave his last Initiation, giving Naam to more than one thousand aspirants. A few days later, on August 1, he addressed a session of the Indian Parliament at the request of its members—the first time in history that a spiritual leader was invited to address the Parliament. Three weeks later he was gone.

The discourses included in this volume were selected and arranged by Malcolm and Kate Tillis from the 48 talks that appeared from 1968 through 1971 in the monthly *Sat Sandesh*; most of them have been long out of print. The first four discourses were given in Philadelphia on consecutive nights during the Master Kirpal Singh Ji's first world tour in 1955. In these talks the Master covers the whole range of his teachings; they serve as a perfect introduction to the Path. The discourses which have been chosen to follow explain in greater detail the necessity for a Master, and the role of the Master on earth. From there the Master expands on the changes which must take place within the disciple by His grace, and goes on to explain the difficulties which are met with on the Path and how they can be overcome. The last discourses speak of how to gain the Master's pleasure, the fruit of his infinite mercy, and, finally, of how the busy householder living in the world can reach the final goal without leaving his work and family—by making the nights his "jungle."

All the discourses, except the first four, were given in India and are translations from the Hindi. Discourses 5, 6, 9 and 11 were translated under the general direction of Bhadra Sena; they were carefully revised from the point of view of the English language by Malcolm and Kate Tillis and the revised versions were approved by the Master Kirpal Singh in January 1974.

# INTRODUCTION

Discourses 7, 8, 10, 12, 13 and 14 were translated by the Princess D. K. Narendra and Eileen Wigg, who were picked by the Master personally for this job. The Princess Narendra and Miss Wigg worked very closely with the Master, who carefully and painstakingly went over the translations word by word, and personally revised them wherever necessary. These discourses are published exactly as the Master left them.

—RUSSELL PERKINS (1975)

*Sant Kirpal Singh Ji*
*(1894-1974)*

# 1

# God and Man

LET ME introduce myself, I have come to you as a man to man. I am just as any of you are. Of course, each man has got the same privileges from God. I developed in a way that concerns my own Self. What I learned at the feet of my Master about my own Self, the real Self, I will put before you so that those who are seeking after Truth may find some guidance.

As a child, I had that awareness in me: "What is the mystery of life?" I sought to find the solution in books. I may tell you that I had the opportunity of going through almost two libraries and also going through the holy scriptures of almost all the religions, or the majority of them, I would say. There were very good descriptions given there, but I could not find the practical solution of my problem.

What I came to know at the feet of my Master, I will be putting before you in the course of four talks. The subject of each talk will be a little bit different.

Today we will deal with "God and Man." The next three talks will deal with "Higher Values of Life," "Kingdom of God," and lastly "The Most Natural Way to Enter the Kingdom of God."

From a careful and unbiased study of the sacred books of the world we find that there is one Reality, which is our goal. That Reality is termed God and by various other names.

---

This is the first of four public talks in Philadelphia, Pennsylvania, in 1955. The other three follow.

God made man and man made worldly religions. Such religions were made for the uplift of man. We have to make the best use of them so that ultimately we may know ourselves and then know God.

Religion has two aspects: One is the social side, or the outward side. The other aspect is the inner religion, the spiritual side. We have to start with outer forms of religions. Man is social; he must remain in some society.

Each society has its own various ceremonies and rituals, its own scriptures, its own mode of saying prayers. This is the non-essential side. We have to remain in some social religion because man is a social being—and to remain in some social religion is a blessing. But that is an elementary step—our going to churches or other holy places of worship, saying prayers, reading the scriptures, observing certain ceremonies and rituals. All these go to create love in us for God.

But if our performance of rituals, reading of the scriptures or attending the churches or other holy places of worship does not even create in us love of God and constitutes mere mental gymnastics, these lead us nowhere. That does not mean that you are not to live in any social religion. You are to do so. If you revolt against it, you will have to form another society.

Suppose there are ten thousand people of your views. Then you will have to form a separate society and make certain rules to go by. After some time you find that a certain rule has proved defective and must be amended. So you go on amending the rules.

All the same this has to do with your outer selves. *The Sabbath was made for man, not man for the Sabbath.* Similarly, social religions were made for man, but man was not made for social religions. The purpose of remaining in any social religion is just to know oneself and then to know God. That is one aspect of religion. The other aspect is the observance of certain rituals and ceremonies. These vary in different religions, but you will find their purpose is nearly the same.

For example, in some churches to sit bareheaded is a mark of respect. In India, to sit with one's head covered is a sign of respect. That is a custom there. Apparently, there is a difference between the two observances, but the purpose is the same. Both signify that whenever you sit in the presence of God, just remembering Him, you should sit in a respectful posture.

These are, however, non-essentials. The purpose is the same, no doubt. Apparently, some differences exist, but those differences do not affect in any way the purpose of the church. Those who follow the letter of the rule, simply forget the spirit and fight only for the apparent differences. In Arabia, where there is a dearth of water, there is a custom that whenever you say prayers, you should just wash your hands, feet, face; and then sit for prayers. In other countries where there is an abundance of water, they say that until you take a bath, it will not be right to sit for prayers. That is only an apparent difference on account of the climatic or geographical conditions of the place.

We have to live in some social religion. So it is better to remain where you are. Do not change, if it can be helped. While there, what should you do? Just read the Holy Scriptures—the sayings of the Masters—you have, and try to understand what they say, and live up to them.

This is what you find: All Masters who came in the past were the children of Light, and came to give Light to the world. They did not come for any special religion or special country. They came for all humanity.

It is now time to cast aside the trivial differences that exist—the non-essentials. We should just look to the purpose for which they were made, and open our eyes to the Reality that we are all worshipping the same God. These were meant to represent that Reality which exists.

Now you will find, from the standpoint of all religions, that God the absolute is beyond what is known and manifested. That is something even beyond what is supporting and creating all creation. That Reality is at the back of every thing. Can we search Him or find Him? No. He cannot be searched. He is unsearchable.

*Canst thou by searching find out God? Canst thou find out the Almighty?* The Almighty is inexpressible and cannot be expressed in words.

Names are simply given by the Masters to express that Reality, which is really inexpressible. He is the Changeless One. You find: "Forevermore, O Lord, Thy Word existed in Heaven." Forevermore—that is the lasting Reality and that is the Changeless One. Ultimately, it is unconditioned and undivided. He is the Nameless One.

All names are holy. We have respect for all names, although God is the Nameless One. By whatever name you call Him with devotion and faith, He will make appearance and you will come in contact with Him. But names refer to a Reality that cannot be expressed in words.

All Masters have tried to express that Reality, each defining in his own way. Almost all definitions of God are parallel. They all say that God is the first and the last, from which nothing can be excluded, and to which nothing can be added. God is omniscient, omnipresent, and the primal cause—the causeless cause—the seat of all things, existence in itself. That cannot be created. That is already in existence.

In the Koran, the Prophet Mohammed says: "There is no variableness in God, since He is eternal, immortal, infinite."

That is unchangeable permanence and everlasting Reality. These words only seek to express, however imperfectly, the great Reality that is at the back of all.

Ever since the Masters first came, they have been trying to express that Reality and chanting praises of the Lord—these have formed the subject of our holy scriptures. But still they say He is as unsaid as ever. For thousands of years, the Masters have been explaining in their own words whatever is possible.

How can the inexpressible be expressed in words? That is the subject of experience you may have, through contact with that Reality. But if even our outer emotions cannot be described in words, how can that Reality be expressed in words? That is why it has always been said that God is inexpressible.

There is the same Reality working throughout all creation. Until we have had some experience of that Reality, we will not know what it is like. What we now know is only what is given in books: we have had no first-hand experience of it.

All Masters say: It is the beginning and the end. In Isaiah it is stated: *I am the first and I am the last, and besides me there is no God.*

Again, we find: *I am Alpha and Omega, the beginning and the ending... which is, and which was, and which is to come, the Almighty.*

These are definitions given to show that Reality is

unchangeable permanence, which has no beginning and no end. *God has no beginning and no end.*

But until we have an experience of Reality, we cannot be convinced. Ever since the world began, Masters have been coming and giving explanations to the best of their ability to the people. But with all that, they always said that He is as unsaid as ever.

Guru Nanak has put it very aptly:

> *He is One, He is the First. He is all that is.*
> *His name is Truth. He is the Creator of all,*
>   *fearing naught, striking fear in naught.*
> *His form on lands and waters is Eternity;*
>   *the One Self-existent.*
> *Through the grace of His true servant,*
>   *continually repeat His Name.*
> *He was in the beginning; He is through all ages,*
> *And He shall be the One who lives forevermore.*

You see that he says the same thing. All Masters, as they have said, had experience of that Reality. Of course, when they gave their descriptions, they expressed it in their own language and in their own way. But you will find that the salient features of whatever they expressed are the same.

Then further Guru Nanak says:

> *He is beyond thought.*
> *No thinking can conceive Him.*

Now the question is: Can we search for Him within the finite pale of our intellect? No, He is beyond thought, no thinking can conceive Him. Not even if the minds of men should think for ages and ages. Then how can we know God? Our bodies, emotions and intellects should first be stilled. Only then the revelation will dawn, you will then know who you are. When you know who you are, you will be able to know and see what God is.

That is why Guru Nanak said if you want to grasp Him within the pale of your finite intellect, He cannot be seen.

It is something like the story of the tortoise of the river, who went into a pond. There was another tortoise there. The river tortoise said, "Look here, the sea is very great and has no end." The tortoise in the pool just stepped back and said: "Is it so much?" "No," said the other, "It is still greater." Then again he stepped back a little more, and questioned: "Is it so much?" And the other answered, "No, it is still greater." Then, he went around the whole pool of water and said, "Is it so much?" The other said, "No, it is still greater."

The tortoise of the pool was all wrong, you see, because his experience only extended to that pool of water, nothing more. Similarly, the Masters have always been saying that Divine Knowledge was limitless and they cannot expect to do justice to the subject.

The Lord is God. If you call Him anything, you simply want to bring Him within the finite ambit of your intellect. When that Reality is infinite, how can we express It in finite terms? This is what all Masters have been saying. Further, Guru Nanak says: *He cannot be conceived.*

The Upanishads say: *To grasp that Reality within the pale of your intellect is as impossible as trying to quench your thirst by drinking wine.* At another place, it is said:... *or just as if you can squeeze out oil from sand.* Both are impossible. Similarly, to bring Him within your intellect, and understand Him fully is not possible.

The Masters did give us something to understand that

which could not be expressed in words. By their grace we can just form some idea about Him. They bring us in contact with that Reality when we enter into the Kingdom of God. Then we have some experience of Him. After that we can say there is something.

Guru Nanak says: *I am just like a fish in the ocean. I do not know which is one end or the other.* Similarly, we cannot grasp Him within our finite intellects.

*Nor can He be known by gaining the worlds, for man's desire is never satiated, even though all the worlds laden with gold fall to his share. No human thoughts can carry man far. The movements of his mind, the thousand acts of wisdom of the world leave him dark, nothing avails. Vain are the ways of man. How then to find Him? Man feels helpless.*

Ever since the world began, all Masters have been saying the same thing. We have so many scriptures at our command, so many pages of the books of God that have been written. There will be many more as each Master comes and describes his contact with God or Reality. From their God intoxication, they pour out whatever comes, of high inspiration, just to give us the knowledge of Reality they have seen. Man has been trying to follow that but has failed.

Then, how can we see Him? Ever since the world began, this has been the fate of man. Unless we see God, the question remains, what is God?

Kabir says there is one Reality in all, supporting all creation, immanent in every form.

With That immanent in every form, why do we differ? Why are there so many wars, so many religions everywhere?

The reason is that when a Master came he had some experience of that Reality. To the people who met him, he simply gave them a first-hand experience of that Reality. When he left the scene—to err is human, you see—some persons gathered together and they had their own way of thinking. So changes occurred.

Again, another Master came, he found dross was added to Reality, to the teachings of the earlier Master. He thrashed out that dross and again let the people know the truth about Reality, to some extent. Again, another religion started.

The Masters never started any creed. They only gave out to the people: *There is one God and you should love Him.*

How can you love anybody until you see him, get some good out of him? Mere feelings or emotions are simply inferences arrived at by intellectual wrestlings. They will not give you any definite satisfaction. They will be wavering. Sometimes you may accept these inferences, but they are all subject to error. Unless you see Reality, come in contact with It firsthand and derive the bliss of It, ineffable and direct, enjoy happiness within—only then will you have love for Him, after having tasted the elixir of that Reality.

When the Masters come what do they tell us? St. John says: *God cannot be seen with thine eyes.* But then you find that some Masters said they saw God. The question was put to Guru Nanak: "Do you see God?" He replied: "I see God. He is everywhere." Christ also said: "Behold the Lord." He pointed to the Lord, saying: "There, behold Him." No reasoning.

The same question was also put by Swami Vivekananda. He was initially an atheist and challenged everybody: "Is there a God? Is there any man who has seen God?"

In those days, there was a man of realization, Parama-hansa Ramakrishna, and he was asked to go to him. Vivekananda went to him and asked: "Master, have you seen God?" The sage replied : "Yes, my child, I see Him as I see you, even more clearly than that." And he came in time to be a great theist. In the latter days of his life, Vivekananda confessed: "Because of that Godman I was saved."

You will find that those who profess to be theists are, truly speaking, not so. We have simply learnt in our scriptures that there is God. We have heard this many times, but we have not seen Him. Unless we see something, we cannot be convinced.

When difficulties arise, the vicissitudes of life come up and we have to pass through them, we are bewildered and ask: "Is there a God?" We become sceptics. But once you have seen, you have had some experience of Reality, you cannot have any doubt.

The Masters say: "We see Him." But what are those eyes with which He can be seen?

Shams-i-Tabrez, a Muslim saint, tells us that we should be able to see God with our own eyes and hear His voice with our own ears. You find in the Bible: *We have eyes and see not.* What are those eyes? Guru Nanak was asked: "You say you see God everywhere." He replied: "Those eyes with which you see God are different." What are those eyes with which you can see God? Those are not outer eyes, but that eye which is within each one of us. That eye is called by Christ the "Single Eye." *The eye is the light of the body. If thine eye be single, thy whole body shall be full of light.* The Hindu scriptures and sayings of other Masters tell us of the Third Eye or the latent eye. That eye is within each one of us. That one eye is not of the flesh and bone, as those we have outside on our faces.

Guru Nanak defines a blind man as not the one who does not have eyes on his face, but one whose inner eye is not open to see the Light of God.

God cannot be expressed. That absolute state can be had only when you rise into that Reality. But when this Supreme Power is the cause of all creation, immanent in all forms, supporting and maintaining them, It expresses itself in two ways—Light and Sound—and that expression of the God-power is an actual experience of Godmen within. It said, *God is Light*. The Mohammedans also say that God is "Noor," i.e., Light. They say that one who goes above and beyond the physical body and sees the Light of God within is a true Muslim. The Christian can also be defined in the same way; one who sees the Light within is a true Christian. The tenth Guru of the Sikhs says the same thing: *Those who see the effulgent Light of God within are true Sikhs, or true "fakirs." They are pure ones.* You will find the same definitions given in all religions, in all the holy scriptures: *Have you seen the Light within you?* Again, they have said: *If you shut the doors of the temple of the body, you will see the Light of Heaven.* It is a possibility.

All the scriptures tell us of the Light of God within. The Voice of God also reverberates in each one of us. There is a way in which we may have an experience of that Reality and its expression. That is the way back to God. Has our closed inner eye been opened or not? That is the question. Unless that inner eye be opened, we cannot see the Light of God within us. It is a question of introversion and inversion.

The ultimate goal of all religions is God, and that we should be able to see God. Leaving the non-essentials, what do they tell us? They say, *Love thy God*. This is said by all the religions. When you see and come in contact with God, only then, truly speaking, can you love God. At present, your loving God is practically impossible. Simply on the emotional side, you sometimes say certain things, but you have no contact with that Reality, and true love does not arise, and does not last.

When the Pharisees and the Sadducees went to Christ they returned in silence, because an intellectual man speaking to a man of realization cannot stand before him. While the latter sees certain things and then speaks, the intellectual man simply quotes verses from the holy scriptures which he has read, and afterwards he cannot reconcile things.

Naturally, when they came to Christ, they became quiet. Then they gathered together and came up to Him.

"Now, Master, what is the greatest commandment in the law?" What did he say? Jesus said unto them:

*Thou shalt love the Lord thy God with all thy heart, with all thy soul and with all thy might. This is the first and greatest of all commandments. And the second is like unto it, Thou shalt love thy neighbor as thyself. On these two commandments hang all the law and the prophets.*

The ultimate teaching of all social religions is just to love God. As God resides in every heart, love all humanity, all creation. For the love of God, you are to love all humanity. If we have love for all humanity, all other commandments follow. He whom you love, are you going to kill him? Are you going to rob him of his property? Are you going to bear false witness against him? No, not in the least.

So on these two commandments hang all other commandments. The Sermon on the Mount, the Eightfold Path of the Buddha, the *Niyama yama* and *Sadachar* of the Hindus all speak of the same thing, in their own languages and, of course, in their own ways.

If we live up to what the scriptures say, there will be peace on earth, and the Kingdom of God will surely come on earth. Then there will be no danger of any war. What a pity: these things are given in our holy scriptures, but we follow, if at all, the letter of the law at the cost of the spirit. That is the cause of discord.

All Masters came to unite men, not to separate man from man. They were the lovers of God, and they taught men how to love all humanity. You will see, this is one side of the thing that we have before us. We are to love all humanity because God resides in every heart.

The holy scriptures, with all the rest of the sayings about the various aspects of God, have not been able exactly to say what God is. Some phase of it, some part of it they did express, out of loving devotion. But from there we can only deduce some idea of God.

Man's highest thought of God never has and never can measure the Eternal, but it constitutes self-revelation. Your highest thought of God is not the measure of God, but the measure of our own hitherto unknown propensities. Each Master has been saying the same thing: *When I attempt to speak of the highest, I cannot. I become as one dumb.* How then can we express it? Even out of the love and intoxication they have of Reality, they give out something, but it still remains as unsaid as ever.

This is what the scriptures lay down. I told you this is the outer aspect of religion—social religions. When you think that God resides in every heart, you will not kill any-one. You will respect each man, when you know for certain that God resides in every heart.

When we live up to what the scriptures say, we should

all love God. Naturally, we will have respect for all others, for all living things.

The human body is a true temple of God, in which God resides. The body is the true temple of God. All Masters say so. If the body is the true temple of God, how then can we destroy or kill it?

Wrong preachings are given by ministers of the various religions instead of giving out the truths which are already in our scriptures. They have been simply proclaiming that their religion, their fold, is the highest and others are in the wrong. The result is, division between man and man and, of course, clashes between class and class. They will be ready, excuse me, just to destroy so many true temples of God—human bodies—for the outer temples which we raise with our own hands.

God resides in temples not made with hands. He resides in the true temple of the body that you are carrying. Of course, we are to maintain our outer temples (bodies) and keep them clean and chaste. These bodies are the temples of God. If the right preaching is given you will see love between man and man. Paid services, in almost all religions, I would say, have gone to make matters worse.

Now, some people think that they have special privileges. Well, God gave equal privileges to all. You see the outer form. Each has two eyes, two nostrils, two ears, a mouth, two arms, two feet and two legs. The outer construction is the same, and the inner construction is also the same. Each man has lungs, stomach, brain. God has given equal privileges to all. They are born the same way; they die the same way.

When men suffer from fever, irrespective of whether they belong to one religion or another, or one country or another, they suffer the same way, and there is the same remedy to cure their fever. When you go to a doctor, an adept in medicine, and tell him that you have fever, he gives you some medicine. He will give the same treatment to anyone else for the same trouble.

I mean that the outer expression, the outer privileges, are the same for each man, as given by God. The inner privileges are also the same. We are souls. God is a limitless Ocean of All-consciousness. We are conscious entities, drops of the Ocean of Life. Of course, our conscious self is hemmed in by mind and matter. It is given over so much to the organs of sense and identified with the body that we cannot now differentiate ourselves from the body.

The inner disease is also the same. Masters are physicians of the souls which have been given over to the influences of mind and matter. They tell us how to analyze the soul from the outgoing faculties, from the organs of sense, and rise above body-consciousness to know oneself, enter into the Kingdom of God and know God. All mankind suffers from the same disease.

Well, for God there is no East or West, no North or South. All creation is one. God is One.

Where do we stand now? We are all one. All Masters, all the holy scriptures say that we are the children of God. Prophet Mohammed says that we are members of the same family of God. The Sikh Masters also say that we are all brothers and God is our Father. The Christian scriptures and all others say the same thing.

Mankind is one, and God is One. We are worshippers of the same God. When we are worshippers of the same God— the archers may be many, but the target is the same—then, naturally we should have love for one another. You will find that two drunkards will embrace each other irrespective of whether they are of the east or the west, or belong to one religion or the other. But do you find that among those who profess to be lovers of God—between followers of one religion and those of another? They are lovers so far as their own faith is concerned. If they are lovers of God, they all should sit together and love one another.

The heads of the various religions are supposed to have contact with God. Whether they reach Him or not, that is another question altogether. But they are supposed by their followers to have seen God and to be one with God. They also profess that they are Godmen themselves. If so, why should they not love and embrace each other? There is one God overhead. It is all one humanity. We all are the same soul—conscious entity.

Man made social religions for the uplift of man. We have to make the best use of them. The best we can have out of the social religions is to know ourselves and to know God. Of course, we have to lead an ethical life. An ethical life is a stepping-stone to spirituality. These are the teachings of all Masters who came in the past.

As lovers of God, we should love all humanity. Having been born in any religion, it is a blessing to remain in it. Nevertheless we should rise above so that we become lovers of God, and then all mankind will have one religion.

Guru Nanak was once asked: "What is the highest form of religion in your opinion?" He replied: "Well, look here. I take all humanity, all men, as reading in the same class, seeking God. We are all classmates and I consider men the world over as classmates for the same ultimate goal." We should love one another.

The tenth Guru of the Sikhs, Guru Gobind Singh, was asked: "What do you think about man?" He replied: "All mankind is one—I tell you the whole truth—whether he is wearing a hat or a turban or is a recluse in a yellow or a black gown." That makes no difference. These are the outer forms.

Excuse me if I ask you: What is the religion of God? He is all-consciousness. He made all men equal. Did He stamp anybody that he was such and such? No.

When you know yourself, you will analyze yourself from the body and discover who you are. When you rise above body consciousness then you will find out. Religions pertain only to the outer forms of our life. We have to make the best use of them.

I have love for all social religions. That is all right. But the point is these social religions should go to help us on the way, to love God and to love all humanity. This is our ultimate goal. And further, to know ourselves and to know God, and have a first-hand experience of that Reality. Although that Reality cannot be expressed in words, still it can be experienced.

True religion is the first-hand experience of oneself, with his own Self and with God. That is the only true religion you have before you. There is the outer religion, and here is the inner religion. When you think everyone is all equal, then you will have love for all.

Our ultimate goal is to have love of God. Those persons or human beings whose souls came in contact with God, became the mouthpiece of God. They spoke as inspired by God. They are called Masters, or Godmen. We love them also for the sake of our love for God.

What did Christ say? He said:

*No man knoweth the Son, but the Father;*
*Neither knoweth any man the Father, save the Son,*
*And he to whomsoever the Son will reveal Him.*

That is why your love goes to them especially. They have had a first-hand experience and they are competent to give us a first-hand experience of that Reality within. They tell us how to rise above body consciousness, to know ourselves and to know God.

Then we see with our eyes, no testimony is required. That is why we love all Masters who came in the past — whether they came here or anywhere else. You have to love God "with all thy heart, with all thy soul, with all thy mind." Those who have loved God that way have merged their will in the Divine Will; they become the mouthpiece or conscious co-workers of the Divine Plan. Therefore, we love all Masters who came in the past.

Further, we revere all scriptures. What are these scriptures after all and what is their value to us? They are the recorded experiences of the past Masters, the experiences that they had in knowing themselves and those they had of God within themselves. They also revealed to us the things that helped them on the way and things that retarded their progress. In short, they gave us an account of their journey Godward. A description of all that formed the subject of all the holy scriptures. All saints deal with their pilgrimage to God. They tell us of the Godway, the halting stations, the various regions they passed through and what they found there; their pilgrimage on the way and their first-hand experiences at each place. They have thus left for us a fine record for our guidance.

All holy books from ages past are but footprints on the sands of time for the love-borne seekers after God.

Those who are lovers of God naturally have love for all the scriptures. Kabir, the great Saint of the East, tells us: *Say not that the scriptures are false, for he who does not see Truth in them is in the wrong.* It is a pity that though we can read the scriptures, we cannot follow their true import until we see for ourselves what those Masters experienced within themselves, or until these are explained to us by one who has had that first-hand experience with himself and with God as those Masters had. Only then will we be following the true import of the holy scriptures. Otherwise, reading of the scriptures from morn till night, without following what the scriptures say, will lead us nowhere.

That does not mean that you should not read the holy scriptures. Read them by all means, but try to understand them rightly. When you have understood them, try to have those experiences in your own self. Only then will you be fully convinced of what they say. They may be likened to records of different persons visiting the same place—say Washington or Philadelphia—and describing it, each in his own language and in his own peculiar way.

We can read all these holy scriptures, but we cannot follow their true import until we seek the help of someone who has seen and had the experience these describe.

I would say that today in the twentieth century, we are rather fortunate. Why? We have all the fine records of the experiences of the Masters who came in the past. Had we come five hundred years ago, the holy scriptures of the Sikhs would not have been with us. Had we come, say 1500 years earlier, the holy Koran would not have been with us. And if we had come before 2000 years, the Bible would not have been with us. If we had come before the time of Zoroaster or the Buddha, or any one else, their scriptures would not have been with us. What I mean is that today we are fortunate in having with us these valuable records of the Masters who came in the past. They tell us what they experienced with themselves and God. The only thing needed now is to have someone who has had that experience which is given in those holy scriptures. He will be able to tell us the true import of things, and also he will be able to give us a first-hand experience of these things.

So for the love of God we love all Godmen. For the love of God, we love all the holy scriptures. There are so many pages of the book of God that have been written to guide the erring humanity. Many more may be written whenever any Master comes.

Further, we love all holy places of worship. Why? Because there people gather together to sing the praises of the one and the same God—in their own ways, of course. If we love somebody and someone happens to be praising him, we stand and hear how he describes him. So we have love for all holy places of worship for the love of God. Also, we love all places of pilgrimage, for they are the spots where once lived some Master, some Godman, who was one with God, who became the mouthpiece of God. It is for that alone that we have respect for all holy places where such Masters lived.

We love God first; God resides in every heart; therefore we love all humanity. For the same reasons, we love all Godmen, for they have known God. We love all holy scriptures, because they speak of Him and are valuable records of the experiences of the past Masters. Again, for the same reason we love all holy places of worship, whether temples or mosques, churches or synagogues. They are meant for chanting the praises of the Lord.

You remember, when Christ came, he entered the Temple in Jerusalem and turned out those who misused or defiled it. He told them: "You have made the house of my Father a business house." Such a man, who is a lover of God, what will he say? He will say what the Vedas say. The Yajur Veda says: *Well, O people, let us all sit together and sing the praises of the Lord and worship the same God.* But there are false ways of preaching that separate man from man. There is no common place where we can all sit together and worship the same God.

Again the Rig Veda says: *Gather ye in thousands, and worship God and chant His praises.* We are all lovers of the same Reality. We are all for the same Truth. There are thousands of lovers, but the Beloved is only one. We may call Him God, or by any name we like. We are lovers of the same Reality. Outwardly speaking, we have different social religions. Blessed you are. Remain where you are. To live in some social religion is a blessing. That is a helping factor. As with a midwife who helps at the birth of a child, so with social religions which help us in that way towards spirituality, in knowing ourselves and in knowing God.

Whenever Masters came, they never touched the outer forms, but simply said: Remain where you are. By changing your outer forms, rituals, this and that, you will not be able to have a first-hand experience of God. Those are only helping factors on the way, paving the road to spirituality. Make the best use of them.

Real religion starts where world philosophies end. All these outer forms of the social religions are limited only to the man's material existence. The Kingdom of God, if you know yourself and know God, will open of itself when you rise above body consciousness. There the alphabet of the teachings of the Masters begins. The true religion starts from there. That is transcendental. That is above the organs of sense. When you come above, you will rise above the senses. It requires practical self-analysis, to know yourself and to know God.

This is the goal before us. The subjective side of all religions is the same. In the objective side you will find some slight differences in non-essentials, but you will find their purpose is the same.

The question remains the same for all humanity—to know our Self and to know God. We have said so much about the outer things, the outer holy places of worship. God made man after His own image, and man made all these holy places of worship after the image of man. Churches are either nose-shaped or dome-shaped, and so are temples of other religions. In mosques, we find places of worship in the form of semicircular arches whose shape resembles the human forehead.

The true temple of God is the man's body and that you have. We just have to tap inside. When you transcend the body, there the ABC of true religion starts. That is the one destiny for all humanity. It has never been different.

The Masters, whenever they came, taught two things: ethical life of clean and chaste living with love for all men and all creation. Be chaste; don't think evil of others even in thought, word or deed. Be truthful and love all humanity— hatred for none and selfless service for all. This is the first part which they take up for all mankind, irrespective of whether they belong to one religion or another.

No religion commends hatred for anybody. The question was put to Christ: "How should we behave with others?" He inquired: "What did Moses say to you?" He was told: "A tooth for a tooth and a nail for a nail." He said: "That was only because of your hard-heartedness." They asked: "What do you say, Rabbi?" Christ answered: "Moses also said, love thy neighbor as thyself." They further asked him: "What about those who are our enemies?" And what did he say? He said: "Love thine enemies."

Now, we all are embodied souls. The lover of God has love for all souls. The soul is a conscious entity of the same essence as of God. In fact, we form a true brotherhood. We are one with God, one in God, and those who are lovers of God, naturally will have love for all humanity. Outward things will not matter. When you know yourself and know God, you come in contact with God; and then you will find Him immanent in every form and naturally you will have love for all. That is the permanent rock, I would say, on which humanity should stand, never to fall. The outer self sometimes gives way and we fall into the error that we preach against. There have been two great wars so far. Fought by whom? By those who were in name the followers of the same Savior and followed the same religion. Then, it comes to this, that they were not living up to what the scriptures of the Masters say. They simply say: "I profess this religion or that."

If we but live up to what the scriptures say, irrespective of country or religion, we get ready to see God. After all, man is man. All religions are comprised of men, and men are the same everywhere. This is just like being students in any school or college. Why do you study? For the sake of gaining knowledge. You may join this college or that, that makes no difference. When you get your degree, you are seldom asked from which college you got your degree. They call you a graduate.

Similarly, all the social religions were made to turn out perfect men believing in the oneness of God. The word university simply means having one purpose in view. And the purpose to have in view is to understand man: who he is, what he is, and what is his relation to God. But this goal has been lost sight of. The means have become the end, and outer knowledge, instead of leading us to inner knowledge, is being studied for its own sake.

The preaching done by paid men in all religions has made matters worse. Otherwise, the men of realization say: "The true temple, if any, is man's body itself." All the scriptures bear this out. All is holy where devotion kneels. Wherever you have devotion, sit down in sweet remem—brance of the Lord and say your prayers.

My Master used to emphasize the need for a common ground where seekers of Truth, irrespective of their faiths, could gather together. There should be no social forms or rituals, there should be no temples or anything of the sort. Let them remain in their own social religions. The purpose of a man's life and the ultimate goal of the social religions is to know oneself and to know God. How to analyze yourself from the body, open your inner eye and enter the Kingdom of God. Those subjects should be dealt with there.

In India, we have an Ashram in Delhi, and we have no temple there. People come to me and ask: "Well, what particular temple have you raised?" I always tell them: "Man's body is the true temple of God. I have love for all temples of the social religions, but here I have none." And for the other temple, the whole world is the temple of God, the earth below and the sky overhead. We have a grassy ground over there where we can accommodate 25 to 30 thousand people. Of course, we have a long shed to give us protection from rain or sun, if necessary. We have all the scriptures over there, for the reason that they speak of the same valuable experiences which the Masters had in their lives.

Men come there. They are seeking after Truth. To follow certain outward observances is not the be-all or the end-all.

They are only the means to an end. Make the best use of them. But until you rise above body consciousness and know yourself and know God, there is no liberation, no return to the True Home of the Father.

These are the elementary steps we take. That is all right. But take a step further from where you are. Rise above the body consciousness, open the inner eye and see the Light of God within and enter the Kingdom of God, reach your True Home, the home of your Father. This is the ultimate goal of all religions.

But there are wrong ways of preaching, I would tell you. Instead of uniting man to man, they are separating man from man; since the ministers themselves have no first-hand experience of that Reality, they must tell their people that man is man and God is God.

All men are equal for God, and the same God is worship–ped by us all. Naturally, we have love for one another. But we find that social religion is like a golden watch, studded with gems and jewels, which does not give us any time whatsoever. We have our social religions. Each social religion has the work before it to turn out perfect men: *Be ye perfect even as thy Father which is in heaven is perfect.* But instead of turning out perfect men, they are simply strengthening their own folds. Naturally, when you say this fold is higher than the other, there is a clash between class and class, and we see no true progress.

My point is, we have one God, the same God. Each religion does not have its own God. The same God is worshipped by all of us. Let us embrace each other and sit in amity, love and accord, to sing praise of the Lord as one family. Since we are lovers of God, we have to love all Godmen, Masters who came in the past or who may come in the future. Our respect goes out to all of them. We have love for all the scriptures, because they speak of the same God and record the experiences that the Masters had with themselves and with God. And we have love for all holy places of worship, because they are meant for singing praises of the Lord.

So all mankind is one, and we are worshippers of the same God. We have different forms, outer forms, we belong to different religions outwardly, but our Beloved is the same. If we only keep that in view before us, we will be at peace, we will have peace on earth and goodwill among men. There will be no danger of war or anything of that sort.

Today's subject was "God and Man." I have put it before you briefly. Next we will see that ultimately we have to know God. But until we know ourselves, how can we know God?

It is the soul that has to have experience of God, because God is All Consciousness, and our souls are also conscious entities. It is the soul that has to experience God, and for that purpose we will have to know the inner man, who we are, what we are. "Know thyself" has been the motto set forth by all sages. They never said "Know others." First if you know yourself, only then will you be able to know the Overself.

That will be the next subject and along with it we will compare the higher values of life—physical, intellectual and spiritual. Next, we will take up the Kingdom of God: where it is, how we can reach that Kingdom, and how to open the inner eye to see. The sages say that God is Light. How can we see God, see the Light of God? That will be the subject of our third talk. After that, we will determine which is the most natural way for having that experience: what other Godmen said, how the scriptures speak of the Godmen, that will be the subject of our last talk.

*Sant Kirpal Singh Ji*
*(1894-1974)*

*Sant Kirpal Singh Ji*
*(1894-1974)*

# 2

# The Higher Values of Life

IN THE previous talk we came to the conclusion that God made man and man made all social religions and that the purpose of social religions was the uplift of man.

We dealt with the outer side of man; we said that man was born with equal privileges from God, irrespective of whether he belonged to one country or another or one religion or another. We have to make the best use of all social religions so that we may know all about man.

Our ultimate goal is to know God. First, we must know ourselves and then we will know God. All scriptures say that we should love God with all our heart, with all our soul and with all our might. As we are lovers of God—and God resides in every heart—we must love all humanity. Those who came into contact with God became the mouthpiece of God—God-in-man or Godmen, because of their love of God. We love all scriptures because they are the treasures of the experiences of the Masters with themselves and with God. We also love all holy places of worship because they are the places meant for singing the praises of the One Lord. We love all holy places of pilgrimage too, for the reason that there lived some lover of God, someone who became one with God and became the mouthpiece of God. Thus, for the sake of love of God, we love all others. If we just love God and hate one Master or the other, or hate one holy book or the other, or if we hate other men, do we truly love God?

This is the second of four public talks in Philadelphia, Pennsylvania, in 1955. The remaining two follow.

Surely not; because God resides in every heart, and our ultimate goal is God. The ultimate goal of all religions too is God. Then, how can a follower of one religion or another hate anyone else? If we would live up to what the scriptures say, that looks an impossibility at first sight.

If we live up to these two commandments—*Love God with all thy heart, with all thy soul, and with all thy might* and, *love all humanity since God resides in every heart*—the Kingdom of God will descend on earth. All other commandments hang on these two commandments. All prophets have laid stress on these commandments. They are all one on these two fundamental tenets.

We would like now to probe further into: *What is man?* Unless man knows himself, he cannot know God. All scriptures which we have with us today say: *"Man, know thyself."* They do not say, "know others." Why?

Who are you? What are you? Are you this five or six foot high body that you have? That is not knowing yourself. You will see for your own self; the time does come when you have to cast away the physical body you are carrying—this muddy vesture of decay. The body remains like a clod of earth and is cremated or buried underground.

If you know so much about your physical self, that is not truly speaking, knowing yourself. The Greeks and the Egyptians had inscribed on their temples these very words— *Gnothi Seaton.* The Upanishads say: *Know thyself.* Christ also said: *know thyself.* Guru Nanak too said: *Unless you know yourself, you are not in a position to know God.* All this delusion through which you are passing cannot easily be set aside. Is it not true that you are deluded? You see bodies like the body you have. You have seen with your own eyes that something left such bodies and they were cremated or buried. You too are carrying a similar body. If you know so much about your physical self it does not follow that you know your own self.

This question has been before us ever since the world began. We have known so much about our outer self—maintaining our bodies, supporting our families, living socially and politically. We have given rather too much thought to the body and bodily relations, but we have never tapped inside to see the inner man, the inner Self, who we are and what we are.

Unless the student opens his own consciousness, the teacher can impart nothing. He can only direct, counsel and define. But understanding cannot be imparted. That must come from within, and through self-development. Of course, he gives you some experience of how to know yourself, how to analyze yourself from the body. You have to start with that, no doubt. But working that way, in accordance with the guidance and the help given by the Master, you will one day come to realize that Reality is within you.

Souls are all divine in nature. They are so many drops of the Ocean of Divinity, but are hemmed in by the mind and matter. They cannot, as they are now, know themselves, differentiate themselves.

What is the greatest study of man? Is it theology? I would say no. Is it knowing the law of Blackstone and other great men who came in the past? Even then the answer will be no. Is it the study of works of men like Shakespeare, Milton, Dickens, Burns? No. Is it occultism or Buddhism or Christianity or Sikhism or any other social religion that we may study? Are such works the greatest aim of man's study? Again I would say that the answer is no. Why?

If you become conversant with all the scriptures left by the Masters, what do they speak of? They speak of man. "Man, know thyself." So, knowing man, both his outer and inner aspects, is the greatest study for us. The greatest study of man is man. Pope, the English poet, has said:

> *Know then thyself, presume not God to scan;*
> *The proper study of mankind is man.*

Until you know man, all else is mere ignorance and superstition. The more you study the outer phase of the scriptures, the more you realize that it is all nothing but accumulation, hoarding up of ideas and opinions expressed by others.

Suppose you become fully conversant with all the scriptures we have today. What does it matter? I have said, we in the twentieth century are fortunate in that all Masters who came in the past left for us their experiences with themselves and with God. What particular things helped them on the way, and what stood in the way of realization? That forms the subject of all scriptures. Even if you know all that, are you satisfied? That is only having something, merchandise just hoarded in your brains—such and such a Master said this, such and such a book said that, such and such scriptures said so. That is not divinity. That is only knowing facts about divinity, about our divine nature the Masters had experienced themselves and with God. Even if you study all the books, you will not be able to know yourself. Of course, you will get some information, you will be able to quote so many things from various books. But will you be able to know yourself? No. Eliot, the poet, says:

> *Where is the wisdom we have lost in knowledge?*
> *Where is the knowledge we have lost in information?*

Knowing the self is a result of self-analysis, in practice, not in theory. We see many people asserting emphatically: "I am not the body. I am not intellect. I am not the vital airs or pranas. I am not the sense-organs." That is all right. But have we ever analyzed ourselves practically by transcending body consciousness and seeing for our own selves that we are something besides the physical body, the intellect, the vital airs and the sensory organs all of which go to make the outer man apart from the inner Self? Have you ever risen above body consciousness, had a first-hand experience of your own Self? You will find very few persons who have really accomplished this.

So your study of man just consists in hoarding certain information in your brain. Sometimes you read the scriptures. The purpose is that by reading the scriptures you get enough information from the study that the Masters made of themselves and of God to help you in just finding your own Self, and nothing more. The reading of those scriptures will create some interest in you to know yourself and to know God.

I do not mean that the scriptures are not to be read. They should be read, and read intelligently. The reading of the scriptures is the first elementary step that goes to create interest in us that such and such Master saw divine light within him. Can we also see the same? Yes, we can also see, for what a man has done, another can do; of course, with proper training and guidance.

I quoted you also that Masters did see the Light of God. Those who followed them, and lived up to what they said, also had the very same experience in varying degrees in their own lives. You should be able, while possessing human life, to see the Light of God. When you have seen that Light, your whole life will be changed. And that you can see only when you rise above body consciousness. It is a practical question.

Now what is to be done? What can be done by under-standing the truth, i.e., by just knowing our own Self and having a first-hand experience of the Self and Overself? That alone will make us free. These things we can have only when we really have risen, we have been born anew. Christ says:

> *Except a man be born again, he cannot see the*
> *Kingdom of God.*

He then goes on to clarify:
> *Except a man be born of water and of the spirit, he*
> *cannot enter the Kingdom of God.*

In Corinthians we have:
> *Flesh and blood cannot inherit the Kingdom of*
> *God.*

St. Paul explains:
> *Being born again, not of corruptible seed, but of*
> *incorruptible, by the Word of God, which liveth*
> *and abideth for ever.*

It is clear that unless we are born anew, we can neither see nor enter the Kingdom of God, nor can we inherit it. In other words, we cannot have a first-hand experience of our own Selves nor of God. We cannot have our inner eye—called the Third Eye or Single Eye—opened, enabling us to see the Light of God.

Reading the scriptures alone will not help. But study the scriptures carefully because they speak of the practical experiences that the Masters had with themselves and with God. Unless we study these scriptures under the guidance of someone who has had actual experiences himself as are recorded therein, we will not be able to follow the right import.

What does Plutarch say? He says: *The same experiences that the soul has at the time of leaving the body are had by those who have been initiated into the mysteries of the Beyond.* You have to leave the body, of course, some day. That is, I think, a very clear proof or testimony that you are not these bodies about which you have known so much. By "knowing the Self" is meant knowing the inner Self, the spiritual Self, the spiritual entity which leaves the body at the time of death. You may say that this physical body may be knocked down by death—the great final change. But you do not die. You must one day leave the body and all things connected with the body, whether you wish it or not.

So the greatest wisdom lies in what? In knowing your Self, who you are, what you are. Unless you know your Self, you cannot know God. He who knows himself comes to know God, too, because it is the infinite soul alone that can know God and not the finite intellect. One cannot grasp Him within the finite intellect.

> *How can the less the Greater comprehend?*
> *Or finite reason reach Infinity?*
>
> —DRYDEN

We cannot see Him. He is unsearchable with our intellect, with our sense-organs, with our outward faculties. With all the imagination, the highest stretch of imagination, He cannot be grasped. It is soul alone to which God reveals Himself. Unless we analyze ourselves, see our own Self—know ourselves—we cannot see God.

Self-knowledge precedes God-knowledge. For that let us see what help may be had.

Looking from without we notice that the body lives as long as soul, the indweller of the house, is with it. But the time does come when we have to leave the body. That is the day of the great final change, or death. But do not be frightened of death; it is no bugbear.

I have told you that the greatest study of man is man. All the scriptures came from where? Of course, from man — a man of realization, no doubt. Great indeed is man. All inventions came from where? From man. Godhood, which gave us a first-hand experience of God, working through the human poles called Masters, also was expressed through man.

Man is great and the greatest study for a man is man himself. Who are you? What is it that enlivens this body, and what is it that leaves it? While that inner Self or the spiritual Self is fixed in the body and working through the body, you are alive, you are moving. But the time does come when you have to leave the body. That is the fate awaiting each one of you, no exception to the rule. All kings and subjects, the rich and the poor, the wise and the ignorant, and even the Masters have to leave the body. How can there be an exception in your case? If so, are you prepared for that final change? If not, you must prepare yourself. And for that, you must solve the mystery of life while there is still time. You must examine your own Self. Who is the real man in the body? Unless you know that, you cannot be at peace.

Buddha, who was first called Gautama, was a prince brought up in a princely way amid luxury and opulence. Once he was visiting the town which was decorated tastefully to welcome him. As he passed through the city in a chariot, he saw an old man with haggard face, sunken eyes, and tottering frame. The old man staggered along with the help of a stick. Looking at the old man, the prince asked his charioteer,

"What was that?" "Old age, my lord; the body must grow old and weak," the charioteer replied. That shocked him greatly. Proceeding further, he saw a dying man, gasping for breath, and again asked what it was. The charioteer replied: "Well, Master, we must die and leave the body. He is dying. He is gasping for breath." That made him still more sad and pensive. The prince wondered if that was the fate of our lovely bodies.  The charioteer took him out of the city to avoid ugly sights. But outside the city, the prince saw four men carrying a corpse. He naturally asked what it was, and was told: "Well, Master, we have to leave the body." This made the prince all the more gloomy and he exclaimed: "It is strange that we must some day leave our beautiful bodies; but what is it that leaves?"

That was the greatest day in Gautama's life. He was awakening, wondering what it was that enlivened the body.

We too have the same sort of bodies. We have witnessed so many cremations and burials. We have attended a great many funerals of our friends and relatives, but the mystery of life has never struck us, as it struck Gautama.

Gautama went home. He had a son. That is generally a very happy day. But he was absorbed with that mystery of life. He left his home, wife and son to seek the solution of the mystery of life—What am I? Who it that leaves the body?"

As long as the inner Self is working in this physical body, we are alive, we are talking, we are thinking, we are moving about. But when that leaves the body, it is cremated or buried. No one keeps the dead body in the house. It is disposed of as soon as possible.

This is the problem before us. We have to consider it very calmly, with due deliberation. We have to look into it to discover what it is: "Who am I? What am I?" Those who know and have fathomed the mystery of life, have done wonderful work. Wherefrom came the scriptures? From within, from within man. All the inventions we have, came from where? From within man; not from without.

The greatest thing before us is "to know oneself," who is the Self and what is the Self. We have seen that the fate of this physical body is death. At the time of this final change, the indweller leaves the house of the body. We are not the body, the dwelling house. We are the indweller of the house that we are enlivening by our presence.

From our very birth, the first companion that we have had is the physical body, now developed and grown up. When we depart, it is left behind; it does not accompany us. Then, how can other things which have come into our contact through our body, accompany us to the other world? If we remember this, the entire angle of vision will change.

Now we see from the level of the body. If we know ourselves—who we are and what we are—that we are the indwellers of the body, the whole angle of perception will change. You will see from the level of the soul and not from the level of the body.

At present, we are working from false premises. We are laying up treasures on earth. We are making so many houses, buildings and gathering other possessions, and hoarding up as much money as we can, never thinking for a moment that we have to leave the body and all earthly possessions. That is why, when Masters come, they simply direct our attention to this most important reality—the inevitability of death—about which we are quite oblivious and ignorant. With all our intellectual attainments, we act as if we never would have to leave the world or the body. That is why, Christ says:

*Lay not up for yourself treasures on earth.* Why? *Where moth and rust doth corrupt and where thieves break through and steal.* What should we do? *But lay up for yourselves treasures in heaven; where neither moth nor rust doth corrupt and where thieves do not break through nor steal.*

What have we done for the other world? We are going to leave this body some day. Have we ever thought of that? If we leave the body what else can accompany us?

We are told that when Queen Noor Jahan was about to die, the physicians in attendance told her: "Well, your Majesty, you now have to leave for the other world." Perhaps she had never known what the other world was. She simply said: "All right, if I have to go to the other world, then how many people will accompany me?" The physician told her, "Your Majesty, none can go along with you. You have to leave all alone."

Just mark the ignorance. Intellectually, we all know that death is inevitable, that it overtakes all, yet have we ever truly realized that we ourselves will also die? Have we ever calmly considered who is it in us that leaves the body and where does it go?

All saints have been stressing the great need to "know thyself." If you know the inner man which leaves the body, you know something; and that will change the entire plane of perception.

I have come here from India. I know I have to go back. Well, on the airplane I can take only forty pounds of luggage. Anything beyond that limit I will have to leave behind. Then what shall I do? Shall I then hoard up too many things to carry along with me? How can I take them? I cannot carry more than forty pounds. Likewise, when going to the other world, even this body does not accompany us; what to speak of all the other possessions.

So, there are two aspects we must remember. First, that we are pilgrims on this earth where we have to spend a certain span of time, be it less or more. After all, it is only a temporary abode and we have to leave it some day. It is something like being on your way to a destination. Night falls on the way, and you stop in some hotel to pass the night, and early in the morning you leave for your destination. Have you ever considered that you live as though you were going to stay in this world forever? Have you ever thought of death?

Secondly, man is composed of the physical body, the intellect and the soul. We know so much about our physical bodies. We know so much about how to maintain them. We know so much about our family relationship, our children, our social life, etc. We have advanced so wonderfully in the intellectual way. We have television, we can fly in the air. All this makes the world like a house. It only takes about 24 hours from India to reach America, from one end of the globe to the other. All these countries are so many rooms in the mansion of my Father, you may say. We have the atom bombs, the hydrogen bombs etc. I mean to say that our advance in intellect and technology has been wonderful.

But what do we know about our own Self—the real Self—that gives vitality to the physical and intellectual aspects of our life? It is the spirit or soul which we really are. Most of the physical side and the intellectual side has the background of our soul. We have developed only in two ways, and know nothing about our own Self.

A Muslim Saint says: *How long will you go on playing with the clay like a child and besmearing yourself with it?* When the soul leaves the body, what remains? Clay. *Dust thou art, and unto dust returneth.* How long will you continue like that?

We are wonderfully developed in two ways, but about our soul we know nothing or next to nothing. We know only so much as is given in the scriptures. We know only that much which we can grasp by our finite intellect. If we want to understand the true import of the scriptures, we must sit at the feet of someone who has practical knowledge of the Self and the Overself, because all scriptures speak of the same thing.

Even if we come across a Master who is a practical adept and he explains to us all the things concerning our own Self and the Overself, still, until we have that experience on our own and for ourselves, we cannot be satisfied.

If at all we read the scriptures, the pursuit in the domain of Self-knowledge is restricted mainly to reading one scripture or the other, attending some holy place of worship, and that is all. These, however, are but elementary steps and by themselves lead to no worthwhile results. Moreover, we will find that many of us go to churches or to holy places of worship, but how many are there who really do so for the sake of having knowledge of God? Very few indeed. Most of us are there to pray for our livelihood or our children or for some other material benefit. We are reading the scriptures for the reason that other circumstances may be adjusted satisfactorily. The majority of us are religious only in that way.

But will such people, by going to the holy places of worship, find God? *Ask and it will be given unto you. Knock and it shall be opened.* But if we are just asking for worldly things, how will we have God instead? *Lord God is kind and what ye ask of Him, that shall He give unto you.*

The story is told of a Persian prince Majnu, who fell in love with the princess Laila. So fervent was his adoration that he kissed the earth she trod. Once people told him: "Look here, God wants to see you." He replied: "All right; if He wants to see me, let Him come in the shape of my Laila." Do you think that such a man will ever find God? He will find Laila, no doubt; but not God.

Similarly, like so many Majnus, we go to the temple seeking not God but the idols of our hearts. How then can we have God? Only they can have God who seek God. For them the way is open; for them there is some Godman to put them on the Path.

So our pursuit of the spiritual way is restricted to that one thing. Those who have a real desire in them to search and find God, He makes arrangements for them to be put on the way.

The elementary step in order to know oneself is to read the holy scriptures we have with us. But they tell us: *Whosoever shall lose his life shall save it, and whosoever shall save his life shall lose it.*

What does that mean? Whosoever is merely living the physical life through the organs of senses, knowing little or nothing about his own inner Self, naturally he will be losing his everlasting life all along. Those who transcend this physical life, know themselves and know God, will have everlasting life.

The scriptures say that very clearly in very simple words. But the intellectual people who have had no practical knowledge of self-analysis, experience with their own Selves and with God, have made it hard to understand. That is all. Otherwise, the truths are very simple.

Again, Christ says: *Unless you be born anew, you cannot see the Kingdom of God.* Be born anew? How? Nicodemus, a very learned man, met Jesus and inquired: "Well, Master, how is it you say we must be born again? How can we be born again? How can we re-enter the womb again and be born again?"

What did Christ say? "Look here, you are a learned man, a very wise man. People sit at your feet, worship you like anything. Don't you see, flesh is flesh, and you are to be born of the spirit?"

This has been a personal problem for all of us. The Masters who came and were capable of giving us the practical solution, gave us the first-hand experience of how to rise above body consciousness and know ourselves.

The whole thing is just topsy-turvy, I would say. We are the indwellers of the house. We have to know and lay up something for where we have to go, but we have identified ourselves with the body so much so that we cannot dif–ferentiate ourselves from it.

Now we are working from the level of the body, knowing nothing but our physical self. We are only considering this outer world and its possessions, as if these were the only be-all and end-all of life. The whole thing is topsy-turvy. That is why Masters have been laying stress: *What is a man profited if he shall gain the whole world and lose his own soul?* Then, they ask: *What shall a man give in exchange for his soul?* You see how important it is.

It is we who have to leave the body, and we know little or nothing about our own Self. We know only so much as is given in the scriptures. But even if we read them for years and years, all through our life, do we have any experience at all?

Of course, we fill our brains with so many facts and theories and the records of the experiences of others. But do they help? It is just like a man going to be married. Afterwards the couple drive away all joyous. But besides them there are many others who join in the festivities; they get nothing thereby. As an Indian proverb goes: *There are two to have a marriage and the rest stand by.*

It does not in any way mean that we should not read scriptures. We should. That is an elementary step. They are valuable records, worth tons of gold and rubies and emeralds, for those who would like to just peep inside, to know themselves and to know God.

We are now merely identified with the body. We are working in the body, behaving from the level of the body; and we are attached to the body and all its environments. The more we are attached, the more we are away from the life everlasting. That is why it is said: *Strive to withdraw from the love of all visible things and direct your attention to the things invisible.* The more we are attached to the outside, to the physical things, the more we are away from our inner Self, our higher Self. Until we withdraw for a while from that place and rise above body consciousness, know ourselves, we cannot know God or come near God or come in contact with God.

When we know for certain that we have to leave the body, why get attached to it? As I just told you, I have to leave for India in a few days, leave the United States and go back to India. I know I will have to go back. I will be leaving you all, of course. I will not be too much attached to the possessions, this and that thing; I have to leave. I have to simply pass my days and go back, that is all.

For this reason, man's life consists not in possessions,

not in the abundance of things he possesses: *The life is more than the meat, and the body is more than the raiment.*

You see how we behave in worldly ways; suppose you are wearing a costly costume or apparel. You meet some accident and that apparel is just spoiled and torn. You say: "Never mind, I am saved." Again, when you are sick and the doctors declare there is little hope of your life. What do you say? "All right, I will spend all the money I have, even all the possessions I have, so that I may be saved." Our bodies are more valuable than all other material possessions. When another accident comes, in which you break your arm or leg, what do you say? "Well, never mind: I am saved." And that which is saved is your own Self, more valuable even than the body.

The Masters have been bringing home to us the fact that the inner Self is the true jewel in the body, the most priceless treasure. We have never known this inner Self. Until we know it, the life being more than the meat, we will not be doing anything for that life.

At present, we consider that our bodies are more than everything, knowing full well that we have to leave them. That is no bugbear, I tell you. But the wise man is he who prepares himself for the change that awaits each one of us, no exception to the rule. The man who "knows himself" is really the wisest man.

We have not cared for that way. Our pursuit has been restricted only to reading the scriptures, and to attending outward observances of certain rituals, ceremonies or forms. Of course, these are the elementary steps we have to take; but that is not the main purpose of our life. What should we do? Just understand the true purpose of life. What is the highest mission of a man? Man is the highest in all creation.

He is next to God. That is what Prophet Mohammed in the Koran says: *God made man and bade the angels bow before him.* So man is higher than even the angels themselves. This is the body, this is the temple of God, in which God resides and you reside. But we have never thought that way. We have simply been looking at the outer man, having outer cleanliness, having good houses to live in and very luxurious furniture. But we have done little or nothing to clean these temples of God (our bodies) from within. We have defiled these temples of God. And whosoever defiles the temples of God is punished by God: *There can be no cleanliness with an unclean heart.*

Cleanliness is next to godliness, of course. We should maintain our bodies clean from outside as well as from inside. *Blessed are the pure in heart, for they shall see God.* We must lead ethical lives, pure lives.

What was given out by Christ in his Sermon on the Mount is parallel to the Eightfold Path of the Buddha; and that is parallel with the *Yama, Niyama* and *Sadachar* rules of the Hindus. That the first step that we have to take. Therein we will also find the Inner Way. He said: *If thine eye be single, thy whole body shall be full of light.*

We have not understood the teachings of the Masters who came in the past. If we but learn how to live up to what the scriptures say, we will have peace on earth and peace hereafter, too. We will have the Kingdom of God on earth, and also the Kingdom of God in the other world, too. *What does profit a man if he gains the whole world, but loses his own soul?*

How do we act in our daily life? From morn till night we are concerned only with the maintenance of the physical bodies of ourselves and of our families. We rise in the morning, answer the call of nature, take some exercise, have a bath, take food and then some go to business, others to their offices, and still others to some sort of labor. The whole day is spent in these pursuits. In the evening we come home. Those married have to take care of their families. Some are sick and need other necessities of life. Some go shopping. At night we take our food and go to sleep. Still others simply eat, drink and make merry. They also go to sleep. That is the usual daily routine we generally have. The next morning the same milling process starts anew. This is how our precious life is frittered away in secondary pursuits. We have no time to attend to the problem and mystery of life.

Masters say: *Well, look here, you have to leave this body one day, it is inevitable. What have you done for that?* We are in great agony. When death overtakes us, we are in agony. If we have seen the fate of a dying man, we must have witnessed the agony of death: crying, having convulsions, etc. No one can help him then. Had he solved the mystery of life, how to leave the body at will, had he known himself by Self-analysis, he would have while alive gone through the experience of death, learned how to rise above body consciousness at will, and he would have just risen to the occasion without any agonizing pain.

Prophet Mohammed says when the soul leaves the body, the pain that man feels may be likened to the dragging of a thorny bush from the rectum through the nostrils. Some Indian scriptures liken the death pangs to a thousand scorpions stinging together. You have witnessed, all of you, how difficult it is to leave the body. Excepting certain cases — very rare cases — say of heart failure, all others have to pass through that agony. If you know how to leave the body at will, a hundred times a day, the Masters say, then death can have no sting.

We ask people: "Look here, dear friend, how have you developed in the spiritual way?" The answer is: "Well, there is no need of it. We will see when we grow old. Let us eat, drink and be merry."

First of all, where is the certainty that you will reach old age? There may be some accident; some disease might overtake you and end your life. Suppose you do reach old age; what then? Your body gives way; your faculties give way; sometimes eyesight is not good; sometimes you are hard of hearing; sometimes you cannot move; sometimes you are bedridden. If you had solved the mystery of life while young, when you had a resolute mind in a strong body, you could have learnt much better.

But you will find you have not paid any heed to this whatsoever. This is the most important, and mostly ignored. A Muslim divine says: *The highest purpose of a man's life is to know himself and know God.* Well, what have you done? If you have known so much of your physical and intellectual things, have you paid any heed to know your inner Self? He says: "Well, what fruit does all that yield? You are a fool. You are not a wise man." A wise man always tries to understand and prepare himself for tomorrow. He prepares for what is going to happen.

Once in India when a certain young man died, his body was carried to the cremation ground. There were about three or four hundred people there, and I was one of them. They wanted me to give a talk, most opportune for the moment.

I told them: "Well, the subject of the talk is lying before you. Something left that body, but that something is still in you. But are you prepared for this change? If not, prepare yourself. Just solve the mystery of life, how to leave the body, how to rise above body consciousness." If death overtakes you, you will be prepared. You will have no sting. That is how you can have victory over death. All of you have to leave your bodies.

The fifth Guru of the Sikhs said: "You see yourselves that such physical frames as ours which others carried, had to be left behind. Where are your forefathers? Where are all those Masters who came in the past? They all had bodies and left them. There can be no exception in your case."

If the government issues an eviction order, that order is carried out, whether you like it or not. There may be some delay in the execution of the order; you might approach somebody and have some concession made. But when the order is issued from God, there is no concession. You have to leave the body and go.

It is wise to learn how to leave the body. What is it that leaves the body? If you have solved that problem, you have conquered the fear of death.

In the *Mahabharata*, the great Indian epic, we have an episode of Yaksha and Prince Yudhistra. When the latter went to a fountain to quench his thirst, Yaksha asked him to desist on pain of death and answer his question first, "What is the most curious thing going on in the world?" Yudhistra answered, "We daily see that people leave behind their bodies which are cremated or buried. We have attended such funeral ceremonies. But we do not believe in the least, nor do we ever take into our head, that we also have to leave the body. People are dying, but we never think that we too shall die." We carry these dead bodies on our shoulders, we cremate them with our own hands. And with all that, we do not have the least thought in ourselves that we have also to leave the body. This is the strangest of all things.

Where are your brothers, your forefathers, and others?

They all lived like you and departed; you too have to leave some day. The wise man is he who prepares himself to leave the body.

That will be the subject for my next talk. In this talk we have dwelt on the higher values of life. The physical body has its own value. This body is a temple of God; maintain it. God resides in every heart; *Visible and invisible too would meet in man.* You have your families as the reaction of the past; maintain them. Love all humanity; that is the second of the greatest commandments that you have in hand. You have intellect; develop it by all means. But even that must perish with the body. *Life is more than meat, the body is more than raiment and all possessions.* But you are acting in quite a contrary way. You consider that the bodies and outer environments are the alpha and the omega of life.

Some people come to me and say: "We do appreciate what you say. We want to know about the mystery of life. We have been in search of that." But when they are asked to attend the discourse, they say: "I have to attend to my job. I cannot come."

I mean to say that for your urgent affairs you have to re-adjust your engagements. When anyone falls ill at home, you take some time off your job. But the highest truth has not taken possession of your hearts. That is the most important thing in life and you have no time for it.

When you leave the body, who is going to help you? If you know your Self, how to leave the body, only then at that time will you be able to leave the body without pain. Somebody who knows that mystery and is competent might be able to help you; but no one else, not even your nearest kith and kin, not even the greatest physician can be of any service.

This is the most important problem of our life. But we

only postpone it to the last. The pigeon may shut his eyes at the sight of an approaching cat; but that does not save him. We too cannot solve the problem of death by turning our faces away from it. We must grapple with it and conquer death or else death shall conquer us.

The end of life must come. That is what the scriptures tell us, that is what all the Masters tell us. But we just do not care. Guru Nanak says: "You are either a child with intellect yet undeveloped or you are stark blind."

The question now arises: Who is it that can help you on the Way? Well, the one who has solved that mystery for himself and is competent to give you an experience of how to rise above body consciousness, opening the inner eye and seeing the Light of God—call him by any name you like.

If you just sit at his feet with a receptive mind and a loving heart, you will succeed in solving this mystery of life. The highest mission of a man's life is to know himself and to know God. But he is engaging in frivolous pursuits. This is seen by those who are awakened and enlightened.

We take the physical aspect as the most precious thing in life. But the awakened one says: "What are they doing? They are not caring for their own real Self. They are not sparing any time for that, and just spending all their hours for the physical body and its environments and intellectual accomplishments."

The reply may be, we have to leave this body, but we are doing everything to maintain it, to procure for it or for its relations every convenience possible. Well, who will tell us what to do then? For that we will have to sit at the feet of somebody who has solved that mystery of life for himself. It is a practical subject.

In the Gospels, we have: *Think not that I am come to destroy, but to fulfill the law.* This fulfillment of the law has ever been, and shall ever be, the mission of all true prophets. This is what all the scriptures tell us. We have been reading all these things. Whenever Masters came, they did not give any thing new to the world. Excellent observers as they were, they saw things in the right perspective and awakened people to Reality. Their clarion call always is, "Awake, O man—what are you doing?"

The Vedas say: *Awake, arise and stop not till the goal is reached.* We are sleeping, as it were. Our superficial life is nothing less than sleep. We are identified with the bodies. We have been receiving impressions from the outside, through the organs of sense, so much so that when we close our eyes we see the same impressions reproduced. When we go to sleep, those very impressions are again reproduced within us in the form of dreams. We live a sort of superficial life, blind to Reality.

We are in physical bodies. We are conscious entities. We are so much tied up with mind and matter that we cannot differentiate ourselves. We have to leave the physical, transcend the astral, go further beyond the causal, supercausal, and reach the true home of our Father. That is the true destination for each one of us.

What have we done for it? We have simply devoted ourselves to the physical bodies and its relationships. This is what the Masters are always telling us. They do not say we should leave the world altogether and sit in the wilderness and follow the life of a recluse. Not the least. They say: "You have physical bodies. Maintain them. These are the temples of God. Keep them clean and tidy from outside and inside." Again, they say: "All right, you have an intellect. Develop intellectually as well. But, remember, you are souls, the indwellers of the bodies. Just know yourself so that you may know the Overself. You will know yourself only when you rise above body consciousness." We are now, as it were, identified with the body. We cannot differentiate ourselves.

So there are different values of life. The physical body has its own value, the intellect has its own, but the spiritual life has the highest of all.

Out of the 24 hours of the day, we pay so much attention and spend so much time for the development of the physical side and its environments and intellectual attainments. We should also devote some time to our development in the way of knowing our own Selves. This is what all Masters have stressed.

Now the question remains: How? All the scriptures speak of the Kingdom of Heaven, and they say that it is within us. How to enter the Kingdom of God? How to open the inner eye to see the Light of God? We will now touch the inner aspect of man. The higher inner possibilities, when we transcend body consciousness, enable us to enter the Kingdom of God.

*There are many mansions in the house of my Father.* There are planes and planes. How to traverse them? That is the subject we will deal with next. How to open the inner eye to see the Light of God of which all the scriptures speak?

I am not advocating any particular religion. You remain where you are. To live in some social religion is a blessing because without it there would be corruption in the world. In the absence of it you will have to form another society. Just follow the right import of the scriptures, what they teach us.

They all tell us to love God, to love all humanity. If you

love all humanity, we cannot rob them, we cannot kill them; other things follow of themselves. Along with that, we must follow ethical lives. We must know ourselves, who we are.

The Sermon on the Mount deals with the outer way of living with your fellow man. Christ also referred therein to the inner light, how to enter the Kingdom of God which is within us. Christ also warns us against the false prophets. They come like lambs, but inwardly they are ravening wolves.

The Masters, who have had that experience with their own Selves, give out all these gifts of God free. They do not charge anything; they are granted free. God's gifts are all free. It is man who sells, not God. This is what has been said by all Prophets and Masters who came in the past.

With all the force of your intellect, you will not be able to follow the right import of sacred writings until you come to someone who has practical experience of this and who is competent to give you a first-hand experience. When you have some little experience that way, then you can go ahead.

Today's subject is over. Next we will take up the Kingdom of God: how to open the inner eye to see it and enter therein. We will see what all the Masters and scriptures have to say on the subject. Lastly, we will deal with the most natural way. There are so many ways and means for that, but we will turn to the most natural way, which even a child can follow.

*Sant Kirpal Singh Ji*
*(1894-1974)*

*Sant Kirpal Singh Ji*
*(1894-1974)*

# 3

# "The Kingdom of God

WHENEVER WE READ religious books or study any subject, there is a certain terminology peculiar to each of them. For instance, in law books, certain terms have a specialized meaning or connotation. If we are conversant with the definitions of the terms used, we are able to under-stand the law properly, and will be able to apply it. If a layman reads the text of the same law, he will not be able to grasp or to apply the true meaning of the law.

We have scriptures, holy scriptures, at hand. Therein we find a certain specialized terminology. Unless we are conversant with it, we may not be able to understand the true import of the scriptures. For instance, there are certain words used in the scriptures, such as "Kingdom of God which is within you." There is "the Light of God." "If thine eye be single, thy whole body shall be full of Light." These are certain terms peculiar to the English Bible.

Because of the special use of words like these, persons not conversant with them are not able to understand the scriptures correctly. They simply interpret them from the intellectual level; and many phrases like "Light within you" or "God is Light" are interpreted by the intellectual people as meaning intellectual light. But the scriptures tell us: *If thine eye be single, thy whole body shall be full of light.* What is the difference?

---

This the third of four public talks in Philadelphia, Pennsylvania, in 1955. The remaining one follows.

Whenever the Masters came, they gave out the truths in a very simple way, so that even the unsophisticated could understand. But, unfortunately, people with no practical inner experience have interpreted them in a way that makes it difficult for others to understand. If we take up the scriptures ourselves and read them, we will find their language always very simple. But the task is rendered difficult if we study them in the light of the controversies raised by different intellectual interpreters who have no knowledge of the practical side of things. Working from the intellectual plane, they complicate matters. Those who read the conflicting commentaries on the scriptures become confused and are spiritually unrewarded.

So the task would become easier if you would read the scriptures directly yourselves. I think the best way to understand any scripture is always to read it in the original language in which it was written. If you know the language, you will probably be able to understand better than by reading how somebody else has translated it in the language which you know. A single error in interpretation may alter much of the essence.

The majority of our scriptures were written in a language different from that in which we read them now. When I was in search of truth, I wanted to read the Persian literature of Maulana Rumi, Shams-i-Tabrez, and other Saints of the Middle East. I read the commentaries of highly renowned interpreters and each gave a different version of the same thing. A commentator tends to give the view-point he holds, not what the scriptures — the real texts of the scriptures — convey. And so the persons who depend on these commentaries are liable to be misled. For this reason, I had to study the Persian language thoroughly so that I might be able to read those scriptures in their original form. And I found them different from what the commentators had said.

The Bible was originally written in Hebrew. Later it was translated into different languages. The translators found here and there something which they could not understand correctly and so those who only read these translations run the risk of going astray.

I have had occasion to meet very intellectually advanced people, who were leaders of thousands of men. When I questioned them about something from the scriptures, just for interpretation's sake, they kept quiet or gave some quaint interpretation of their own, on an intellectual level. Their conception of God, soul and scriptures answered to the level of their intellect and interests.

Wherever I speak, I always ask the heads of various sects what they understand by scriptural quotes like *God is Light* and *Ye are the temple of the living God,* etc. But they, not having gone within, interpret "the Light of God" as the light of reason and intellect.

The other day I met the head of a large religious society and questioned him about the significance of words like: *If thine eye be single, thy whole body shall be full of light;* and *The Kingdom of God is within you. It cannot be had by observation.* "Well, does it mean anything?" No reply to that.

The point is, the truths are there in the holy scriptures. The pity is, that not being conversant with what lies within, we cannot interpret correctly.

I have had a series of talks in a church in Louisville. The clergyman in charge was very open-minded and admitted that though what I said was borne out by the Bible and other scriptures, yet he had no practical knowledge of the truths mentioned therein.

What I am telling you is not anything new. It is all there in the scriptures. I simply had the good fortune to sit at the feet of a Master in India who was a practical and perfect Saint. At his feet I learned not only the theory but also the practice—seeing the truth for myself.

When you see things for yourself, you are fully convinced. Generally, what do you find? We take God as a matter of something in the way of feeling or something emotional, or just as a matter of inference arrived at by intellectual striving. All these are subject to error. But the scriptures tell us that we have "eyes and yet see not."

"Blessed are your eyes for they see... many prophets and righteous men have desired to see these things which ye see and have not seen them and to hear those things which ye hear and have not heard them." Our scriptures say so.

Well, what did they see and what did they hear? That is the point. The scriptures tell us God is Light. They saw the Light of God. But where and how?

God made man in his own image, and man made places of worship after the image of man. Churches are nose-shaped. All temples of other religious sects are dome-shaped, like the head, and the places of worship in Mohammedan mosques are forehead-shaped. All these are made after the image of man. What do we keep in them? First, the symbol of Light, and second, the symbol of the Sound Principle. This is only to show to the seekers after Truth that in this temple of the body that you are carrying, you will find the Light of God. This light you can see if your inner eye is opened. You will also hear the sweet symphony of the "Music of the Spheres," as Plato puts it, that is reverberating throughout all creation.

So the physical body is the true temple of God, and after

this image of man the outer places of worship were made, in which you find the symbol of light and sound.

When I was in service, I had a Roman Catholic office superintendent working under me. I asked him to go to the Bishop of Lahore (in Punjab) to ask him about the symbolism of the big bell that is rung in churches. This symbol you also find in all other places of worship, whether they are Hindu or Sikh temples or Jain or Buddhist. (We also find the symbol of light in the churches in the form of lighted candles—which is also a common symbol in all other places of worship.)

I just explained all this to him and asked him to inquire of the Bishop who was considered to be the most advanced in India, what the ringing of the bells stood for. He did go to the Bishop, who replied that it was meant simply to call people to church. But if that were correct, how can we explain this custom in the temples of other religions where every visitor when he enters, tolls the bell? Among the Hindus it is a common practice to light earthen lamps and ring bells at prayertime. These symbols stand for something about which we are ignorant.

When you look within this temple of God—the human body—you find the Light of God. Where to find God? Does He reside in the holy scriptures? The holy scriptures merely contain a very good account of the valuable experiences that the Masters had themselves, within this temple of the body. They saw the light of God within, and heard the Voice of God within. The reading of the scriptures will inspire in us a desire to know Truth.

Does God reside in the holy temples? We have respect for all temples because there we all sing the praises of the Lord. These holy temples are made after the image of man to remind us that God is to be realized within the human body and not outside it.

Where then does God reside? In the true temple of the body. We find in Corinthians: *Know ye not that ye are the temple of God, and the Spirit of God dwelleth in you?*

All is holy where devotion kneels. The true temples are these bodies we are carrying. The whole world is the true temple of God, the earth below and the sky above. There is no place where God is not present.

These temples were made to enable us to sit together and join our hands in prayer to the Almighty. For that reason, we get together in temples. But God does not reside in the temples made by human hands. He resides in this human frame which truly is the temple of God. We must keep it clean and chaste. How clean we keep the temples of brick and mortar, both without and within! But what about the true temple of God—the human body? It must above everything else be kept pure and chaste. In Corinthians we have:

> *Let us cleanse ourselves from all filthiness of the*
> *flesh and spirit, perfecting holiness in the fear of*
> *God.*

But we only defile this temple of God. Again I refer to Corinthians:

> *If any man defile the temple of God, him shall God*
> *destroy; for the temple of God is holy, which temple*
> *ye are.*

These scriptures are all ours. They were produced by the holy Masters who found God within themselves. Whatever experience they had, they recorded for our guidance and help.

Again we find in the Bible: *Now, this I say, brethren, that flesh and blood cannot inherit the Kingdom of God.* The phrase "flesh and blood" signifies the life of the senses. Until we know how to rise above the physical body, we cannot inherit the Kingdom of God. Saint Paul wrote: *Flesh and blood cannot inherit the Kingdom of God. Neither doth the corruptible inherit the incorruptible.*

*The Lord of heaven and earth dwelleth not in temples made with hands.* That is what all scriptures say. This does not in any way mean that we have no respect for the places of worship; we have respect for them because these are the places meant for singing the praises of the Lord, Whom we are enjoined to love, with all our heart, with all our soul, and with all our mind. Because we love God, wherever we sit together and chant His praises, the atmosphere of that place gets charged with the loving devotion of the devotees. But God resides in us; that is the point I am bringing out.

A Mohammedan Saint says: *Whom you worship, Whom you are after, He resides in you and you are seeking Him elsewhere, in the outer things; how will you find Him?* That is what the scriptures and all the Saints tell us.

The body is the true temple of God, wherein God resides. How can we worship Him? The scriptures tell us: *God is spirit and they that worship Him must worship Him in spirit and in truth.*

The elementary steps that we have in all the religions begin with the body. These lead or pave the road to true spirituality, and are helping factors. They are means to the end; they help us, just like a nurse helps in bringing up a child. We have to make the best use of them, and, with due deference to all the social religions and their immense importance to man's social life, we must go beyond them. It is a blessing to be born in a temple but not necessarily to die in one.

I told you earlier that we in the twentieth century are fortunate in possessing the records of the spiritual experience of all the Masters who came in the past. We are fortunate that we have all these words of wisdom, the invaluable records of their teachings, of the experiences they had with themselves and with God. Had we lived before those Masters came, we would have been without them. The only thing that now remains is that we have to view these scriptures in their right perspective; and to begin with we have to learn the terminology of the scriptures. If you read the scriptures under the guidance of one who has had no experience with the Light within, who has not known God as a first-hand experience, it becomes almost impossible to understand the otherwise simple and accessible truths taught by the Masters.

In Revelation it is said; *Behold, the tabernacle of God is with men, and he dwelleth with them.*

Some people will ask: "Where should we find God?" For that purpose, we shall have to look within our own self, which, the seers say, is the true temple of God. We have to make the best use of the scriptures and of the places of worship. We must understand the true import of the scriptures we have, but we cannot do so until we sit at the feet of one who has himself experienced what they describe and is capable of giving us that experience. Only a true Master is competent to give us all that.

What do the scriptures say? Again they speak of the true home of our Father and pray — *Thy Kingdom come.* I am not going to give you examples from all the scriptures; I have simply laid before you the gist of what they say within the short time I have at my disposal in order to bring home to you the truth as it is given in them.

What do we find in our Bible? *The Kingdom of God*

*cometh not by observation. The Kingdom of God is within you.* If we have to enter the Kingdom of God, we have to enter the Kingdom of God within us and not go outside in search of it. Other scriptures say:

> *The Word is beyond all physical perception and limitations.*
> *The Word, the source of all blessings, dwells within the human frame.*
> *If you ascend within, then alone you will experience the Word.*

In the Bible we find: *Whosoever shall seek to save his life shall lose it.* Those who are just leading the life of the physical senses and do not know how to transcend body consciousness will not have everlasting life. But *whosoever shall lose his life shall save it.*

Losing one's life does not mean committing suicide; it means coming above body consciousness while alive. Let me relate to you a sad incident that took place in India due to an ignorance of the real meaning of the scriptures. We read in the Bible, that the Kingdom of God is within us. It can be gained by death-in-life or in other words by taking a new birth for we have in the scriptures: *Whosoever loses this life shall have life everlasting.* This is what a certain man had read in the scriptures. The ministers had given him to understand that by just dying he would enter the Kingdom of God, for the ministers had no practical experience of the truth given in the scriptures. So what did the poor fellow do? He took a glass of wine and put in it a big lump of opium. He placed it on the table before him and said: "O God, I am now coming to you." With these words he drank the deadly potion, killed himself and thus brought ruin on himself and his family.

This was the result of blind faith in the teachings of blind priests. The scriptures never meant this. Of course, they tell us: *Unless you lose this life, you cannot have everlasting life.* But "losing this life" means just rising above body consciousness at will. It is a practical subject that we can learn at the feet of someone who has had that experience and is a real adept in the theory and practice of the science of spirituality.

Further, it is said; *Verily, Verily, I say unto you, except a man be born of water and of the spirit, he cannot enter into the Kingdom of God.* The scriptures explain the whole thing precisely; provided there is a real teacher to expound it from personal knowledge and practice and be a guide on the Godway.

"Baptism" or initiation at the hands of one competent enough to impart the life-impulse and grant an experience of the beyond is an absolute necessity on the Path of the Masters. By personal attention, the Master can make one rise above body consciousness and give a first-hand experience of the "Kingdom of God" within.

Again, you will find: *Except a man be born again, he cannot see the Kingdom of God.*

The Kingdom of God does not come by observation. It is just a question of "being born again" of the incorruptible seed, "by the word of God, which liveth and abideth for ever."

Again, we have in scriptures: *seek ye first the Kingdom of God, and all these things will be added unto you.* "Seek ye the Kingdom of God" is the first and foremost thing—the rest will follow. Unfortunately, we have been seeking the Kingdom of God without.

For entering the Kingdom of God, and for seeing the Kingdom of God, we have to invert, enter within the temple of the body. We have to tap inside and peep within. It is a regular process of inversion. Our body has been likened to a mansion with ten doors. The outer organs of sense constitute nine of them: two eyes, two ears, mouth, two nostrils, the rectum and the genital organ. These are the outlets of the body. These are the doors with which we live all the time. Besides, there is a tenth door. It is within and latent. It leads to the Kingdom of God. But very few find this out about which it is written: *strait is the gate, and narrow is the way, which leadeth unto Life, and few there be that find it.*

About this, it is said: *Knock and it shall be opened unto you.* But we do not know where and how to knock. This is something practical. The tenth door in the body is the entrance into the Beyond. Until you know all about it, you cannot enter into the Kingdom of God.

How can you find your way to the Kingdom of God within you and not without? You can enter into it and see it only when you are able to rise above the physical body at will. So the scriptures say: *Learn how to die so that you may begin to live.* Bear the cross and the cross will bear you. Though the outward man perishes, the inward man is renewed day by day.

Christ, in unmistakable terms speaks: *Take up your cross daily and follow me.* The life which can be saved, the ever-lasting life, can be had only when we learn to die while alive. Dadu, a Hindu saint, says: *Dadu, learn to die before death comes, for in the end everyone has to die.*

What is death? Death is not something terrible; it is a mere change, a transference from one plane to another. What happens when you leave the physical body at the time of death? This physical body is knocked down. We shake off this mortal coil. As we do not know how to shake it off, it eventually overtakes us and we are overtaken unawares.

We think ourselves to be just the body, and we are attached to its environments. But death comes and we must leave all this behind, and therefore, we are frightened and confused. What is more, we do not know where we have to go or who is going. And as we do not know how to leave the body, we have to pass through the agony of death.

I quoted from Plutarch to you the other day: *The experiences that the soul has at the time of leaving the body at death, the same experiences one has who has been initiated into the mysteries of the beyond.* This is the meaning of "Learn to die so that you may begin to live." And unfortunately this we have not known yet.

Again it is said: *Forsake the flesh for the spirit.* Mark the word "forsake." We live in the physical body all the twenty-four hours of the day. We have the physical body, the intellect, and the soul. We know a lot about the physical body and its environments, our families, our social connections and political affiliations and the like. We have also advanced much on the intellectual side. But we know little or nothing about our soul—the real inner self in us. There are values and higher values of life. Each thing has its own value. *Is not life more than meat, and the body more than raiment?*

I told you the other day that in our daily life we unwillingly act wisely. When a man meets with an accident, and his very costly apparel is spoiled and torn, he says: "Never mind, I am saved." Again, when he is in the grip of a deadly malady and the doctors declare his case hopeless, what does he do? He says: "All right, spend all the money I have so that I may be saved." If there is no money in the house, he says, "Well, sell all my possessions so that I may be saved." Thus the body is to us more than all the possessions we have. Again, if he accidently breaks his leg or arm, he cries out: "Well, never mind, I am saved." This shows that there is something even more valuable than the physical body. This something is the actual life in him—the active life-principle of which he is not yet actively aware, though he feels its presence in him.

In worldly affairs, we act like this. But in spiritual matters we behave quite the other way. We act like little children with all our care for the physical body and its environments, for attaining intellectual advancement. We pay no heed whatsoever to our inner self—the real one in us. Isn't it most strange? This is the grand delusion in which we live through all our life.

The most important aspect of a man's life is his own self, and he does little or nothing in that direction. Whomsoever you meet, you may say: "My dear fellow, have you ever considered this? You have to leave the body some day."

But that is no terror. It is just leaving this body and entering into the Beyond, about which we know nothing so far. And who is it that leaves? That is what I was explaining to you in my previous talk. "Know thyself" has been the theme of all the scriptures. Even the old Greeks and Egyptians inscribed on their temples "Know thyself."

You go to temples so that you may know yourself—not others; not books, religions, social forms, rituals. But they said: "Know thyself." You go to churches only for that very purpose—to know yourselves and to know God.

The human life is the golden opportunity that you have. The highest mission of man's life is to know himself and to know God. If he has not done that he has not achieved the object for which man's life was meant. You may be an excellent engineer, you may be a great astronomer, you may be a famous doctor, you may be anything, but unless you know something about your own self, you have done precious little. Why? Because, after all, you have to leave the body. All your intellectual attainments and all your outer possessions cannot help you towards self-knowledge, which alone shall make easy the passage from this world to the Beyond.

This is the desideratum of all religions. Kabir tells us that this is the only true devotion, the only true religion that you may know how to die while living. And this you will learn at the feet of some living Master who is a practical adept in the line. He will be able to give you a first-hand experience of how to go beyond the body consciousness—how to die while living. Once he gives you some experience, you can develop that from day to day by regular practice, with proper guidance and help which shall be readily given.

This is the most important subject, and unfortunately we have ignored it too long. *Seek ye, therefore, first the Kingdom of God and His justice, and all these things shall be added unto you.* All these things to which we are devoting the major portion of our daily lives will be added, when we seek first of all our own selves.

After all, we have to leave the body. When? Nobody knows. No time is fixed that we know. The sooner we solve the mystery of life, the better, because who knows when the time may come for us to leave the body? Each one of us has to leave the body. That is no bugbear, I assure you. Certainly, it is a change but is no calamity. I assure you it is only for the better, if we know how to leave the body.

These are the things we read in the religious books, all

our life, but we have not cared about them because we have had no knowledge of their inner meanings so far. Our social religions teach us only to observe certain rituals, certain ceremonies, the daily recitation of hymns, offering prayers, and adopting particular modes of life. These are the elementary steps, no doubt. We cannot ignore them. But these are only meant to pave the way to spirituality, and not spirituality in its true sense.

What then is spirituality? To know oneself—who you are, what you are. Are you this five or six-foot high physical frame of flesh and bones or something else? Certainly you are not the body nor the senses nor the vital airs, all of which constitute the outer man. You are the indweller of the body. You possess the senses and the vital airs as aids in your physical existence. The time does come when you have to leave the body, and all the rest. You must know the inner man that you are. Until you know the inner man, you are lost.

That is why it has always been stressed: *Verily, verily I say unto you, if a man keeps my sayings, he shall never die,* and *The last enemy that shall be destroyed is death.*

How can we destroy the all-powerful death? By knowing how to leave the body while alive, at will; this is what all the Masters stress.

What is death? It is simply "leaving the body." If you know how to rise above body consciousness, naturally the sting of death is gone, all fear of death is vanished.

The holy books of the Sikhs say: *If you are afraid of death, just go to the feet of some Master.* He will tell you how to die while living. He will give you an experience of death in life.

Everybody wants to live on. Guru Amardas, the third Master of the Sikhs, tells us:

*Everybody is afraid of hearing the name of death.*
*Why? First, we do not know how to die. Secondly,*
*we do not know after death where to go. And third,*
*we do not know ourselves that we have to leave*
*the body. These are three things which awe us, and*
*cause us to dread dying.*

God gave us different vestures of the body—physical, astral, causal and super-causal. We find that the macrocosm is in the microcosm, on a miniature scale in the body. At present we are identified with the physical bodies so much so that we cannot differentiate ourselves. We pass our lives in the enjoyment of the senses, never given to understand what it is to die while alive.

In our places of worship, this ought to be the most important subject to be taught, but this point is never even touched upon. We are simply told to observe certain rituals, certain rites, certain forms, this and that; and we shall be saved.

But with all this, we are still where we were. If we acquired great learning, will we retain it after death? If not, we remain as ignorant after death as when alive. Death by itself does not mean heaven. It does not make gods of us all.

Now what should we do to conquer death? Guru Amardas tells us: *Just sit at the feet of a Master-soul by whose favour you may learn how to transcend the body.* When you have learned to transcend the body at will, you become a conscious co-worker of the Divine plan. If you know how to die while living, if you know this much, you will have life ever-lasting.

So this is what our scriptures say—this is the way by which we can overcome death. If we know it, we are prepared for it. I know I have to leave Philadelphia, I am prepared for it, and ready to leave at any moment.

During the last war, an Indian Air Force pilot was given six hours notice to prepare himself for the front. In panic he came to me and said: "Well, please tell me how to die." He was panic-stricken for he was not prepared for death.

My point is, if we are prepared in advance, then there is no danger. Fore-warned is fore-armed. After all, we have to leave the body one day. When death overtakes us, can we do anything at that hour? If you are prepared for death, there is no fear, no panic.

I will tell you of an instance in India in 1919. There was a friend of mine in Peshawar. At that time influenza was sweeping the country. I went to see him. He was then reading a book on Yoga. When I asked him what he was doing, he said since death was overtaking everybody, he was reading that book to find the Yoga-way. "I may as well learn something about life after death and am reading a book on Yoga," he added.

I told him: "Is it not too late now? How can you begin to dig a well when you are dying of thirst?" A week after this conversation I went to see him again. It was Sunday and the gentleman lay on his death-bed. My words had proved true. It had indeed been too late.

This is the most important thing in life, the most important subject, but we have ignored it altogether. *Seek ye first,* say the Masters and we have not even made it the last. We have simply been ignoring the great importance that all the scriptures attach to this subject. A saint of the East has said: *All must die at the time of death, but thou, my friend, learn to die while living.* If you are prepared in this way death may strike at any moment and you are prepared for it. Once you have traversed the inner planes, you know where to go after leaving the body.

Maulana Rumi says: *Look here, be not afraid of death, for death is not the end of life, and thou hast bodies more than just the physical.* We are at present working through the physical bodies and sense-organs. We feel that outer life is the only reality. If we learn to leave the physical body, work in the astral body through astral sense-organs, we will come in contact with the astral world, just as we are with the physical world. He who can transcend that way, why should he be afraid of death?

This is no miracle I am telling you about. This is a practical subject, which can be learned just as any other science. And I think this is by no means a very difficult one. Why? In other things, when you have to learn, you have to begin with some hypothesis and then work up to the solution. But this way—an adept giving you a first-hand experience of transcending physical consciousness—is direct. Who are the true Masters—their qualifications and their competence— and how can we distinguish the genuine from the spurious? This subject will be discussed in my next talk.

Coming back to our present theme, all that I say is how the scriptures have put it. Rumi says: *Don't be afraid, because you have another body to live in.*

Again, he lays much stress on it. He says: *Look here, poor friend. Die while you are alive, if you would like to have the true profit of a man's life.* That we also find in the scriptures. *What does it profit a man if he gains the possessions of the whole world and loses his own soul?*

I do not mean that you should leave the world and go to the wilderness and lead the life of a recluse.

God has given you physical bodies. Maintain them. These are the temples of God. Maintain your families. Fulfill your duties. God resides in every heart. Others, as members of your family, have come in contact with you as a result of your past karmas about which you are not aware. God brought you together. Maintain your relationships. By love serve one another. Do all that you can do in that way. This is an essential step.

Earn your livelihood by honest means, by the sweat of your brow. This is also part of the show. You must maintain your physical frame. It is the temple of God, wherein you may discover Him—a rare privilege indeed.

The Masters have said: *You have intellect. Develop it, become intellectual giants. But you are souls. You must know about your own Self as well.* They simply say, out of 24 hours of the day, you should devote some part of it in search of your own Self. Man's greatest search is man. Just search your Self. When you know your own Self, only then can you know the Overself.

Is there any reality, other than God, which we can under- stand, which is defined by the name of God and so many other names? Truly speaking, we are not really theists. How? When we talk of God, we do so on hearsay or from our knowledge of the scriptures. We have no first-hand experience of it.

Unless we see and experience for ourselves, unless we have a first-hand experience of our own Selves, and come in contact with that Reality, unless our inner eye is opened and we see the Light of God within us, we cannot be convinced. We may read the scriptures. We may come across a Master and hear his words of wisdom on the subject, yet we will not be really convinced. We may accept what they say, and make it the basis of our search for God. But till we see and experience God within ourselves, we can never be fully convinced, and thus become real theists.

But who is to know God? It is our own Selves. Self-knowledge precedes God-knowledge. Until we know ourselves, how can we see God?

This is why so much stress is laid on Self-knowledge. In all the scriptures, ever since the world began, the Masters have always been emphasizing *know thyself.* Unless we know a drop of water, we cannot know the ocean. We may not get full knowledge, but we will have some idea of what the ocean is.

It is the soul that can know God, not intellect, nor physical body, nor sense organs. God is an ocean, a limitless ocean of all consciousness. Our souls are a drop of that ocean. We are conscious entities, conscious beings. Unless we know our Selves, we cannot know God. God will be known only when we know our Selves by a process of self-analysis; who we are and what we are.

Kabir says: *Learn to die at will, a hundred times a day. Transcend body consciousness and enter the Kingdom of God.* This is a regular way.

All Masters have laid stress on this point, but we have been ignoring it altogether. We think that by observance of the outer forms, rituals and ceremonies we can reach God. They are helping factors, no doubt; but Self-knowledge is the real road that leads to God. Only then shall we come to know God.

Let me give a concrete example. Once in Lahore, there was a man who loudly proclaimed God, His generosity, His love and His Infiniteness. However, he had not had any practical experience of God and what he taught was mere hearsay from the scriptures. Then came the partition of the country into India and Pakistan, entailing great hardship on the people. He lost his possessions and many of his relations were killed. When he met me again in Delhi, he asked me if there really was a God, after all. And how many of us are like him?

When misfortunes overtake us, we begin to question the existence of God.

But if we have had a first-hand experience of God, then how can we doubt His existence? You see how important it is to have practical experience of Reality, and that you can have only by self-analysis, by knowing your real Self. Unless you do that, you cannot see nor enter the Kingdom of God.

The question again and again arises: "How can we know the Self?" You have seen the difference in faith born of firsthand knowledge and that arrived at by belief in hearsay. Seeing is believing. Direct perception is far better than inferential knowledge. That is why the scriptures say: *Blessed are they that see. You have eyes and see not.* All the scriptures say that there is a Kingdom of God and that it is within you. You can enter the same and see the Light of God if you transcend body consciousness. The Kingdom of God cannot be had by observation; it can only be had by inversion, by tapping inside, as Emerson puts it. But how to tap inside? This experience you will have, as I have said repeatedly, at the feet of a Master—an adept in science. He will give you at the time of initiation some experience which you may develop by daily practice. You may learn how to leave your body. Until your inner eye is opened, you cannot see and be convinced. *Truly, we have eyes and see not.* Guru Nanak says: *He is not a blind man who has no eyes on his face, but one whose inner eye is not open to see the Light of God within.*

How many of us are there who are not blind? We have heard about the Light of God. Have we ever seen it? Can we see the Light of God, and how?

Again I refer to the scriptures. Most of the sayings are taken from the Bible, as you are most familiar with it. However, let me tell you that Christ belonged to the East where the people are more conversant with the spirit. If you only learn those scriptures through the eyes of an Easterner you will come nearer the Truth. I do not mean that the West is in any sense opposed to or different from the East. What I mean is that the terminology of the Holy Bible is Eastern. Therein it is said: *It is better for thee to enter into life with one eye.* With one eye? We have two eyes. What does Christ mean? He says further:... *rather having two eyes and be cast into hell-fire.*

When I was on my way from Chicago to Washington, in the plane, some children came to me for autographs, which I gave them. An old lady also came up and said: "Will you please write something for me and give me your autograph?" I simply wrote these words: "It is better for thee to enter into life with one eye" and signed it. She read it. She wondered what could it mean? Her son was a bishop. He was also travelling in the same plane. She took it to him and asked if he could explain it. He read it exclaiming: "It is from the Bible, of course." But even he could not understand its meaning. Practical knowledge is different. To ask people to observe certain rules and regulations, rituals and ceremonies, is something else. The bishop asked one of my companions if he could talk with me. He was of course welcome. He came over to me.

The words I quoted are from the scriptures. I am not telling you anything new. They are not given in the Bible only, but in all other scriptures of which you probably know very little. If you are broad-minded and interested in the subject, I would suggest that you undertake a comparative study of different religions to find Truth, but not for finding fault with them for then you will gain nothing. The kite though it soars high in the sky, yet its eyes are fixed on the carrion flesh. If you begin to look for flaws, you will be able to find fault with everything; but you will miss the truth.

Kabir, a great saint of the East says: *It is not the scriptures that are false, but they who do not understand them.* Christ says: *The light of the body is the eye. If thine eye be single, thy whole body shall be full of Light.* The "Single" or "one eye"—in the East they call it the third eye, or the latent eye—is in each of us, even in the blind who have no outer sight. But the single eye is closed. We have to open it. When it is opened, you see the Light of God which is already within you. You do not have to create it.

Some people simply visualize. They light a candle, they look at it, and imagine it within. You need not visualize any such thing when you enter this temple of God—the human body. You will see the Light of Heaven within you. It is already there. You are not to visualize, not to pre-suppose, not to imagine.

These are concrete facts, which are experienced by those who enter this temple of the body, such as you have. The difference is that you are leading an external life and have never known how to invert and tap within.

The fact is as Jesus says: *But if thine eye be evil, thy*

*body is full of darkness.* The Light is there. It has been there. But do we see it? Have we ever heeded the solemn warning? *Take heed that the Light in you be not darkness.* It does not mean that you will have to create the Light. It exists already. You must see that it is not darkened. How can the Light be darkened? Merely by not paying heed to it, by externalization, by neglecting the inner life, if you could abstract yourself from the outer world, you would see the Light of God, here and now.

God is everywhere. The Light of God is everywhere. The whole world is made of Light, but only for those whose inner Eye is opened.

How to open that Eye? This is a practical question. These things are explained by others too, besides Christ. Tulsidas and Guru Nanak tell us that only a true Master can put us on the way to God. What can he give to us? He opens our inner Eye. He enables us to see the Light of God. *Take heed, therefore, that the Light which is in thee be not darkness.* That is what we read in St. Luke. But how to find that Light?

In the East we are told that there are two ways in this life. One, called the "Pire Marg," a very beautiful way, and the other, "Share Marg," very dark and narrow to begin with. When you enter the way of the world, you are lost and reach nowhere. But if you were to go the other way—the way of the spirit within you, you may have to start in darkness; but ultimately you will enter the Kingdom of God. The Gospels express it very simply: *Strait is the Way.* And when that opens up, you will find worlds and worlds within you.

There are two ways in this life. One taking us into the outside world, away from the Kingdom of God, the other taking us within towards the Kingdom of God. One leads to death, the other to life.

That is why it is also said: *Enter ye in at the strait gate.* This you will find in Matthew: *For wide is the gate, and broad is the way, that leadeth to destruction, and many there be which go in thereat. Because strait is the gate and narrow is the way which leadeth into life, and few there be that find it.*

There are few who take to the latter course. So Jesus stresses: *Strive to enter in at the strait gate, for many, I say unto you, will seek to enter but shall not be able.* Again, *It is easier for a camel to pass through the eye of a needle than for a rich man to enter into the Kingdom of God.*

This then is the way to enter into the Kingdom of God within you. This then is the way to open the Inner Eye.

At present you see two eyes. How to have the Single Eye? It is a practical matter which you have to learn at the feet of some competent Master, who can, by giving you the preliminary lift, enable you to have that experience from within. The Gospel compares it to the lighting of a candle: *If the whole body, therefore, be full of Light, having no part dark, the whole shall be full of Light; as when the bright shining of a candle doth give thee light.*

Now you may understand the significance of the lighted candles placed in churches; they symbolize the Light within. The Master enables you to see that real Light. That is why we are told about the Masters who came in the past that they could cure the blind—physical blindness in some cases perhaps, but for the most part spiritual blindness, the inability to see the Light of God. Jesus further says: *Blessed are your eyes, for they see, and your ears, for they hear.* We have eyes and see not and ears that hear not.

This is what the scriptures tell you. There is the Inner Eye to be opened and also the Inner Ear to see the Light of

God and to hear the Voice of God which is reverberating throughout the creation.

The subject of this talk was: Where is the Kingdom of God, where to see the Light of God, how to enter the Kingdom of God, and how to see the Light of God? All is within you when you rise above body consciousness. As long as you are leading this physical life of the senses, you are identified with the body; you do not know how to transcend the body consciousness, to open the Inner Eye and the Inner Ear; you cannot see the Kingdom of God or the Light of Heaven and you cannot hear the Voice of God. You can learn all these things when you sit at the feet of some competent living Master. But Christ warns us: *Beware of false prophets, which come to you in sheep's clothing, but inwardly they are ravening wolves.*

The world today is full of pseudo masters so much so that the people are fed up with the very word "master." Men are willing to sacrifice everything—their money, their possessions, just to see the Light of God. They are fed on hopes and promises and then they are told that they are as yet not fit for the way. Ultimately, they find that those "masters" (so called) are after material wealth like themselves; they lead the same life of the senses as themselves. Naturally this causes revulsion and the people say that masters are all a hoax. This is only an erroneous result of the sad experiences that they have had.

All the gifts of nature are free. Spirituality is also a gift of God, not of man. Why should it be sold? It is not a marketable commodity. Knowledge is to be given away free. Do we have to pay for the sun that shines on all of us? Why then should we pay for the knowledge of God? It is God's gift, and it is to be distributed free and freely, so no true Master will ever accept anything in return. He gives freely.

Once, some people in America wrote to my Master in India; "We have sufficient worldly wealth. We will give you this wealth, and in exchange, will you kindly give us the wealth of spirituality?"

What did he write? He replied: "Spirituality is God's gift, and all His gifts are free. This too will be given free. I don't want any material wealth in return."

What does a spiritually rich man care for worldly riches? But many of the so-called masters have made it a source of profit. I have had occasion to meet some of them. A few do concede their fault, but add that they must live, and living costs money. But it is sinful all the same. You will find there are heads of various sects all the world over, who, we are prone to assume, have reached God. Whether they have reached God or not, is another question. But we do assume that all the religious leaders have reached God. If this be true, then why can they not be friends with each other? Two lovers of wine, two tipplers can sit together in a tavern but two professed God-men cannot even brook the sight of each other.

Humanity is ignorant, and therefore, it is exploited by so-called God-men. We must learn to distinguish the genuine from the false, and find the true Master. He would give us a first-hand experience of the Inner Reality. As Shamas Tabrez, a Muslim mystic, says: *We should be able to see God with our own eyes. We should be able to hear the Voice of God with our own ears.* He should make us see the Light of God and hear the Voice of God; and he would do all this for love and not for money. This is what all the scriptures say and what all true Masters grant.

*Sant Kirpal Singh Ji*
*(1894-1974)*

# 4

# The Most Natural Way

IN CONTINUATION of my talk of last evening, I proceed further. Yesterday I told you that we were here to understand and to have a wider and more purposeful knowledge of the teachings of Christ and other Masters who came in the past. They taught the truth in a simple and unvarnished way which is possible for everyone to understand.

This subject relates to the practical science of the soul which is to be practiced and experienced by all. Even a child, if he is put on the way, can see things for himself. It is not a matter of intellectual unraveling but of first-hand experience; for seeing is believing, and *Blessed are they who see*. True religion begins with the opening of the inner eye to see the light of God, and of the inner ear to hear the voice of God. This was the conclusion we arrived at last evening. As to how to open the inner eye and the inner ear, quotations were given from the Bible and from other scriptures. Truth is one, and the way leading to it is also one. You will find these parallel thoughts in almost all the scriptures that we have with us today.

For the opening of the inner eye and ear, ethical culture is of paramount importance. Ethical life is a stepping stone to spirituality. Right conduct is a prerequisite for spiritual progress.

*Blessed are the pure in heart, for they shall see God.*

---

This is the fourth of four public talks in Philadelphia, Pennsylvania in 1955.

85

Purity of heart is very necessary for a pilgrim on the Path, for without it one cannot see the Light of God and hear the Voice of God. All scriptures speak of it. The Sermon on the Mount is clear enough on this point. In it Jesus deals with the realities of life. References to the "single eye" and the "Kingdom of God within," etc., pertain to the inner life. The inner and the outer are interdependent. Jesus has dealt with both the aspects of life: outer as well as inner. We have therefore to go step by step.

Buddha also laid great stress on right living and enunciated the Eightfold Path of righteous living for his followers. In fact, he never uttered a word about God, as he knew that the God experience would follow of necessity when the ground was prepared. The Hindu scriptures too say the same thing.

I came across a book the other day which a Buddhist scholar brought to me. The author tried to show that Jesus Christ was not unacquainted with the teachings of Buddha. This is a matter for research and not for discussion. Nevertheless, the Christian teachings are almost parallel to the teachings of Buddha, so much so that the two seem to be almost identical.

Ethical life, as said before, precedes spiritual life. It consists of righteous living with life dedicated to the highest ideals: to wit, (1) Chastity or purity in thought, word and deed, for chastity is life and indulgence is death; (2) Universal love or love for all living creatures—in this way the self expands and tries to embrace the totality in one single sweep; (3) service, or service before self, which stems from the great reservoir of love for God, the very source and fountainhead of life; (4) Love and service naturally lead to *ahimsa* or non-violence, even in thoughts and words, what to speak of deeds; (5) Truthfulness—It comes in as a natural efflorescence from the above, for then one begins to be true to one's self. Of truthfulness or true living, Guru Nanak says: *Truth is higher than everything but higher still is true living.* These, then, are the five cardinal virtues or the five aspects of ethical life and these above all else pave the way Godward. Christ emphatically speaks of these in his beatitudes for he himself was an embodiment of purity and love and truth.

Suppose you said that you had reached the higher spiritual planes, that you were the mouthpiece of God, but you were having the qualities of an ordinary man, then how could anyone believe you? That is why Nanak says, *True living is higher still.*

True living is the stepping-stone to having the spiritual experiences which are recorded in the scriptures.

All Masters who came in the past were the children of light. Whenever they came, they gave light to all the world. They came not for one nation, for one country, for one social religion or another, but for all mankind, to lead them back to their Father's home. Whatever they found helpful on the Godway, they recorded in their scriptures. *I am the light of world, he that followeth me shall not walk in darkness, but shall have the light of life,* said Jesus.

All these scriptures are with us. They are all true and contain the experiences with Truth which these Masters had in their lives. When you look into them, you will see that their thoughts are all parallel and at places even the wording is similar. Of course, they used different languages; but the import is the same.

These scriptures or holy books we have to understand. But how? We can do so only at the feet of those who have had the same experiences described in the scriptures. Suppose some people come to visit Philadelphia from abroad. When they return to their different countries, they record in their own particular language what they have seen. If you were to read their accounts, you would find that they agree on the salient features, but in certain matters there may be differences in details—one giving a full description of one particular thing and another omitting the details altogether. If you have seen Philadelphia yourself, you would find no contradictions at all in the various accounts, but if you have not, you may be confused and bewildered and be unable to reconcile the differences in the different accounts. Similarly, the scriptures we have with us are travelogues of those who trod the Inner Way, describing how they rose above body consciousness, what they experienced on the Way, what helped them in their journey, and what retarded their progress. The description of all these things is given in the holy scriptures. Now the man who has himself traveled on the Godway knows what the scriptures are speaking about and can explain them to us, logically reconciling what may appear to be inconsistencies to the novices on the path who have not yet learned to delve deep beneath the surface.

In our last meeting, I told you something about the Light of God and the Voice of God, both of which reside in the temple of God which we are. This is what the man of realization would say, for he has actually experienced these within himself. But it would be quite different with the man of intellect, with no face-to-face realization of the Reality. He, with all his learning and knowledge only of outer forms and formalities, rites and rituals, knows next to nothing of spiritual matters and talks of things empirically on the human level. The man of inner attainment, on the other hand, besides ironing out apparent differences, grants us an experience of the Reality, dispelling all doubts; for when one actually sees things for himself, one gets a deep-rooted conviction born of practical experience.

Christ tells us, *If thine eye be single, thy whole body shall be full of light.* The Light of God is within each one of us and so is the "single eye." But how to develop the single eye and how to witness the Light of God is the problem within us, and none can solve these problems for us but a living competent Master who, like Christ, has had an actual living experience of them in his own person and makes it manifest to us by means of actual experience.

All the scriptures at the most relate to us the spiritual experiences of the Masters: what they have seen within and how. Those who have not had the same experiences cannot even correctly interpret the scriptures to us. They would simply ramble and miss the most important part, for it is not a matter of intellectual grasp. The intellectuals often gather round the Masters, put silly questions to them, but what does the Master tell them? Once some learned people came to Shamaz Tabrez, a Persian Saint. He plainly told them, "My friends, if you see the Midnight Sun, you are most welcome. If not, do not waste your time and mine." The people were bewildered. What could he mean by "Midnight Sun?" They said, "The sun is only seen at daytime, not at night!" The sage replied, "The sun I speak of never sets, and they alone behold its glory whose hearts are pure."

A very similar anecdote is recorded in the life of Guru Nanak, the Indian mystic. One night he declared that the sun was ablaze in the heavens. His family thought that he had gone crazy. When his beloved disciple, Bhai Lehna (who was to succeed him as Guru Angad), came to him, Guru Nanak repeated what he had said earlier: "The sun is ablaze in the heavens." And Bhai Lehna at once said, "Yes, my Master, it is so." "How far has it risen?" was the next question, and he promptly replied, "As far as you make it."

These instances I have quoted from the holy books.

Now I will tell you a similar incident that occurred before my very eyes. My Master, Baba Sawan Singh Ji, once during his last illness asked those around him if people in the neighboring towns could see the sun that he beheld. Everyone thought that he had lost his reason and the doctor in attendance, an eminent Swiss homeopath, declared that the Master was suffering from uremia, i.e., urine poison was affecting his brain.

When I visited him in the evening, he laughed heartily and asked me the same question: "Look here, the sun is ablaze in the heavens. Do the people living in other stations see that?" I told him: "Master, distance is immaterial. A man may be living in America or in Europe. If he were to turn within, he will see the Light of God." "That is right," said my beloved Master.

References to the same Light may be found in the most sacred of the Vedic hymns, the Gayatri Mantra. It speaks of the *savitar* or the sun shining within, and exhorts the religious-minded to attend to the all-absorbing influence of "that glorious orb," but how many of us who daily recite this mantra ever know its significance and practice what the Vedas speak of?

God is light, more brilliant than the light of countless suns put together, a light that is at once uncreate and shadowless, very sweet, very soothing, *a light that never was on sea or land*. It is always there. But externalized as we are on the plane of the senses, we cannot see it. To see it, we must invert and rise above the body consciousness. This is a practical subject.

An incident in the life of Kabir brings out the difference between a merely intellectual and a practical man very clearly. Once a learned pundit came to him for the sake of pointless argument. The sage put him off, saying, "My learned friend, why argue when we can never hope to agree? You speak of something you have not seen, of something you have only read; while I speak only of that which I have seen."

Jesus Christ once said, *Verily, verily, I say unto thee, we speak that we do know, and testify that we have seen.*

One of the Sikh Masters also said the same thing: *Listen ye to the true testimony of the Saints, for they speak of that which they have seen.*

Of course the man who has seen the Reality himself will say, "I have seen it and I know what it is!" He speaks with confidence and conviction. There is force and weight in what he says. When one has experienced what he describes, the words spring from the abundance of the heart and they carry their own testimony. They have about them an air of certainty and definiteness that does not admit of any doubt and suspicion.

Kabir further says, *I tell the people to wake up from their slumber.* It means that we are asleep. But how? The fact is that we are asleep as regards the Reality that is within, because our inner eye has not yet been opened and we have not witnessed the Light of God. We have never risen above the body consciousness, never developed the "single eye" that alone pierces into the Beyond. We are, as it were, asleep from within, and are identified with our bodies and the bodily impressions. We are leading a superficial life on the sensual plane. It because of this that Kabir asks us to wake up from the deadly spell of the senses.

The Vedas also say the same thing: *Awake, arise and stop not until the goal is reached,* meaning thereby that our goal is elsewhere and we are not even aware of it; and that it is high time for us to know of it and strive for it.

Thus we see that even the rishis of old used the very same words as Kabir. Again the fifth Master of the Sikhs stresses the same thing: *Awake, O Traveler! and hasten toward thy destination which is a long way off.* What a long journey we have before us! And yet we have no knowledge of it.

We are all the time confined to and concerned with the physical bodies. But we have to reach the True Home—the home of our Father. We must first come above the physical consciousness. It is from there that the long journey homeward begins. *Strait is the way,* but when once you are put on it you have to traverse further and further. *My father's house has many mansions.* There are many planes and subplanes in the Kingdom of God, which you have to pass through, one by one, before you reach your home. That indeed is the ultimate goal of human life, and all our endeavors must be directed to that end. It does not mean that we should neglect our duties of daily life. It only means that we must wake up from our self-complacency and gradually try to rise to the reality of things and devote some time to knowing the Self within us. This can be done, no matter where we are, what we are, what religion we profess; provided of course we have right direction and proper guidance from a real adept in the line. This is the point that Kabir raised in his discussion with the pundits: "My friends, you think that just by being a Hindu you will reach God. But that is not enough." No doubt, allegiance to a particular religion is no bar to entering the Kingdom of God. All social religions are good in themselves and serve a useful purpose in their own way, yet each will have to work out his own salvation by himself and nobody else can do this for him by proxy. The ultimate aim toward which all religions converge is salvation; but the means to salvation lie within, and we shall have to traverse the way back to God, and that way back is one and one only for all mankind—the way of death in life.

All the Masters who came in the past spoke of this way—the way of inversion or entering within. If we traverse on this way, and learn to die at will—as Kabir puts it, *hundred times a day*—or as a Christian saint tells us that he died daily, then death can have no terror for us and we will not be taken unaware when it comes and will not get lost at the last moment, but smilingly kick off the mortal coil and march ahead as a matter of routine.

Sant Kabir further told the pundit: "I tell the people to remain in the world *and* go to the wilderness. I only tell them to face life and to fight the battle. I only say: Maintain your bodies well, for they are the true temples of God. Maintain your families, for they have been given to you by God's grace. Maintain them. God resides in every heart. Have love for your family, for all the social religions, nay, for all mankind as a whole. This is what I mean when I say: "Remain in the world and yet out of it.""

From where do our attachments arise? They originate with the body. We are attached so much to it that we cannot distinguish our true self. When we have to leave it all of a sudden, we feel lost. Therefore, Kabir says: *Remain in the world, but enter into the Kingdom of God, see the Light of God by opening the third eye or the single eye within. When you rise above body consciousness, you will find this physical frame to be mere dust, a clod of clay.*

*Dust thou art, and unto dust returneth.* You are then cut off from the body from within, and consequently from the outer environments. You will be in the world, yet out of it.

Sant Kabir compares such a life to that of the stately

swan that, living in the water, takes to its wings, soaring high and dry. Nanak speaks of it thus: *So we should live in the world and yet out of it.* But we are simply attached to the body itself. We know nothing beyond this life. We say: "Right here now and forever, eat, drink, be merry, for this life is all in all."

At times the Masters have to tell the truth, bitter as it may sound, in very clear terms because they have love for humanity and they wish all to reach the goal.

When Christ entered the temple, do you remember what he said to the money changers there? "Take these things hence; make not my Father's house a house of merchandise!"

Similarly, Kabir said to the pundit: "O learned man! You are like a maid that has no husband of her own and yet goes about telling other people that she can give them what she has not known all her life. You just try to work upon their emotions by high-sounding words and hypocrisy. But how can you show them the Reality when you have not seen it yourself? If you want to see God, come and follow me."

The truth of the matter is that those who have not seen God themselves cannot make others see. When their own inner eye is not yet opened and they do not see the Light of God within, how can they open the eyes of others or make manifest the Light of God?

Sant Kabir further told the man of learning: "You have frittered away your life and lost life's purpose. The human body occupies the highest place in all creation. It was given to you to know yourself and to know God. That opportunity you have frittered away. You are not only deceiving your own self but deceiving all those who come to you. Had you kept to yourself, it would have been much better; for then you would have lost life's game only for yourself, and not made others lose theirs. You have never married—how can you tell others what marriage is? You have lost your opportunity; why waste that of others? Why are you making others lose their golden opportunity?"

In the Upanishads, a story is told of King Janak, a seeker of Truth. He gathered together all the sages of the time and said, "My dear friends, I want to know the way back to God. Can you teach me its theory, since theory precedes practice?"

It is said that one Yajnavalkya, a rishi, satisfied the king on this account. He got the price fixed for the purpose. But then another sage, Gargi, who had realized the truth, questioned Yajnavalkya: "Look here, O Rishi! Have you seen the Reality that you have spoken of, and expounded so well, with your own eyes, just as you see those cattle grazing in the meadow?" And what did he say? Yajnavalkya, true to his own self, unhesitatingly admitted, "No. I have only understood the theory; I am not a man of realization myself." Naturally, Janak had to search elsewhere for the practical solution to the problem.

We must be sincere. If you have seen the Truth, only then ask the people to follow you. "Dear friend, come and see and have it!" But if you have not seen the Truth yourself, then why, like the proverbial blind man, lead others into the pit along with you? We must be sincere to our own selves and to our fellow men and women. If you only know the scriptures in theory, say so. If you have seen the Light and can rise above body consciousness, and are also competent to give others some experience of it, well and good. Go and tell the people so.

You see, that is the difficulty. People speak so much about the scriptures. You must have heard so many speakers holding forth on the subject. But how many of them are there who have had the first-hand experience of Truth, and are competent to give you also that experience? To talk of spirituality is just like giving a learned discourse on the principles of business without having any capital or practical capability to start the business.

While here, each morning people sit for meditation and get some experience of the inner Truth. When you get experience inside, however elementary it may be, you are convinced of the Reality and can develop it to any length you may like, by regular practice.

Preaching was meant to be done only by those who had the first-hand experience of Truth. But preaching has become a source of income; and paid service in all social religions has made matters worse. I am not talking of any particular religion, but what I say is true of all religions. People have made a business of religion and so many have taken to it just as a means of livelihood.

But God's gifts are all free. They pretend to serve Him, but at bottom it is all mercenary. The world is full of them and that is why we are fed up with the very word "Master." But a real Master does not seek worldly gain. He gives God's gift—spirituality—freely and free of cost. He has realized God. He is the perfect man. He has transcended the physical consciousness and has seen the Light within. What did Kabir tell the pundit? "O learned pundit, if you want an experience of the Reality, go to some competent living Master."

"What sort of Master?" asked the pundit. Then Kabir went on to define "Master" as one through whom God speaks. This is what all the Saints, including Kabir, have said.

Thus we have in the Bible: *Holy men of God spake as they were moved by the Holy Ghost (II Peter 1:21)*. Guru

Nanak says, *Poor Nanak only speaks what he is bidden,* and *O Lalo! I only say that which my Lord speaks through me.* A Muslim divine also says the same thing: *The words of the Prophet are the words of God, though they may seemingly appear to drop from a human tongue.*

You too have the same possibility in you. But you have not yet come in contact with the Power working in you, because you are still bound to the physical body. As long as you do not lose this body consciousness, you cannot enter into the Beyond. The Bible says, *Flesh and blood cannot inherit the Kingdom of God.*

You must seek out one who has risen into cosmic awareness and is a conscious co-worker of the Divine Plan. He will no doubt be a man like any of you. But he has realized his own Self and experienced God within. When you sit with him, you will find him quite a different being, full of love and compassion for all: a radiating center of the Divinity in him. The very atmosphere around him is charged with the radioactive rays of spiritual bliss.

A man who has attained the highest degree of mastery in any field of activity will at first appear like an ordinary man. He is essentially a man first and last. But he has developed in his own particular way. When you sit with him, you will find him a giant in his own field. This is exactly the case with a Master-soul. When you meet him, you will find him just like any other man at first sight. He himself will tell you: "I come to you as a man to man. I am a man just like you. I had the good fortune to sit at the feet of my Master and progressed in the spiritual way. Those who are in search of the Godway are most welcome."

A doctor is a man first and then a doctor. An engineer is a man first and then an engineer. Similarly, a spiritual man, a Master, is a man first and then a spiritual guide.

All possibilities are within man. Great is man. He who has developed in a certain line and has an experience of it, is able to guide you also if you are seeking the same way.

I told you in our meeting the day before yesterday: *Is not life more than meat, and body more than raiment?* And yesterday: *Seek ye first the Kingdom of God.* That is what I emphasized: *Seek ye first,* i.e., that this is the most important thing in life, the thing that concerns you most.

*Know thyself* has been the theme of all the Masters who have come so far. Know about yourself and not about others, they said. Know thyself: who you are and what you are. That is the most important thing before us. Those who have known themselves—call them by any name you like—will be able not only to put you on the way but give you some experience of the way. Then you can go ahead. That is why Sant Kabir asks us to seek such a man. That man is not an ordinary man, 1 tell you. He has of course a human body like any of us. But he has come in contact with the Truth within and become its mouthpiece. *Holy men of God spake as they were moved by the Holy Ghost.* What they say is not premeditated; it is all unthought of from the human level, and as Emerson puts it: *The thoughts which come of themselves from within are always perfect.* The Master is not the physical entity. He is the Divine Power working at the human pole. What did Jesus say? *Lo, I am with you always even to the end of the world. I will never leave thee nor forsake thee.* This is what all the Masters say. I am not going to quote you references from the various scriptures, but am only giving references from the Bible because you are so conversant with it.

The Master Power never leaves you. It not the human body but the power working through it that remains forever.

Christ Power has been working through the ages and shall continue to work; but through different divine instruments and according to the needs of the times. The body alone perishes, but that Power remains. Those who have really seen the Truth within can open your inner eye and make you see it. If they give you some inner experience, however little it may be, you can develop it. One of Christ's parables illustrates this beautifully: A rich man going out on a journey distributed among his servants some talents—twenty to one, ten to another, five to the third. When he came back, the man who had had twenty talents had made them thirty, the one with ten had made fifteen of them, and the last who had gotten only five had never touched them but had kept them safe buried underground. As no use was made of them, the Master thought it prudent to withdraw them. What I mean to say is, that when you are given some experience, you have to develop it as you do your learning in a school. Initiation does not mean observance of any ceremony, or ritual, or anything of the sort. It is just a practical experience of the science spiritual. The theory is explained first, and then the experience is given, and that is to be developed from day to day. That Master Power overhead which gives the experience protects both within and without, and keeps a constant watch over the disciples.

You will find that such people have been coming to the Masters and asking them as Philip asked Jesus: "Lord, show us the Father and it sufficeth us." And what did he reply? He grew indignant and said, "Have I been so long time with you, and yet thou hast not known me, Philip? He that hath seen me hath seen the Father; and how sayest thou then, Show us the Father? Believest thou not that I am in the Father, and the Father in me? the words that I speak unto you I speak not of myself: but the Father that dwelleth in me, He doeth the works."

Christ was a conscious co-worker with the Father or Divine Power within him. Only he who is conscious of the Power working through him can bring you in contact with the Power within. That contact is possible only when you rise above body consciousness and not otherwise.

It is something quite apart from intellectual activity. Intellectual attainments may serve as an additional aid to a practical man, for then he can explain to you the same thing in so many ways, very graphically. But the man who is only intellectual with no practical inner experience is, as Sheikh Saadi, a Muslim Saint, rather strongly puts it, *an ass carrying a heavy load of books, quite ignorant of their value.*

A Sikh Master has said the same thing in a milder way. He says, *The ladle moves briskly in the pudding but never tastes its sweetness; even so you revel in an intellectual knowledge of the scriptures, but have never experienced what they describe.*

This does not mean that you should not read the scriptures. Reading is a help. Those who have entered the field of the intellect and are determined to know the why and wherefore of things, ultimately find the way. But the way that they have to follow is the same that the unlearned follow. The path is the same for all mankind and it begins when you rise above the physical plane and that, as said so often, is a practical subject.

To have intellectual attainments is also a blessing. Once it so happened that Keshab Chandra Sen, the learned head of the Brahmo Samaj in India, went to Ramakrishna, a man of realization. He went to him just for the sake of understanding things, and Ramakrishna told him, "If you are ready to learn by a few words, then come to me. And if many, go to my disciple Vivekananda."

Intellectual knowledge is a good thing in itself. It is a feather in the cap of a practical adept, but with some people it becomes an obsession and they not only deceive themselves but they also deceive others, for they have no access inside.

When the Masters come, they tell us of God and the Godway. They remind us of the Reality within. Man is the teacher of man. Can past Masters help us? Yes, we do need them. They are helpful in their own way. We have respect for them, because they gave out the Truth and their experiences of it. Those who came in contact with them were put on the way, and they also realized the same Truth. The scriptures are the treasures of the experiences that they had with their own Selves and with God and we are fortunate to have them with us today.

If we had come two thousand years earlier, we would not have the New Testament with us and I would not have given you these beautiful quotations from it. All scriptures deal with the same Truth. But we are familiar with one or another scripture only. When I quote the Bible to you, you have no difficulty. So it is with people of other faiths. They follow easily what is said, when I offer quotations to them from their respective scriptures. All these scriptures make my task easier, as well as that of my listeners. The sacred books are just handy aids in the hands of a man of realization for they all deal with the selfsame subject, viz., God-realization.

What we need is someone who has the experience within himself of what is spoken of in the scriptures, and who is competent to give us some taste of that experience right now. Call such a man what you will—*pir, murshid,* Saint or Master—that is immaterial.

We have respect for all such persons who came in the past or who are here now in the present age. Those who have seen the Reality can put us on the Path and give us a first-hand experience of it. The need of such a Godman has been felt ever since the world began.

Some people say that they don't need any Master. Well, they will have to rely on books, the holy scriptures. These scriptures are, of course, more reliable than the intellectual commentaries on them by the learned. If the commentators have seen the Truth, they will interpret the scriptures correctly, but if not, they will confound and confuse the reader in spite of all his wits and will lead him nowhere.

When you rely solely on books, you ultimately rely on some Master, for the scriptures were after all written by somebody. Instead of this indirect approach, would it not be better if you could meet a man of realization directly? He has practical experience of what the scriptures describe and can give you much more than you can ever get from books; he can give you first-hand experience of the Reality itself. This aspect has been stressed by all the Saints. They enable us to understand how we may have that experience in our lives. In the Gospel of Matthew we have, *All things are delivered unto me of My Father, and No man knoweth the Father save the son, and he to whomsoever the son will reveal him.* Thus, the son knows the Father and the Father knows the son, and all others to whom the son reveals Him, for he becomes a conscious co-worker with the Father, on the Divine Plan. This is why Christ said: *I and my Father are one. It is not I that am doing it. I am the way, the truth and the life. No man cometh unto the Father but by me. If you had known me, ye should have known my Father also.* In what a forceful way he has put it: Through the man who has known the Father (God), you can also know God.

The alphabet of the teachings of the Masters starts where the world philosophies end. That is the beginning of true religion. It begins when you come above body conscious-ness and not before.

Naturally, the man who has experience of the Truth is the only one competent to put you on the way. You may be able, in the company of such a righteous man, to understand the true nature of things, the real significance of what is highly abstract.

So all Masters who have been coming from time to time have been giving out the Truth. The question now arises: what sort of *yoga* (spiritual discipline) do they teach? We have so many yogas, so many ways of coming to the home of our Father, to reach the state of unchangeable permanence, all peace, all joy, all happiness, which never decays and is not subject to Dissolution or Grand Dissolution.

That was the goal which we set before us in our first meeting. I also gave quotations from different scriptures. The ultimate goal of all religions is God. We are worshipers of the same God, no matter whether we belong to one country or the other, East or West, to one religion or another; for that makes no difference. All religions say the same thing: *Love God;* and further, as God resides in every heart, *love all humanity.* This is the best way of leading our outer life. If followed naturally, the Kingdom of God would surely come on earth—for which we so often pray but are disappointed.

Next we have to enter into the Kingdom of God, reach our true home. The way to it starts when we rise above body consciousness. But how are we to achieve this? All scriptures speak of the Way that leads back to God. We have to find this Way.

There are so many different methods that we may follow! But which of them is the most natural, the most easy and can give us the quickest results?—so that we can realize the

Truth in this very life and not have to wait till after death.

I met a man in California who came to me and told me that his Master had said that his inner eye had been opened. I asked him if he saw anything within, to which he said, "No." I asked him, what made him believe this? He replied that his Master had said so and therefore it must be so. I advised him not to follow blindly but to see things for himself.

Another man came up and said, "My Master says I will have salvation after death." But I asked him, "Where is the proof that you will have it?" People are after Truth, I tell you. I quite see the search for Truth everywhere in the world. Men have been seeking for Truth for years and years, through books, through rituals, and through countless other means. But they have not gained practical experience of the Reality.

I met a very learned man in San Francisco; he is the organizer of all the international religions conferences that are being held now in Japan, France, Germany, and other places. He heard one of my talks in which I dealt with this subject. At the end he admitted that what I said was true and that he had not seen the light within. The people are after it, no doubt, and many of them are quite sincere, broadminded and open to conviction.

The question arises: Of the many yogas, which is the best, the quickest and easiest, and the most suited to our times?

The Masters teach you the most natural way. Natural ways are the easiest. Easy things can be followed by anyone anywhere. Even a child should be able to see the Light of Heaven within.

There are so many yogic practices: We have Hatha Yoga. It gives us physical fitness, a strong body, for one thing; and for another it prepares the way for another type of yoga, the Prana Yoga. Prana Yoga gives control over the respiratory system in the body, and enables one to withdraw the motor and sensory currents together to the seat of the soul within. The body is simply left as a clod of earth, without breath or motion; this is technically called *kumbhak*. When we achieve this withdrawal of the pranas (vital airs), we see the Light of God and hear the Voice of God within. This is a difficult and arduous way. Everyone is not fit for it. Everyone cannot follow it. The body must be sound and strong. For this we have to take to the Hatha Yoga practices for a long time to make our body fit, and then we can take it up. Those who are physically unfit, if they take it up, they fall a victim to different diseases.

Next there is Laya Yoga, which is concerned with the awakening of the *kundalini* or the serpentine power. That is also practiced through controlling one's breathing. We have to awaken all centers in the body and go up step by step.

There are other forms of yoga as well, which enable one to control his mind. They ask us to visualize within some outer object so that we may have something to concentrate our thoughts upon.

Then there is Jnana Yoga for grasping the reality within by the sheer force of intellect—a very difficult path indeed, I may say.

Brihadaranyaka Upanishad says, *To grasp the infinity by the finite intellect is as impossible as to quench thirst by taking wine or to extract oil from sand.*

How can the finite intellect grasp the all-pervading Reality within its narrow compass? That is a sheer impossibility. This is why Confucius said: *The reality is something which cannot be grasped, cannot be understood and cannot be comprehended.* This is why he turned from the spiritual to the ethical side of life.

Can we possibly come in contact with that Reality? All the Masters with one voice emphatically say, "Yes!" Guru Nanak says, *The Lord God of Nanak is visible everywhere.*

Swami Vivekananda, who came to America some years ago, began life as an atheist. He would challenge people to show him God. He would question: Is there anyone who has seen God? He was told to visit Dakshineswar (in Bengal) and meet Ramakrishna Paramhans.

He went there, all puffed up with his intellectual attainments. Ramakrishna appeared to him like an ordinary man. You see, the Masters do not act and pose. They do not believe in any show. They just behave like ordinary individuals. He found the sage first on the grassy plot adjoining his hut and put to him his oft-repeated question: "Master, have you seen God?" And what was the reply? "Yes, my child, I see Him just as I see you—only more vividly." At these words coming from the heart of a man of realization, Vivekananda bowed down. And throughout the rest of his life he always declared, "Only through that Godman was I saved."

How then is salvation possible? All Masters say, *If thine eye be single, thy whole body shall be full of light.* For salvation then we must develop our "single eye." But how to find it and how to develop it?

Guru Nanak tells us that the "single eye" spoken of is not of flesh and bone, as are our outer eyes. It is the inner eye— the eye within you. And this is to be opened. But how? One who has his own eye opened and has seen the light of God is also capable of giving you first-hand inner experience of it. Seeing is believing, and when you see for your own self, you will require no further testimony. On the other hand, the blind cannot lead the blind. An awakened soul alone can awaken souls slumbering on the plane of the senses. As light comes from light, so does life from life. A man of realization can grant an experience of the Reality to others. He who has risen in Cosmic Awareness, can make others rise in that Awareness. So it is not an impossibility. All Masters have testified to this. Shamas of Tabrez says : *We should be able to see God with our own eyes and hear the voice of God with our own ears.* This is no new thing. It is the most ancient science and the most authentic.

Another Muslim Saint, Mojeen-ud-Din Chishti, tells us: *You have to open the inner eye to behold the glory of God within. It is already there.*

A true Christian must know how to cross over the body consciousness to see the Light of God. A true Muslim must witness the glory of God from the top of Mount Toor, which is our body. The prophet Moses used to go up Mount Sinai to hear the Decalogue in the midst of lightning and thunder. Similarly, a true Sikh (Khalsa) is one who sees the light of God in his own person. The scriptures tell us that *Guru* (Master) is one who can dispel darkness in man by revealing the light of Heaven. The Christians figuratively call this spot (where the light is seen) the mount of transfiguration.

This is the goal before us. It is possible and within the reach of everyone. When? When you come in contact with some practical adept. He will be a man as any of you are, but he has inner experience of Truth and is competent to give the same experience to you. If he gives you some experience at the very outset, you can expect more from him.

What type of yoga do the Masters teach? I have just mentioned certain types of yoga. There are other types as well, which enable us to concentrate and dwell on the lower ganglions in the body. They aim at awakening the different supernatural powers thereby. But the true aim of life is to know one's Self and to know God, and not to have supernatural powers. To one who practices the highest type of yoga, by following the Path of the Masters, all such powers come of themselves: one has not to work for them. But a true seeker of God bypasses all such temptations.

What then is the most natural yoga? What do the Masters teach? The Path of the Masters is known as *Sehaj Yoga* (the natural yoga) or the *Surat Shabd Yoga* (the yoga of the Sound Current). What is surat? It is the soul within each one of us, the outward expression of which is the attention or what is known as consciousness, awareness or wakefulness. When you open and close your eyes successively for some time, you will feel a kind of wakefulness and consciousness behind the eyes. This wakefulness or consciousness is the "Self" in you, and that you are. In the waking state it is diffused in the body and is engaged in outer pursuits of the world through the agency of the senses. But it can be withdrawn and concentrated within. The Master helps in withdrawing the sensory currents, collecting them at one center, and gives an inner contact with the "Word Power" within—the divine link in each one of us. This God Power is known by different names. St. John speaks of it as the "Word." It is the "Holy Ghost" of Christ. The Muslims call it *Kalma* or *Ism-i-Azam*, while the Hindu Rishis called it *Sruti* or *Udgit*. Zoroaster gave it the name of *Sraosha* or the "Creative Verbum." Guru Nanak speaks of it as *Naam*. It is the great Creative Power of God which is controlling the Universe. This Sound Principle or "Divine harmony" is the core of all that is.

And what is God? You find the same thing mentioned in the Bible. St. John begins his Gospel with the memorable words, *In the beginning was the Word, and the Word was with God, and the Word was God. The same was in the beginning with God. All things were made by him, and without him was not anything made that was made.*

Dryden, a great English poet, in his poetic fancy calls it "Harmony," and ascribes the creation to the great "Power of Music."

This Word existed even before the Creation came into being.

God the Absolute is Wordless and Nameless. When that Absolute came into manifestation, it was given different names as said before: Word, Kalma, Naam, Sruti, Udgit, etc. This first and primal manifestation of the Absolute (in the form of the Sound Principle) is the Divine Link within each one of us, and this Power is all-pervading and everlasting. *Forever, O Lord, thy Word is settled in heaven.* The Bible further tells us: *By the Word of the Lord were the heavens made.* That is the creative power: *Upholding all things by the Word of his power.* The Bible calls that creative principle the "Word." As I told you yesterday, unless you know the specialized terminology of the Masters, you cannot know the true import of the scriptures. The Word, as used throughout the Bible and especially by St. John, is one example of such terms; and so are many others in different scriptures. That Word is lasting, everlasting and abiding forever and forever: *The grass withereth, the flower fadeth, but the Word of our God shall stand forever.*

The "Word of God" does not mean the words uttered by the Masters. Their words of wisdom simply express the Word of God and its creative, controlling and sustaining power over all that is visible and invisible. This Power existed right from the beginning. *The Word was with God and the Word was God.*

That Divine Link is within every man. The Epistle to the

Hebrews (in the New Testament) speaks of the Word of God as: *For the Word of God is quick* (which means living) *and powerful and sharper than any two-edged sword, piercing even to the dividing asunder of soul and spirit and of the joints and marrow, and is a discerner of the thoughts and intents of the heart.* That power is denoted by the term "Word."

So God is the Nameless or the Wordless One. When that Power came into being and assumed a manifest form,— "God-in-action"—it became the primal cause, the Causeless Cause, of all creation in the higher and lower spheres. And that first manifested form of the Absolute is the only Way back to God.

What we have to do is to contact that Divine Link which is the supporting power of all creation. We owe our very existence to this powerful link within us, which is uniting the radiant soul with the gross physical body. When that power is withdrawn, the connecting link snaps and the soul departs, leaving the body a lifeless clod of clay. This we call death—the dissolution of the microcosm. When this Power is withdrawn from the world, there follows Grand Dissolution.

This Divine Link is in every heart. With that we have to establish contact—a real and living contact. But how? You can find it by transcending physical consciousness. The Bible says, *The Word was made flesh and dwelt among us.* One who is Word personified will naturally be able to join you with the Word within. That Power ever abides in us. It is the Bread of Life, and verily we live by it, though we have never recognized it. Christ tells us, *Whosoever partaketh of this bread will have everlasting life.* He never meant his body but the Word personified and within him. It is often described by the sages as the Water of Life. Christ says, *Whosoever drinketh of the water that I shall give him shall never thirst; but the water that I shall give him shall be in him a well of water springing up into everlasting life.*

But how to get this Bread of Life or Water of Life, that bestows life everlasting? How to sip this elixir? All the scriptures tell us in one voice that it can be had from a living Saint who is an embodiment of this active life principle. It will not cost you anything, not a farthing. It is as much a gift of nature as light, air and water. This experience of Truth you can get through the grace of a living Master, competent enough to contact you with the Divine Link within.

What is this experience like? The Bible says: *If thine eye be single, thy whole body shall be full of light.* And further it says : *Thy Word is a lamp unto my feet and a light unto my path.* That shows there is some experience of light within.

And then there is something else as well—the Sound Principle. *Being born again not of corruptible seed but of incorruptible, by the Word of God which liveth and abideth forever.*

You will have to rise above body consciousness before you can come in contact with that Word Power within. It means an experience of light—the Light of God within you. And this is the beacon light that saves: *The righteous runneth into it and is safe.*

To those who are just put on the Path of the Masters, there comes a marvelous change in their life and conduct. Steadfast in the Power of the Word, they are saved by it and escape from the cycle of births and deaths. The Dissolutions and Grand Dissolution have no effect on them. It is then said: *Man shall not live by bread alone, but by every word that proceedeth out of the mouth of God.* Mark the words *out of the mouth of God.* This experience (revelation of light) comes about by the grace of an adept in the science of spirituality. The Master has to transmit his own life impulse when he puts us on the Way and gives us a contact with the all-powerful, live and vibrant chord within. With this manifestation within, we learn the significance of the words of the Master Christian: *The son knows the Father and those to whom the son reveals.* And again: *The wind bloweth where it listeth, and thou hearest the sound thereof, but canst not tell whence it cometh and whither it goeth; so is everyone who is born of the Spirit.*

What I mean to say is that the Word Power has two aspects: one is of Sound and the other is of Light. This is the natural way. The Masters do not touch the breathing system. They do not invoke the aid of pranas, for the simple reason that pranas have an independent function in the body, and do not in any way interfere with our daily pursuits like walking, talking, eating and drinking. If we can ignore the pranas otherwise, they can safely be bypassed in spiritual sadhnas as well. The work of God can as well be performed without the intervention of pranas or vital airs. They have eliminated that part of the show altogether to make the system easier and in accord with the present times. Even a child, if he is made to sit, is given an experience. He begins to see light and hears the tinkling of bells.

This then is the natural way that is given by the Masters. It is the most suitable for these days. The secret of success lies in the conscious entity within us. The concentration of attention is all that is needed. Whenever a thing is done with undivided attention, the result is sublime. Even physical exercises with an eye on body-building processes will make you strong and healthy. Similarly, when your attention is directed to the centers of the brain, you become intellectual stalwarts. When you fix your attention or soul on the Divine Link within called the Word, you become spiritually great.

Everything can be achieved by the direction of attention. It is why Emerson said, *The key to success is one's own thought.* All that is required is the proper direction and guidance. For this, you need no outer ceremonies and rituals; you can remain wherever you are. The way is within you. The easiest way, the natural way, to go back to God is therefore by means of contact with the Sound Principle.

This is the most natural yoga which befits our times. On account of our short span of life and other inherent infirmities, we are not hereditarily and temperamentally fit to take up the harder yogic ways. There are other ways as well, but this is the simplest, easiest, and the most profitable.

I visited a village in India where a man had been engaged in Prana Yoga practices for over forty years. I went to him. He was a thin emaciated figure. (That type of yoga requires a stout and strong body, for which you must have Hatha Yoga practices and others to make you strong before you take to that way.) His body was so weak that he could not even talk or move easily. On being questioned as to the results achieved in forty years of Prana Yogic discipline, he informed me that at times he would see a streak of light and occasionally hear some sound (indistinguishable) within. Just compare the strenuous labor with the insignificant results achieved! When he was told of the natural way and asked to experiment, his joy knew no bounds and he discovered quicker and better results in shorter time.

What I mean to say is that the natural ways are always easier. The natural yoga does not interfere with the pranic system, which is a complicated affair. I do not deny the efficacy of the prana yoga. But are we fit for it? As explained above, we are not. The Masters, therefore, simply taught: "Let pranas do their own function in the physical frame. Ignore them altogether as one does when engaged in various activities. Withdraw the spirit currents and see within." That is all.

The Surat Shabd Yoga or Yoga of the Sound Current needs Initiation or first-hand experience from some competent Master in the line who is capable of giving some spiritual experience. When he puts you on the way, you see things for your self. If you can have a little from him in the beginning, you can also expect more from him later.

Moreover, the Master being in tune with the Infinite is an unerring guide on the Godway and an unfailing friend both within and without. He has the competency to appear to you within, as some of you had an experience of this morning, and guide you on the inner spiritual planes as well.

A Mohammedan Saint says: *He who can give you instructions outside when on the physical plane, and go up voluntarily while alive, as at the time of death, has the competency to appear to you within and give you guidance there.* Such indeed is the Master!

That is what I have told you. I have not given you any rigmaroles, but facts from the scriptures. Until we come to and sit at the feet of some practical Master, we do not see things for our own selves. When we see our own "Self," no further testimony will be required.

Of course, for that certain prerequisites are necessary. And what are these? To restrict ourselves to a strict vegetarian diet, for the reason that we should have normal lives. The diet which excites passions has to be avoided altogether. It is better to have a light, simple and natural diet, which is an aid to spiritual *sadhna* or practice.

Those who take up the practices concerning the lower centers in the body, do take meat—the Mohammedans and people of other religions also. But those who are anxious to rise above body consciousness and go into the Beyond have of necessity to eschew all that. This is the Path that I have put before you. Liberation or salvation is something which starts only when you rise above body consciousness. For that reason, vegetarianism is the first essential.

Another is that of abstention from intoxicants. You are a conscious entity. You have to rise in cosmic consciousness, and go beyond into the super consciousness. The things which go to muddle your consciousness or make you morbid and lose your consciousness are to be avoided; therefore, leave off all intoxicants, liquors, narcotics, smoking and all kinds of drinks unnatural and artificial.

The third requirement, of course, is good character and ethical life, in thoughts, words and deeds.

These are the essential requirements which qualify a man to tread the Godway. If you do not detach yourself from the above things, your further progress on the way will be retarded. Moreover, even in ordinary life, if you observe these instructions, that will give you a blessedness unknown hitherto.

*Sant Kirpal Singh Ji*
*(1894-1974)*

# 5

# Guru, Gurudev and Satguru

*I have heard that many have seen you. But actually none has known what you really are.*

O SATGURU, myriads upon myriads of people greet you and bow in obeisance at your feet, but few recognize your greatness in the measure in which you may choose to reveal. *Son knows the Father and those to whom the son may reveal.* He is a living embodiment of the Father of Light and it is only through His grace that he manifests this Light of God in others. I shall now tell you what the Guru is. It is best to know of him from some Gurumukh, that is, one who has become a mouthpiece of the Guru, for it is said: *A prophet alone can recognize the prophet.*

All great Masters the world over have presented the same eternal truth each, of course, in his own inimitable way. They say that the divine Power-of-God resides in every human heart, but the heart wherein it is manifested the most is worthy to be adored. A perfect living Master is an embodiment of the Power-of-God and as such he is much more than what he appears to be. He does live in this world but is not of this world as the soul in him is in tune with the infinite.

"O Lalo," Nanak says, "I do not speak anything on my own but whatever I utter, I am inspired by Him."

Though physically He, like us, may look to be a denizen

of this world, yet inwardly His soul is free from the shackles of mind and matter and is in perfect harmony with the universal life-principle. All great Masters bear testimony to this sublime truth. Who can give us the tidings of God? Who can unite us with the living life-lines as provided by Him? Since He is peerless, self-created and the causeless cause, how can we possibly get to know Him and realize Him, and with whose help? It may therefore be taken for granted that merely by our own manifold efforts, we cannot get near Him. If there is God, there must also be a God-way which in turn leads to the irresistible conclusion that there should be a Godman who has practiced God and is competent enough to lead us on the God-path. Without such a human pole-star we cannot know of the Pole. It is just plain talk. It does not involve any reasoning nor is there any ambiguity about it. Sages and seers have always spoken in the third person for our guidance. *Kabir says that he is conversant with the Mysteries of the Beyond and has brought a message from the Most High.*

My Master, Hazur Sawan Singh Ji, also was a true messenger of God. If we were to hear directly such Master-souls, we would get from them sublime truths illustrative of their inner greatness. Once He said: "Whenever we come to this physical plane, we bring with us our own staff to work with us. When our work is finished on one side, we are deputed on to the other." You can well understand what this signifies. Similarly, all other Masters in the past have said the same thing. The tenth Guru (Guru Gobind Singh) says: *Having become one with Him, I had no intention whatsoever to come back to this world, but willy nilly I was made to do so to fulfill the divine purpose.*

Christ also said the same thing: *I and my Father are one. He who has seen me, has seen the Father. Father knows the son and the son knows the Father.*

# GURU, GURUDEV, AND SATGURU

Guru Arjan says: *Father and son are dyed in the same color. The Father and son have entered into a divine partnership.*

All Masters have given their own version of the same thing. Shams-i-Tabrez says. *O, people of the world, do not look at my tattered clothes, just try to peep into the innermost recesses of my mind for then you will know of the vast Kingdom of God to which I belong. Do not take me as a poor mendicant or a helpless being like yourself. I am much more than what I appear to be and am blessed with untold treasures of spiritual riches.* Continuing in the same strain he says: *We may be likened to an experienced physician. We need not feel the pulse or test the urine of the ailing patients but through their eyes we look deeply into the deep-rooted maladies of the mind. We have with us a panacea for all ills of life and freely dispense the same.*

During my second tour in the U.S.A. I happened to give a talk on Christmas Day. I told the congregation that Christ lived long before Jesus did. It is just 2,000 years ago when Jesus came into the world but the Christ-power was always there working for the spiritual welfare of humanity at large. Significantly enough Christ remarked: *I am that I am.* The Master-soul never dies. It is eternally present from end to end. The great divine Power when manifested at some physical pole is known as the living Master. Just try to understand that Guru-power is nothing but the Power-of-God.

In the Gurbani it says: *He who is the ever-living God-power is called a Guru when it adopts some human-pole for working in this world.*

*Satguru is the great immaculate Power; do not mistake Him for the human-pole from which it works.*

*The servant of Hari (God) is like Hari Himself. Please do not be mistaken by the physical raiment of the servant.*

As explained so many times, Hazur was the sun of spirituality. He is ever with me and lives with me.

The spiritual stalwarts come whenever the world is in need of them. Guru Nanak came when there was a tremendous rift between Hindus and Muslims. Kabir also came in the same period. Both of them preached: God is one and all mankind is one. All persons are ensouled bodies. The soul is of the same essence as that of God. The various religious orders were set up for just one purpose: spiritual emancipation. But, alas, they have degenerated into strong fetters and manacles for our hands and feet.

*We had started Godwards, but unfortunately got stuck fast on the way.*

We had entered into religious orders for God-knowledge and God-realization, but became contented with the labeled liveries of socio-religious forms and formulas. The result is that we have failed hopelessly in our search for God. We had joined the different social orders just to equip ourselves for the realization of God but side-stepped God and got engaged in internecine quarrels with each other in the blessed name of religion. Millions of people have been sacrificed on the altar of religious fanaticism. Hazur too came at a critical juncture when many sects, at variance with each other, were at loggerheads.

Guru Nanak, when questioned as to who he was, replied: *If I say that I am a Hindu as apparently I happen to be with all the outer hallmarks of Hindus, you will surely kill me, but at the same time I am not a Muslim either, in the sense in which you take it to mean by outer signs. My real character is that my physical being is made of five elements of nature, while within me God's divine power is at work.*

As we are usually apt to forget this great lesson, the Masters come to revive it as and when necessary. The first problem the Masters tackle is to knit the children of God in the silken bonds of love, sacrifice and service of one and all. They have to bring all children of God together to one common platform. My Master came to the earth-plane when there were many diverse sects in Christianity, Sikhism, Hinduism, Islam and many other creeds. He delivered his message to the people — to learn to sit together with love and to try to understand the basic concept of the one divinity that is working in the entire creation. In the Gurbani it states that, *The wisdom of the seers is all alike.*

Those who have realized their own self regard all mankind as one. The various sects, creeds and religions are like so many schools of thought and outward forms like so many hall-marks adopted by us. But, all the same, in spite of these seeming differences, we are basically human beings and the soul in man has the same attributes on a miniature scale as those of God. From this lofty viewpoint all are alike. It was Hazur's great desire that there should be some common platform for teaching the science of the soul to all, despite differences in their outlook on world, color or creed. Ruhani Satsang was the name suggested by Hazur for such a forum. He was a Jivan-Mukt, a liberated Master-soul, and had come for the liberation of humanity.

It was once suggested to Hazur that he should form a distinct sect or religious order dealing exclusively with spirituality. You will be surprised to know how gracefully he replied:, "What earthly good will it do to dig more wells where too many already exist?" All that was needed at the moment was to find out the Water of Life already referred to in various scriptures. Truth or divinity is already existing in man and those who have realized it say the same thing. But those who have not seen the Reality are vainly engaged in fighting the varying ideological beliefs and doctrines. The principal aspect of his teachings was that we should be able to sit together in love for understanding the divinity which forms the common bed-rock for humanity. We are already one and must try to know the One in us. We are blessed with the same type of eyes, ears, hands, feet, etc., and from the level of the soul we are also one. The God we worship is one for the whole human race. He is the Lord of us all. As we are likely to lose sight of this fundamental Truth, the Masters come from time to time to revive it. So the first lesson which we get from the Master is that we should, while remaining in our respective religions, strive to realize our true Self and then realize the Self of the universe and finally the great Truth which is the very life of all creation. To find this Truth it is necessary that we should know what is "true living."

Guru Nanak says: *True living is higher than knowing the truth.*

A truly blessed life flavored with divine love is above everything else. Such a life is conducive to spiritual uplift. Just as an electric bulb when clean and neat sheds clear light, so does a life free from all blemishes. The purity of life—or man-making, as it is called—was the outer work which my Master accomplished and it is admittedly the only way that leads to the welfare of humanity and prepares the way for spiritual development. It is spirituality alone that offers any hope for the security of man.

I once happened to talk with Pandit Jawaharlal Nehru, the first Prime Minister of India. He listened to me with rapt attention for about fifty minutes. And since then in his speeches he used to emphasize that spirituality was the only common ground where mankind could live in peace and amity. Spirituality then is the only remedy for all ills of mankind; and leaders of all thoughts, social, political or religious, could derive their inspiration from it. We are all worshippers of One God. As men we are all alike.

It is on this common ground we can meet irrespective of differences in religious creeds and beliefs, social customs and living habits, which are of little consequence. The Rig Veda exhorts us to participate in congregational prayers in which thousands may join to glorify the Lord. This great lesson of the Vedas has once again been revived by the great Master (Hazur). It is not something new. It is the ancient science. Since we had forgotten it, he came to remind us of it. Historically the Vedas, which contain the wisdom of the ages, are the oldest of all scriptures, whereas the Guru Granth Sahib is the latest compendium incorporating the teachings of as many great souls of different times and climes as could possibly be collected at that time. We have great respect for all who have enriched our spiritual heritage and have left for our guidance a valuable record of their personal experiences with the great "Self within."

All great Masters have, in fact, said the same thing, of course, in their own language. The holy Koran says that God sent His prophets to different parts of the world. A true Muslim is one who believes in all the messiahs of God. Similarly, a real Sikh is one who accepts the teachings of all Masters as recorded in the Guru Granth Sahib, a veritable banquet hall of spirituality. If this divine message is carried to all, then peace and harmony will reign supreme in all homes, societies and countries.

In my second tour of the West, I had an opportunity to meet political leaders of different shades of opinion and I always dwelt on the principle of "Live and let others live."

God had put so many children of His in their loving care, and it was their duty to serve them as best they could. If one country could not, for one reason or another, properly look after the welfare of its people and attend to their legitimate needs, let others extend their helping hand to them. Why resort to violence and shed the blood of millions of His creatures? By the grace of God, the timely realization of this basic truth actually helped in preventing a crisis on two different occasions, when things were getting out of hand. I received an S.O.S. from a third place as well. I am placing these facts before you just to stress the importance of spiritual unity which is the only way out from our present difficulties, as it will enable us to get nearer to each other and be able to solve our problems. But here there is one difficulty: differences in views and cross purposes. Guru Arjan has therefore suggested a remedy: *Let us put our heads together and in a spirit of friendliness iron out all our differences with a determined will born of burning faith in God.*

Just learn to sit together in love, leaving aside all thoughts of duality for we all are children of God. Do we not worship one God who is God of all, though our modes of worship may be different according to the environments in which we are born and brought up? When we are already one on the common ground of spirituality, like rosary beads of different designs and colors, then where is the scope for conflict?

The Gurbani tells us: *Let us get united in the name of the Lord, for we are not apart from Him.*

So this is the way that leads to unity in diversity, for diversity circles around the center, the unchangeable permanence. Guru Arjan has also emphasized: *Sit together shoulder to shoulder in the company of one who has become Gurumukh.* Gurumukh means the mouthpiece of the Guru, who is the human pole from which the Power-of-God works. I would like to stress the importance of spiritual understanding. Kabir says: *In this world there is none more munificent than the Guru; in fact, he alone is the giver of all gifts.*

The blessings of the Master are indeed very precious. Let us see what He actually bestows upon the disciple. Gurbani says: *Satguru has granted me a priceless boon* (the Holy Naam) *and has explained to me the mysteries of the Beyond.*

This is something which lies beyond the pale of the senses, mind and intellect. He alone is in a position to grant such a boon, and no one else can, for none can give what he does not have himself. It is something which one cannot acquire by mere learning and wisdom or by study of the scriptures. Who else could give the wonderful gift of the Power-of-God?

We find also in the Gurbani, *He grants us His own life-impulse and makes manifest the saving life-lines within. Who can do this? None but a polarized God on earth.*

Guru Arjan also says like this: *Having manifested Himself in the Master, He Himself distributes the holy Shabd.*

On the one hand there is the absolute God and on the other is the Power-of-God or God-in-action and unless the Power-of-God becomes manifest in us, we cannot possibly have a contact with God. As it is the living Master who can grant us this contact, His importance to begin with surpasses that of God Himself. Though the two are but one and the same, yet in finite terms, we have to differentiate between the two. Kabir says: *When the Master and the Lord both are standing before me to whom should I offer my obeisance? Definitely, I will bow to the Master who has been the means of uniting me with the Lord.*

God the absolute is an abstraction which no one has and can know and hence we can bow only to the personified God where God's Power works. Just as there is a powerhouse which you have not seen, but you see in your house a small switch which serves your purpose, similarly, the living Master is in possession of all the divine virtues and powers granted to him by the absolute God for the spiritual welfare of humanity. Thus it is quite clear that we have to adore a living Master, for the physical body of the Master is superbly divine, having been made by invisible hands for a specific purpose—to work through him in bringing about a union of human souls with Himself. If with all this we still regard the Guru just as any one of us on the human level, it is our misfortune. Kabir says those who take the Master as nothing more than a mere man being, will come again and again in lower forms of creation. Again he says: *Kabir's mind has become so subtle and pure that even the Lord is now after him.*

One whose mind is pure and intellect is at rest will surely reflect the Light of God. We are to be worshippers of the Light of life, no matter to which social religion we owe allegiance. Every religion speaks of this truth.

Guru Gobind Singh tells us: *In whom the Light of God shines in its fullness, he alone is Khalsa* (the pure in heart). *Khalsa is my own form and I reside in him. Khalsa is the true Master all powerful.*

When such great souls come, their mission in life is to unite all mankind in one great family of God. One who views all beings from the soul-level is really a great Master, for God works through him.

What does he give after all? He gives something which the senses cannot comprehend. We have to find out such a Guru who can do this.

# GURU, GURUDEV, AND SATGURU

This quest is one of supreme importance for all of us, irrespective of sex. The physical relationship between man and woman ends with the holy wedlock. Next comes the spiritual relationship: the wedlock of the soul—whether of male or female—with the Oversoul. The scriptures tell us that Paravati, the consort of Shiva, accepted Narada as her Guru. Sita, the consort of Rama, took Anasuiya as her Guru. Those who consider that there is no necessity of a Guru for women are mistaken. Both men and women do need a Guru for the emancipation of their souls from the meshes of mind and matter. The spirit of each one of us cries for liberation no matter in what bodily raiment it may be clothed.

The institution of marriage only provides us with a life companion, a standby in weal or woe in life's journey. This stage of a householder (Grihastha Ashram) is an important integral phase in one's life and must therefore, be gone through happily. Marriage is no bar to spirituality. It rather helps in spiritual advancement when both are engaged in spiritual sadhna (practice). Procreation is one aspect of married life. In the bygone days the married people were contented with just one or two children and thereafter they would renounce the world and retire into jungles for meditation and God-realization. Christ has emphasized that husbands should love their wives as Christ loved the church. It is good to be married but after begetting one or two children, the rest of the life-span should be dedicated to the highest purpose of life—God realization. It a pity that we regard marital life as a means of sense-enjoyment. Some Masters in the past were householders and had children.

In ancient times there were gradations in *brahmcharya* (period of celibacy), the minimum being that of 25 years. These days we can hardly find one who observes complete chastity—in thought, word and deed—for even one year.

With this sad state of affairs how can we aspire for a truly spiritual life?

The one great lesson that we learn from the life of Hazur is that of his continence. He married before attaining the age of 25, but his wife died before consummation of marriage. He married a second time after he had attained the age of 25, which meant an observance of complete brahmcharya for all these years. His wife lived with him intermittently for brief spells which hardly totalled six months. Besides, he had in him all Godly virtues. God is immortal and so are our souls. He is all truth, all wisdom and all bliss and our Self too is endowed with all these attributes. But the Self in us, environed as it is by mind and matter, has forgotten its essential pristine nature and has so identified with the body and bodily adjuncts that we cannot see anything beyond this physical world. Whenever great souls come, they tell us of the right path and give us right understanding and a correct lead.

Now, where lies the path homewards? There are so many yogic systems; some aim at physical development, others provide the means for prolonging the life span. There is Bhakti Yoga which tells us how to develop love and devotion. So long as man remains in constant search for spiritual enlightenment, he does not descend to lower gradation of the creation. Ramakrisna Paramhans was the worshipper of God as a divine Mother and he saw Her immanent in all creation. He thus remained in a state of duality and could not transcend into the beyond. When he went to Guru Totapuri, the latter gave him the secret of the eye-focus, behind and between the eyes, and then hit him hard in the forehead with a piece of glass and directed him to meditate at that point. It was then that he was able to transcend body consciousness and pass from duality to oneness. Then there is the path of Gyan Yoga, of logical reasoning and inference, fit only for those gifted with strong intellectual powers. It cannot be practiced by everyone. How are the young, old and imbecile people to benefit from it?

The great sage Patanjali has defined yoga as *yogish chittavriti niroda*, ie., stilling the vibrations of mind. In reality this too is but a preparatory stage that paves the way to God-realization. The sage Yajnavalkya has defined yoga: *yogish atma Parmatma sanyog* (the union of soul with the Oversoul). But, there is something beyond this. It is Self-realization or constant awareness of the Self which comes as you rise above body consciousness; gradually cast off physical, astral and causal vestures and develop cosmic and super-cosmic awareness. And last of all you are a wave of the Ocean of all Consciousness. How can this be achieved? Guru Nanak says: *Without self-analysis the miasma of delusion does not disappear.*

So long as you do not rise above body consciousness, you cannot even get an idea of the Self within. You have to uncover your Self from the various enshrouding sheaths of physical, astral and causal, all of which are illusory. Even the great Shankara hinted at something far above and beyond when he said: *O Lord, I know that there is no difference whatsoever between you and me. I am yours. Yet you are not mine for the river has its waves but the waves do not have the river.* On the one hand, there is Self-awareness and on the other is cosmic-awareness and yet transcending them is the state of super-cosmic-consciousness. Saints have always referred to this state of super-cosmic-consciousness. All great Masters have done the same and are known for their catholicity. Hazur used to tell us that he was for all and accepted all, and that it was the foremost duty of a real Master to unite all the children of God.

All human beings, all religions, all nations, and all

countries are His in spite of seeming differences due to geographical and climatic conditions, because they live on the same earth and under the same blue canopy and are charged with the same life-impulse. Saints give to all alike the same inner contact with the overflowing ocean of divine intoxication, lying hidden in every soul and long since forgotten because of the heavy pressure of the work-a-day life. The Master helps us to gain access to the divine nectar by raising us a little above body consciousness. A great Master has his soul-currents well under his control, while ours are flowing out through the sense organs. The sun's rays do not ordinarily burn, but when made to pass through a convex lens, these are collected and burn anything on the other side of the lens. It is our own attention that gives life to mind and intellect. If instead of flowing outward through the senses, it could be collected at the center of the soul, you could well understand its potential. It is a subject of actual experience and not of theory only. The living Master then is a great ocean of divine bliss and harmony: *A Godman is ever in a state of divine intoxication.*

Those who really become men of God, they need no outer aids to get lost to themselves. This is why Mira Bai exclaimed that she remained in a state of constant intoxication without any wine.

Christ tells us: *It is not by bread alone that man lives.* Guru Ramdas tells us: *The mind remains fully engrossed in the music of the soul.*

The living Master is just like a blooming tree laden with fragrant flowers and luscious fruits. Blessed indeed is one who happens to meet such a Master. Please remember that the eyes are the windows of the soul. The power that a saint has within is imparted through the eyes. His soul is charged with divinity. This realization one can have from him.

Every Master has had his own *bola* (a chosen form of remembering God) and whatever the bola, it is charged with all the magnetic force of the Saint. Guru Nanak very often used to exclaim "Sat Kartar" meaning that the Creator was all pervasive. Similarly, Chaitanya Mahaprabhu went about saying: "Hari Bol" (take ye the name of the Lord). Once he happened to pass by a pond where washermen were busy washing clothes. He asked one of them to say "Hari Bol" but the latter did not pay any heed, taking him to be a beggar. But when Chaitanya once again emphatically asked the washerman the latter could not resist but repeated the words "Hari Bol" and began to dance in ecstasy with the refrain of the words. Very soon other washermen nearby caught the rhythm of the charged words and the whole place began to ring with the merry chant "Hari Bol" in rhythmic union. You see, my point is that the words of a Master-soul, no matter whatever they may be, are highly charged on account of his personal contact with the God-head within him and as such cannot but profoundly affect the hearers and help them in spiritual advancement. The eyes are the windows of the soul and a single love-laden glance from his God-intoxicated eyes is enough to raise the spirit to heights immeasurable.

Shams-i-Tabrez prays, *O Master divine, give me just one draught from the holy vintage which may bring peace to my lacerated heart.*

*O Master give me that elixir of life which is not available even in paradise.*

Bhai Nandlal says: *A single tumbler from the Water of Life is more exhilarating than two thousand barrels of wine.*

And from Guru Gobind Singh we learn, *It is not a subject of discussion on the intellectual level but one of seeing yourself.*

Bhikna declares, *He who knows does not speak out as it is not given to mortal imagination. It is a subject of seeing only. Those who speak out that they know, they really do not know.*

Maulana Rumi tells us, *If I were to tell something of this state, then all the infidels of the world would instantly turn into Godmen.*

After all, what do the Masters give? It is something supremely divine and defies description. The great Maulana Rumi then goes on to say: *If after my death, manure were made of my body, and if that manure were scattered in a field of wheat, the cook and bearer of chapatis made therefrom will dance in ecstasy, and even the very oven will start emitting the flames of love.*

The Maulana has said this much, without telling us what will be the state of one who partakes of the food thus prepared, for that is ineffable.

The path of the Masters is a straight one involving no physical yogic practices. He gives a direct contact with the strands of life within. This consists of linking the soul-currents with the Power-of-God in which we actually live, move about and have our very being. It is a matter of direct inner perception quite apart from all kinds of reasoning, feeling, emotion and inferential knowledge which are all fallible. Actual seeing is believing, leaving no place for scepticism. Guru Amardas came to this rich heritage at the fairly advanced age of seventy and when he experienced God, he said, *If one is fortunate enough, one may get in touch with a Master of Truth, a Satguru, and get from him communion with the holy Word or contact with the inner Sound Principle, the Light of life.*

While philosophical treatises deal with theoretical

aspects of religions, mysticism brings you face to face with the divine Power-of-God.

Even small children can be attuned with the Light of God. Nothing is taken for granted and no make-believe is required. It is simply a direct and conscious contact with the God-into-expression-power within, the primal manifestation of Light and Sound principles. Hazur was an adept both in the theory and practice of Surat Shabd yoga. In this modern age, this science started from Kabir and the Sikh Gurus, and in turn came to Tulsi Sahib of Hathras and on to Swami Ji, Baba Jaimal Singh Ji, Hazur Sawan Singh Ji and the same power is now working through the living Master. It is Hazur's divine grace that everybody without exception is being blessed with inner experience of Light and Sound. It is indeed a priceless gift. Guru Nanak speaking of it said: *Nanak remains all the time in a state of continuous ecstasy.*

I was talking to you of meditation and the natural question you would like to ask is: what should one meditate upon? One cannot meditate upon something one has not seen. In other words how can we meditate on the abstract and absolute God? Contemplation is a dangerous thing. If you are lucky enough to get in touch with a perfect Master then it may be well. But if perchance, and God forbid, your teacher is not competent to fulfill his promise and you contemplate on his form, you will be lost in the wilderness. During the early days of my discipleship, I once questioned Hazur as to what one should fix one's attention on after the withdrawal of one's sensory currents. He smilingly replied: "We all the time usually think of our children, friends, and other worldly possessions. So where then is the harm to contemplate for some time on the form of a *Sadh* (Master)?"

In the Gurbani it states, *God Himself comes in the form of a Sadh.*

After some time, when I once again questioned Hazur about *dhyan* (meditation) he lucidly explained: "When the Master initiates a person, he, in his radiant form, becomes a constant companion of the disciple. You may, while sitting for contemplation, think of his form or may not, but when you will progress within, you are sure to meet him there. The Guru after all is not a human being as one may generally take him to be, but something much more than that for in him works the Power-of-God in its plentitude, for the benefit of humanity. He does not leave nor forsake his chosen souls till they are safely led to the true home of His Father." Fortunate are they who had the privilege of getting holy communion or inner contact from Hazur Maharaj Ji. The contemplation of his holy form is all that is needed.

But herein comes another great obstacle. We can easily contemplate on any human form like our own, but it is not possible to visualize the form of a highly advanced soul like the Master's which is one with the Divine. We may try to visualize his form within by thinking of his milk-white flowing beard, his radiant face, his turban, his tall stature, his regal gait or anything else associated with him, but it will be our make-believe and not the real form and hence of not much benefit. It is because of this that I do not advise anybody to contemplate on any form, even of the Master, but to look straight ahead into the eye-focus and therein see intently whatever comes into view—light or darkness—and mentally repeat the charged names very, very slowly, maybe at intervals, so that the inner gaze is not disturbed. As the loving gaze will grow steadily in intensity, the divine form of the Master (the radiant pole at which God is working) will appear of itself within and begin to stay, at first momentarily and then for a longer time with the development of inner perception. On initiation here in India, it generally happens that some 25 to 30 per cent of the initiates do see within them the radiant form of the Master and of Hazur Maharaj, even those who had never met him at all. The appearance within of the Master may therefore be left up to him. It is his job. He is God-in-man and knows best the level from where and how to work. He may come alone or along with his Master or any other benign soul for they are all children of the Light of God. Guru Arjan says: *The Gurudev* (the radiant form of the Master) *has opened my eyes* (the inner eye) *to see His Light. I have now no delusions and all my strivings have come to an end.*

With the coming in of the radiant form of the Master, half the bhakti, devotion, is accomplished. We must, therefore, unceasingly pray to God to bring us to the divine pole or the live switch board where His power is fully manifest. The immutable law of demand and supply works equally at all levels. There is always food for the hungry and water for the thirsty. There are instances of lovingly devoted souls who got inner experience of the Master's form much before they actually came in contact with him on the physical plane. In Pakistan there are still many persons who used to see the radiant form of Hazur though they had never met him before. In my case, Hazur's lustrous form often visited me inside, seven years before I actually met him and got my initiation.

I was telling you that our prayers must spring from the bottom of our hearts. Frankly speaking, I did not favor the idea of having a Guru, though I knew that without a competent Guru one could not make headway in spirituality. I was, however, afraid of the fake Gurus in which the world abounds. But how was I to find a true Master when there was a swarm of them and each held out high hopes and was ready to bless you for a pittance? So I used to pray earnestly: "O God, grant me inner guidance in my quest." My humble prayer was granted and Hazur began revealing himself to me and continued to do so for seven years before I was formally initiated. I did not know then who he was, and always took him for Guru Nanak. I also composed some verses in praise of him.

I was extremely fond of rivers. Wherever I happened to be, I would look for a stream nearby and find a solitary spot for my meditations. When I went to Lahore, I had the river Ravi. And so it was at Jehlum. For hours together I would sit by the river-side absorbed in thought. While at Lahore it struck me to see Beas river. It was this lure of the flowing water that led me to Beas. It was a fine Sunday morning that I took a train for Beas. I enquired from the station master at Beas the location of the river. Surprisingly enough, he asked me if I had come to visit the sage of Beas. I exclaimed as to whether there was any sage living there. He then told me of Hazur. Thus the visit to Beas was amply rewarded. It gave me an opportunity to see both the river Beas and to meet my Master-to-be.

On reaching *Dera* (colony) my surprise knew no bounds when I discovered in Hazur the likeness of the radiant form that had visited me in my meditations all these years. I imploringly enquired as to why he had delayed our meeting for such a long time. He, with a benign smile, replied that that was the most opportune time for the meeting.

A competent Master reveals himself even before initiation. There is hardly any need to conjure up any images while engaged in spiritual practices. The Master plants his own image at the time of initiation and his radiant form comes in of its own when we completely get into the eye-focus. The secret of success lies in entering into the eye-focus completely and entirely and the real Master's form does come regardless of any invitation. This is a comparatively easier, and the most natural, way of God-realization. Guru Bhakti is the surest way back home to God but the path is quite slippery as well. When the end of Maulana Rumi approached near, he said: *Little dost thou know of the great king within me, see thou the radiance in this house of flesh and bones.*

When a disciple rises to this level and becomes a Guru-man, he becomes truly blessed. I have told you just two things that the Guru does: First, he teaches that all the children of God should sit together for this is the only way out for the entire human race to escape from the trials and tribulations of the world. Secondly, he gives us such a divine wealth as cannot be had from anywhere else. It is therefore, of supreme importance that, while looking at the physical form of the Master, one should be conscious as well of the spiritual radiation emanating from that form. Maulana Rumi says: *O Shams-i-Tabrez, if I see anybody other than God in the mirror of your face, I would be worse than an infidel.*

To meet a real Master is to get closer to God, whereas to be away from Him is to be away from God. Whenever the Masters come into the world, they do so to serve us with the nectar of life. It is said: *The scriptures are useful to the Guru for teaching the masses. Without a living Master, we cannot even get the right import of the sacred books.*

It is God alone who can lead us into Him. The Master is the true lover of God and is competent to narrate the story of his Beloved.

Bhai Nandlal says, *Get hold of a perfect Master and follow his instructions fully, then shalt thou gain salvation even while engaged in worldly duties. God is with thee from eternity, thou hast but to turn thy face unto Him.*

For Guru Arjan, Ramdas (his guru) was not only a mere human being, but was an embodiment of God Himself and God verily dwelt in the form of Ramdas.

A disciple who does not see in his Master the Power-of-God, is not yet a true disciple. He is yet on probation and continues to be so until he sees in Him the glory of God, and this in the true sense happens only when the Master reveals His radiant form within the disciple. It is this resplendently luminous form that guides the soul from plane to plane in the spiritual journey Homewards. When this radiant form comes, you may converse with Him for then many problems will resolve of themselves. The Guru, who works as a human guide on the physical plane, is known as *Gurudev* when He manifests Himself in His astral radiance and the same power, when it escorts the soul on to the highest region of unalloyed bliss and harmony, is called *Satguru* (Truth personified or Master of Truth). Those who are *Gurubhaktas* see something superb in the living Master.

A Sikh disciple truly lives in sweet remembrance of the Guru. Just as an infant depends for his very existence on the milk of his mother, so does the disciple depend on the "Water of Life" or the "Bread of Life" with which the Master continuously feeds him. He loves the disciple with every breath of His life and constantly takes care of his well-being in diverse ways which the poor infant does not know. How fondly the mother takes care of her baby, herself undergoing all sorts of privations to make him comfortable. A Master does much more than this. It is a pity that we do not realize the greatness of the Guru. We know only that much which He may, in His grace, choose to reveal to us. If a mother were to ask her child if he knew her, he may say "yes" but how much can he know? Similarly, we the disciples cannot possibly fathom the greatness of the Guru.

After all, why all this adoration? What do they give us to merit such praise? They impart to us their own life-impulse and transmit to us that divine ecstasy of which we have read so much in the scriptures. All this is done through their magnetic eyes from which highly charged spiritual currents pass on to us. Life comes from life as does light from light. A really living reservoir-of-life can help us to find the fount of life, and nobody else can do this. This is the immutable law of nature and it admits no exception whatsoever. Our Hazur was a limitless ocean of the life-giving water.

We find in the Gurbani: *The teachings of the great Masters are the same for one and all. Listen ye to the direct testimony of the saints for they speak of what they actually see with their inner eyes.*

The testimony of saints, then, is direct and immediate and not one based on hearsay or on the authority of scriptural texts. In succinct and lucid terms they tell us of their inner experiences with their own Self and with God. Having a direct contact with the Power-of-God within, they are able to give us the correct interpretation of the various scriptures, ironing out the seeming differences, and present an integrated picture of the Reality as seen by sages and seers of all times. It is said: *Those who see God face to face, shall all tell the same thing.*

The differences come in only because of the means of approach in each case, the language of the time employed, the mode of expression then prevailing and the intellectual level of the age. Again, these differences are not in essentials but only in non-essential details.

To "sit together" is a sovereign remedy for all the ills of mankind. What the Masters give is an invaluable gift of pure spirituality which cannot be taught but may, like an infection, be caught from the radioactive rays that emanate from them.

I may tell you that spirituality too is a kind of science not unlike other sciences. It is a science of metaphysical experiences, the results of which can be verified with precision and exactitude. The credit for presenting it as a regular science and for the scientific approach to the abstruse and abstract subject that has ever baffled mankind goes to Hazur. With the change in the temper of the people in this scientific age, it was he who conceived that it could appeal most only if it was presented in a spirit in conformity with the present times. It is an age-old subject, the most ancient, coming from time immemorial. It is to our advantage that Hazur revived this as a science of soul. Though spiritual awakening is given by many, yet the divine revelation is granted by few. It is due to his good grace that so many are acquiring the inner experience of holy Light and Sound principle which can, of course, be developed by practice with loving concentration.

Let us strive to be worthy sons of our Father. Try to understand the facts of divine life. Hazur has not gone away from us. His divine power is ever with us in spite of an ostensible change of covering. And even now the same divine grace is working in abundance.

*Sant Kirpal Singh Ji*
*(1894-1974)*

*Sant Kirpal Singh Ji*
*(1894-1974)*

# 6

# Let Us Reform Ourselves

THE SIGNIFICANCE of Satsang has been explained on a number of occasions. This is a sacred place (Sawan Ashram) and must be taken as such. Whenever you visit a Gurudwara or a temple, you do so with a feeling of reverence. If you go there without such a feeling and keep thinking about worldly affairs, what will you gain? The purpose of your coming here is love of God: His remembrance and communion with Him. Come here with a clean mind and pure heart remembering the Lord. Then alone you will be able to derive full benefit from Satsang. The more attentive you are, the greater will be the benefit. Whatever you understand you must practice. Otherwise, the result is sorrow.

Swami Ji Maharaj has aptly explained the significance of Satsang. Kabir in a couplet says: *The heart is somewhere else, but the body is with the saint. How can an unbleached cloth be dyed like this?* If you just sit quietly and attentively, even if you are not able to follow the Satsang fully, you will derive some benefit. By thinking about mundane matters, you not only harm yourself, but also spoil the atmosphere for others. We do not assemble here to make friends, but to establish a true relationship—the relationship with God that does not break even after death. It cannot be snapped during one's lifetime. It only because of our lack of understanding, false sense of ego and such other ideas that we are amidst this conflict. Where does this conflict lead us to? To suffering.

There can be no salvation by visiting this place as a

routine. The more you put your heart into the Satsang, the happier you will be. If you do this you will get something which is not available elsewhere. You have been asked to maintain a diary, but you remain adamant and do not do so. If we keep a diary regularly, we can become angels. We are not saints, but have come here to become saints. This can happen only if we put our hearts to what we understand here.

Swami Ji pointedly tells us: *For years we have been having Satsang, at least now leave old habits.*

If we do something for a number of days or months, it becomes a habit. Habit so formed should be unraveled. Bad habits—falsehood, deceit, enmity, intrigue, back-biting etc. should be discarded. It is to shed these old habits that we come to Satsang. If that is not done and we make only a show of it, then, what is the point of coming to Satsang?

We come to Satsang to form such habits and adopt such ideas so as to forge a link with the truth (Sat), to give up negative ideas and to assimilate positive thoughts in our lives. The holy Koran says that even God does not care about a person who does not think of reforming himself. By reforming ourselves, we can change the whole world

The worst of all bad habits is to criticize others. One must observe non-injury (non-violence) even in thought. All religions are good, but the observance of non-violence is the highest. Forget the past and discard all bad habits. Otherwise, we will only harm ourselves and remain entangled in the whirlpool of births and deaths. Thus, saints lovingly exhort us to give up obstinacy now. Swami Ji says, *How long are we going to deceive the Master? It is high time we get to know him.*

"Deceiving the Master" means that we think whatever

we do (good or bad) is all right and that He is not watching us. But the Master-power is always within us and is watching all our actions. The Master is not an ordinary human being. The Master is a divine power manifest on a human pole. That Power is always watching us, although physically He may not be seeing us. So, recognize the Master-power. The Master loves all, even those who may consider themselves as His enemies. He wishes everyone well. Even if someone threatens to kill him, he will not wish ill of him. Why? Because of the Master-power in him. If we recognize this Power in him, we must obey him, for he will never give us bad advice.

Swami Ji reminds us that Satsang is done by the Master, who is not an ordinary human being. Then who is a Guru or Master? He is God Himself. You should come here in His remembrance and go out remembering Him. Adopt whatever things are helpful to reach Him, and reject those which become obstacles. To reach God is not difficult, but difficult it is to become a man. Although we may appear to show great reverence and understanding, we consider ourselves to be wisest of all. That is why Swami Ji Maharaj has said that we must leave our old habits.

Everyone judges things from his own level. Unless you concede someone as your superior and obey him, you cannot get anything. Anyone who has not attained a higher level will take you downward. He who is at a higher level will unite all. All human beings are liable to make mistakes. If someone commits a mistake, forgive and forget.

Kabir says that if someone considers the Master an ordinary human being, he will get the lowest birth. The manifest God-in-him is the Master. If you consider him a superior individual, you must listen to him. If you do not agree with him, he may not contest it, and may say that he might have made a mistake. Even then, if he is blamed, it cannot result in happiness and will cause suffering. There is not an iota of doubt about it. The purpose of Satsang is to increase happiness within ourselves. When a soul gets a link with God, it will acquire all His virtues. The Master is full of compassion and washes our sins away. For example, a mother lovingly cleans the dirt off her child before embracing him. She does not harm him. We come to Satsang to become saints. We can do so if we practice what we are able to grasp. Swami Ji, thus, very lovingly explains that we are committing a blunder if we see the Master from our own level. He goes on to say: *Do not take the Guru to be merely a human being. He is the essence of the Lord.*

The question now is: Who is a Master? This is not a new question. Guru Nanak was asked this question. He replied that the WORD is the Guru or the Master and soul is the disciple. The Lord Himself is the Master and our souls are His disciples. Kabir also gave the same reply when this question was put to him. When the soul establishes a contact with Him, it is the human-pole on which the Light of God is manifest. He can show Light to others. That is the only proof of his being the Master. Christ has said: *I am the Light of the world, those who come to me shall never walk in darkness.*

The Master's word is the real Master. Those who obey what he says, achieve salvation. He can give us some experience of Light. If this is done, then there is no scope for doubt. Swami Ji says that the Master is the essence of God. That Godpower, working through the Master, never dies. He also says, *Make the mind understand somehow, and contemplate on Him with loving confidence.*

Swami Ji means that somehow we will have to understand that the Master in whom the God-power is manifest can give us the experience of that power. This is the only touchstone to remove any doubt. Anyone can lecture, act and pose, but few can give the experience of Light within. Someone who can give this experience proves adequately that he has the divine Light in him. Then, whatever he says must be accepted. What he says is that we should have communion with God who is within us all and, therefore, we should love all. The mind may refuse to understand this, but you will have to make it understand.

So it is not difficult to find God: it is difficult to become a real man. Dr. Iqbal, the famous Urdu poet, once said that Moses went to Mount Tur in search of God, but he did not know that God Himself was in search of a real man. Baba Jaimal Singh Ji found Hazur, my Master, in the Murree Hills of Punjab. Was there no one else for him to find in the whole of Punjab? What I mean to stress is that mind will have to recognize the Master. Then only we will be able to obey Him. Otherwise, we will remain entangled in a maze of doubts and the purpose of human life and of coming to Satsang will not be achieved. Now Swami Ji tells us, *He discourses with compassion and grace. He is God personified.*

The Master's mission is to teach us with compassion and grace. All are the Lord's children. What is that Power which creates such compassion and love in him? It is the God-power, which compels Him to love all. He is love personified. He teaches love and spreads vibrations of love. His words are meant for increasing love. Swami Ji thus exhorts us to obey the Master. If we developed love of God, enabling us to see Him in all and all in Him, there is no reason for us to come to this world again and again. When we forget the Lord, our ego naturally gets bloated and we are caught up in our conflicts. The karmic law is supreme—if you cause suffering, you will suffer; if you do violence, you will face violence and, similarly, if you usurp somebody's rights, your rights will be usurped. Thus, you will keep coming and going in this world. Hence the need to change ourselves. Saints always teach us with love, but, if necessary, they may punish also to reform us. Swami Ji, therefore, says, *The Master-power works on a human pole. He will liberate you anyway.*

So man is the teacher of man. The Master comes in a human form and becomes like us to teach us. He is a human being like us. God is hidden in us and is the source of our lives, but in Him, the Master, God is manifest. This is the only difference. Excuse me, old Masters cannot come back to guide us, although we can benefit by reading whatever they have said. The living Master, who has passed through life just like us, has the experience of life. He says he has done it and you can do it likewise by strictly following the principles. What are those principles? They are: *Truth and love of God. You should love all and ignore others' mistakes with love. Blood cannot be washed with blood, but it can be washed with the water of love.* And Swami Ji advises, *Serve and worship Him. For He is not different from Guru Nanak.*

Keep ready to serve. What is service? Obey his commandments and mold your lives according to his teachings. He says: keep your lives clean and thoughts pure. Never think ill of anyone. Adopt truth. Love all for the Lord resides in all. W are fortunate to have this human life, and we should derive full benefit out of it by linking our souls with the Oversoul.

Now Swami Ji tells us, *He is Kabir, He is Sat Naam. Know all the Masters as Him.*

The Master power has been working on different human poles. When one electric bulb is fused, another replaces it, but the power remains the same. People brought a sinner before Jesus Christ and asked him to punish the culprit.

Christ agreed to do so and asked the people what was the normal punishment for such a crime. On being told that the accused should be stoned to death, he told the people that only those who have never committed any sin should throw stones at the accused. No one came forward. Then Christ asked the accused to *Sin no more*. So, try to recognize the Master power which never dies. *I shall never leave thee, nor for-sake thee till the end of the world.* Christ, the Master power manifested in him, said this and not the human pole of Jesus. The Master will explain with love, show sympathy and even at times shed tears, somehow to bring us on the right path. His aim is to ensure that we attain the Truth.

At least those who come to Satsang and especially those who have been initiated by the Master should have love for others. Christ asked his followers to live with love so that others should know that they were associated with him. If we are able to remove even one man's suffering by sweet words and sympathy, we have done a big service.

Swami Ji goes on to say, *You can achieve your Goal only through Him. Cast away delusion and vanity.*

Swami Ji now asks: *What is your goal in life?* To find God. You can find God through right understanding. Your real friends are those by meeting whom ignorance can be removed. What is ignorance? God has made all of us alike. All are embodied souls. Soul is the essence of God. He is present in all. This realization is the means to removal of ignorance and to get the right perspective. So, he pulls you out of delusion. You cannot succeed in your mission without him. Your life's mission was to realize God and not to lose yourself in materialistic pursuits and struggles. We continue to sow new seeds of karmas, which we will have to reap. *As you sow so shall you reap.*

Do away with false pride and self-veneration and keep your mission in view. By doing so, not only you, but the whole world can be happy. Thus, to find God is the real mission of our lives. Only God can fulfill this mission. Swami Ji has stressed this point by saying that we should go and fulfill our own mission and not get entangled in the material world. Think before acting whether your actions will result in happiness or suffering. It is very easy to increase pain, but difficult to remove it. Love alone can wipe out sorrow. There is no other remedy.

Dhritarashtra once abused Arjuna's bow, for which the latter had high regard. Arjuna stood up and aimed his arrow at Dhritarashtra. On Lord Krishna's intervention, Arjuna said that he had taken a vow to kill anyone who abused his bow. Lord Krishna then asked him whether dharma (duty) should cause happiness or sorrow. Happiness, Arjuna replied. Lord Krishna then told Arjuna to ponder over the obvious result of his intention to kill Dhritarashtra.

What is Dharma and what is its test? Both Vyas, the author of the Mahabharata, and Christ were asked these questions. The common theme of their replies is that we should treat others in the manner in which we ourselves like to be treated. We have to decide, therefore, whether our actions will result in happiness or sorrow. Saints aim at increasing happiness. Obey them and you will reach the goal. Otherwise, you will go on groping in the dark as before.

A Saint or Master is a lighthouse of both worlds. In association with him you can get communion with God—the real goal of life. Swami Ji, therefore, entreats us: *Do not let go this opportunity. There is none greater than Him.*

We are very fortunate to have this human life. If we miss this opportunity (to realize God), who knows when this opportunity will come again? Engage yourself in activities which can be helpful to realize God. All other worldly activities which cause self-veneration, cleverness and sense of ego are useless. It is hard to find a man who aims at all-round unity. It is the saints' mission to unite all. If you are able to find such a saint, and you obey him, you can accomplish your mission. Swami Ji explains: *If you miss this opportunity to follow the Master now, you will be deluded and remain entangled.*

Human life is a great boon. You have been able to find a Master. If you let go this opportunity and fail to take advantage of his association by not obeying him, by not shaping your lives according to his teachings, the obvious result will be the endless wheel of life. For, what you think, so you become.

Bharat, after whom India has been named as Bharat, was a king who renounced the world and became a hermit, but he developed attachment for a deer. Consequently, he had to take birth as a deer. The Master's only concern is to see us all happy. He tries to set right our mistakes. His ideal is love for all. Swami Ji now emphasizes, *You will never find such a Master, understand this once for all.*

Why is gurudom in disrepute today? Modern gurus are generally political at heart. They have an axe to grind—to make money and get honor and respect. They are not concerned with the well-being of the people. Their object is to impress the people by their hypocrisy, deceit and false-hood. You may be taken in by these methods. On the contrary, the saint will talk to you frankly and lovingly and point out that you are making a mistake. He will make you see the difference between truth and falsehood. Such a Guru is a great blessing. Our soul at one time became separated from the Lord and to be reunited is the foremost mission of our lives.

Swami Ji warns us, *By endless reading of scriptures and singing of hymns, do not inflate your sense of ego.*

What are you proud of? Is it because you sing well, or you can exhibit your knowledge, or you are a good orator? These things lead you nowhere. Ravana was said to be proficient in all the four Vedas and six Shastras. Still he is popularly shown with an ass's head. Why? All his learning proved useless due to his wrong action.

Intellectual pursuits, cleverness, and indulgence in tall talk is easy. It is difficult to control your senses, to rise above body consciousness, to keep thoughts pure and not to think ill of others. If we accomplish these things, it is not difficult to realize God.

Swami Ji through his writings has been exhorting us for about one hundred years now that we show only superficial respect for the Master instead of respecting his teachings, in which lies our salvation. Saints do not spare anyone, including themselves. He goes on, *It is this pride which has ruined our lives. It is this pride which is harming us now.*

Swami Ji says that our ego makes us come to this world again and again. Do not follow your mind; follow your Master. This will bring happiness. Now Swami Ji says: *I am explaining to you fully. This carelessness is not good for you.* He adds, *Your carelessness in failing to change your old habits or reforming yourself is harmful to you. Make haste in discarding deceit. Increase your sense of devotion.*

Discard deceit. What deceit? You say something and do something else. Only by doing away with hypocrisy can we increase our sense of devotion. Therefore, deceit and hypocrisy should go first. Then give up tall talk and inculcate humility. A person with such virtues will automatically get the Master's grace.

Swami Ji, therefore, now warns us: *Even now if the mind fails to understand, you suffer the consequences.*

If you refuse to listen, then what can be done? Even Saints cannot help you. In that case, you will be miserable and unhappy. He goes on: *The Negative Power rules over you and will not let your mind understand.*

*The Negative Power will delude you. The compassionate Lord alone can save you from doubts and delusions.* And further he says: *One thing is clear, brother, that you are a man of no principle.*

You have no principle in life. What can be done to such a person?

*If you keep the Master's association, perhaps your mind may gradually understand.*

If your mind agrees, you go on making efforts to reform yourself. What is true will always remain true. Even if your vision is clouded, the Master's image will not be blackened. Try to understand gradually; do not despair. There is every hope that the delusion may ultimately disappear. To give up heart after making flimsy efforts is not the solution. The solution lies in reforming your inner self. Once you have satisfied yourself about the competence of the Master, then you must persist in making efforts to understand. Do not listen to your mind, listen to the Master. This will make you understand. Now Swami Ji finally warns us: *The Master has explained fully that such souls will have to suffer.*

The human pole on which the God-power is manifest is called Radhaswami by Swami Ji Maharaja. The Master explains that if you do not understand you will grope in the dark.

*Sant Kirpal Singh Ji*
*(1894-1974)*

# 7

# Oh Mind, Listen for Once

YOU MAY CALL IT the heart, or you may call it the mind; but through its hands people are selling themselves. Under the control of mind, one remains but a man of the world, for mind is not made of consciousness but matter. Each and every thing has its source and is naturally drawn to that; you can demonstrate this for yourself by throwing a ball of clay in the air as far as your strength will allow, yet it will return to its own source, the earth. Or you can try to keep a flame upside down; it will not burn downward, but will rise upward, for its source is the sun.

Anyone whose soul is under the mind's influence and control becomes an image of the mind, for he forgets his true self. We call this *ego* or *I-hood* for one thinks "I am everything." Yet, one does not know that true "I." If one has forgotten one's true Self, then who is it that will realize the Lord? The heart is a huge ocean of unlimited waves of desire, rising and falling; many great swimmers have drowned in it. It is impossible to cross this ocean without a very wise boatman. *The ocean of heart cannot be crossed without the Competent One.* Maharishi Vashisht said to Lord Rama, "O Ram, if someone tells you that the rivers have stood still, you may perhaps believe it, or if someone says that the heat has left the fire, you may also believe this; but if a person declares he has controlled his mind, never believe this until you have seen it with your own eyes."

All Masters stress that one should know oneself, for having identified ourselves with mind, which in turn has identified itself with the senses, indeed complete forgetfulness has taken place. Birth after birth, the soul thrashes itself to pieces at the hands of the mind, and as long as the mind does not emancipate itself from the senses, and the soul gain freedom from the mind and come to know itself in truth, it is impossible to know God. One great Master says that if you are willing to make a strong resolution to realize the Lord, then put one foot on your mind—to make it still—and without any effort the next step you take will take you to your Beloved. *To win the mind is to win the world.*

You will find that even great Rishis and Munis have suffered through the mind. The important thing is to make it understand the true facts, for this life is but for a few days; no one has ever lived here permanently, or ever will. To sacrifice one's spiritual future just for a few days dancing to the mind's tune—is this intelligent? The Masters try to help us to see the true facts, and bring our attention to the soul—that we *are* soul, the indweller of the physical body. This world is not our world. *O beloved soul, your true home is above the illusion; you have burdened yourself with illusion's company. It is said also, Yours is the caste of Sat Naam.*

My Satguru used to say that the soul's marriage should have taken place with an Emperor, but instead she became attached to a garbage collector, for the whole time she is submerged in dirt and filth. What else is there to enjoy under the senses' influence but filth upon filth? The dirt comes out from all orifices of the body; even the pores exude a perspiration which smells unpleasant. So what can we call him who ever remains in this body, but a garbage collector? We have forgotten who we truly are. We should feel ashamed to hear the words of one Master, who says, *O soul, you are a dweller of high regions; why are you stuck in the mire of mud and water?*

The mind is difficult to understand, for its net is strong and it has many departments. There is the *Pind* or physical mind, lost in the outer enjoyments. Then *And* and *Brahmand,* astral and causal mind. If one transcends all three, one realizes who one is. Mind is no small thing, and is not easy to conquer, but we should start by changing its direction. While its face remains turned toward the worldly things, the soul will be worldly, but if it turns around and faces the soul, the soul will become spiritual. We *must* turn it around. Like fire, it is a good servant but a bad master. While you are in control, fire can do any amount of work for you—it will drive machines or cook your food and many other things; but once out of control it can consume you to ashes. You may remember the story of the man who was given a genie as a present, and was told at the time that the genie would do all his work for him, but was not to be allowed to remain idle, for it would eat him up. After one or two days, all the work was finished, and not knowing what to do, the man consulted a great Mahatma. The Mahatma advised him to erect a tall strong pole, and order the genie to continue climbing up and down the pole until told to stop. It illustrates that a vacant mind is the home of the devil, and if left vacant, it will devise some mischief or other. To fully control it, Naam is the only solution. In the Koran it says that he who has recognized the beat of his mind has recognized his God. Many great Rishis, Munis and Mahatmas have remained in the domain of the mind's illusion: causal or astral. Only the Saints— the True Masters—succeed in unraveling the mystery, by going beyond the mind and thereby gaining the knowledge of how the mind tricks the soul into miserable unending imprisonment in this world.

As I speak on this subject, a certain hymn of Swami Ji comes to mind, in which he has described with great beauty the tribulations of soul and mind. I have never taken this hymn before—listen attentively, for the Masters open up the subject with deep clarity.

*O mind, listen to my words!*

If any man looks into his heart, he will have to admit, if he is honest, that it is filled with unhappiness through the mind's dominance; yet he knows no remedy for it. If you know that someone is stealing your money, one way of controlling the situation is to praise his honesty and work, and make him your treasurer. Swami Ji advises us to *Make a friend of the mind.* It is our cruel enemy which will go on tormenting our life, but by making friends with it we take the first step toward gaining the desired control. If one makes friends with an enemy, he may not immediately cease his enmity, but it will lessen the lengths of his cruelty. In this way there are chances of his becoming stilled, during which time you will be more awakened.

Here the soul is pleading to the mind: "Just listen to one word of mine! You are unhappy and I am unhappy—listen, and you will gain peace as well as I." After all, the mind is rarely happy—do we not say so often, "My heart is so sad"? When we are restless, he is also restless. So this is an appeal from the soul, asking the mind to listen carefully.

*I have been thy slave birth after birth;*
*And you have been my lord.*

"From the day we were separated from God and came into creation, I have been your slave and have ever danced to whatever tune you chose. I have always been completely yours—please listen to me for once. I did not even obey God's word, or the Guru's; but whatever you ordered I obeyed. I read page upon page of holy scriptures, but threw them all away and turned my face from the Lord—just to obey you. Never once did I become God's servant, never once did I serve the Guru; I served only you. So today I pray you, listen to me."

*You are called the lord of the three regions;*
*Wherein even the gods are your disciples.*

"You are the lord of the physical, astral and causal regions; you are the master there, with control over all the gods and goddesses." If you read authoritative books on the subject, you will find that the mind's orders are carried out on every plane; he is a great lord, and all due respect is paid to him. Even when you rise above the physical form, you are still under his orders—*Andi* or astral mind—and then also in the causal plane, you are under the Brahmandi mind. It is his habit to again and again bring about your downfall. If the gods and goddesses bow down to him, what is the poor condition of Man?

*Rishi, Muni, all are under your orders;*
*Renouncer and righteous alike are in your territory.*

You are not even aware of what you are before transcending all three regions. The gods and goddesses are anxious to get the human form, and it means only that the human form is the highest in all creation due to its great spiritual possibilities; but man, who has been given this desirable boon, is selling himself to the mind. But one cannot say that it is entirely his fault, poor thing. *O Nanak, mind can be controlled, but only through His full mercy.* When God showers all His mercy and takes the soul above all three regions, then mind is powerless. Up to this point, the danger from the mind remains, to lead the poor soul astray.

During the time of Guru Gobind Singh, a certain story

tells that there was a rishi who left everything and went into the forests to do his meditation. Now there was also a certain king who had conquered many people and places, but whose greatest ambition was to conquer the rishi and make him obey his wishes. This strange ambition arose from the fact that the rishi was formerly a great king before he had renounced everything for a spiritual life. So when the king's advisers told him to go and conquer the rishi, he prepared himself and his army for battle and marched into the deep forests. On approaching the rishi, he found he was in meditation, but undaunted he accosted the holy man and told him, "Prepare yourself for a fight, I have come to do battle with you." The rishi calmly surveyed the king and his mighty armies, and replied, "Fight! I ran away from the worldly life for fear of my one great enemy, and hid myself here in these woods. My soul yet shivers to hear the sound of his name—even to take his name myself, my heart is quivering." The rishi went on describing his enemy to the king, until finally the king grew angry and shouted, "Is he stronger than me, this enemy of yours?" The rishi replied, "Even the thought of him almost destroys my soul—I have left everything to escape from him." The king then demanded to know the name of this fearful enemy, "What is the use?" said the rishi; "you will not be able to conquer him." The king boldly replied, "If I cannot conquer him, I will burn myself to death." The rishi then told the king that the great enemy he spoke of was the mind. From that very day the king tried everything possible, using all manner of means to gain control over his mind, but found that he could not. Finally, after admitting that he had failed, he burned himself alive at a place called Katasraj.

*Within Your control are brave men and yogis;*
*No one can disobey your word.*

Because of its vast area of rule, everyone is under the mind's control, so among those who practice meditation, very few rise above even the first region. Even fewer rise above the second, and to rise above the third is really something rare.

*You bind whoever you wish to this world;*
*Whoever you wish becomes free.*

The means of freedom lie in leaving the outer enjoyments of senses, but if these outer tastes are not cast aside, one remains imprisoned here. Just look at the condition of the world today: Whatever the mind orders is carried out unquestionably, and what is more, those very orders are highly praised throughout the world! The Guru's word and holy books are all ignored, but the mind's desires are fulfilled.

*Such high praise of you have I heard!*
*So now I plead to you.*

If one has served a person devotedly, one can claim at least some rights from that person. So — "Will you not listen to me just once? You are unhappy and so am I... just grant my one request, and you will also accomplish something worthwhile... only one word must you hear." All Masters have explained this situation in their different ways, to help the dear souls to realize the facts. Swami Ji Maharaj has personified the soul and the mind and has given expression to the plight of both.

*In this town (body), in this valueless place (world),*
*Why remain imprisoned in the darkness?*

"In this body full of filth there is only dense darkness, so why remain imprisoned here?—you who are lord of all three regions! Have you forgotten how great you really are?

You are really an emperor, yet you have become a garbage collector. Think! Awaken!"

The mind is also a brilliant magistrate who sits in judgment upon his own actions.

*Satguru told me one thing:*
*"Take the mind with you."*

The Satguru advises the soul to take the mind along if it wants to return home. He never says to ignore the mind, or leave it behind, but that the soul should make it understand and make it agreeable. As long as man does not kill the physical mind and withdraw from the sense level, he cannot proceed. One must leave all sense attractions and rise above body consciousness, otherwise it remains impossible to go higher and taste the Nectar of the Lord. Excessive eating and drinking, frittering away the attention on worldly sights, sounds and sensation—all these are outer enjoyments which deny one the bliss of the inner enjoyments. Lord Buddha said we should *Be desireless*, for desire is but sense enjoyment. Only by stepping aside from all this can one truly take a step ahead. If you can take the mind with you, it will be easier, but if you forget yourself and your aim in the mind's enjoyments, you will lose all desire to progress. Make it your companion, and make it understand the situation, for the mind *is* unhappy—so much so that at times it cries out in torment.

The world is a mere nothing—a place full of illusion and wrong-doing—valueless, with no virtue, a place where the darkest deeds are carried out. What is there here that can hold any real value for either the soul or the mind? Make it understand these realities, for at present it is strongly attached to all the falseness of the world, and it simply has to turn and face the truth to become attached to something higher.

If the soul does not leave the senses, how can it transcend the body? If it does not transcend the body, how can it realize what it is? It is a straightforward matter, requiring no special philosophy to understand. Where the world's philosophies end, there religion truly starts.

So the very first step is to withdraw from outer attractions and learn to lead a life of tranquility; only then will you be able to gain steady progress toward the Truth. Nothing can be gained by cursing the mind, for the mind is no small thing; so the Master's advice is to befriend it. There is the story of a clever man who was traveling alone with a huge load of valuables, when he encountered five or six men whom he knew to be rogues and tricksters. With dismay he thought to himself, "These men are rogues and will take all my goods, for I am alone and helpless." So as the men drew close he said to them, "My friends, I am so glad I have met you—kindly look after my things for me until we reach the destination."

The mind's habit is to drag everything downward, yet as your friend, even if it wants to hurt you, it will not do so. Under such an arrangement, he might even cooperate with you. If he desires food, then agree— "Yes, I will give you food, but first let us do a little meditation, then we will have food." If you immediately refuse the food, he will be tormented with the desire for it. He is like a stubborn donkey; the more you restrict him, the more stubborn he becomes. It is a very accurate definition of the mind. If you make a note in a book, "do not read page so-and-so," it will be the first page people will read; they won't be able to resist the temptation! So make your mind a companion; don't fight with him.

*So I plead with thee:*
*Why delay? Transcend body consciousness.*

There is no Truth in this world, no righteousness, no justice. Why not rise above and place all your attention in the Ineffable One Lord? Until this happens, that eye is not developed through which you will have true perception.

Two very powerful forces are anger and lust. They rule over everything. If the attention dwells on lust, the soul falls very low; in anger, the ego expands. The soul cannot be linked with Naam until it withdraws inwardly and rises above the senses. Our attention has instead become like an image of the mind. We want to enjoy all the low, worldly things, yet we say we want the highest thing of all—the Nectar of Life! It is all wrong—how far do we think we will go? Do one thing at a time; but do not remain under this false impression. One Saint says, *Where there is Naam, there is no kam* (lust)—*where there is kam there is no Naam; Two cannot remain at once—light and darkness.*

Most of our precious time is wasted in indulgence of jealousies, ego, scandal, criticizing, backbiting, possessiveness, etc. There are other degrading pitfalls, but remember that lust and anger are the most powerful, and a soul under their influence can never go very far within, for there is no tranquility, serenity or oneness. *He who has no lust and anger is the image of God.* Just think, the merest glance from such a person can still the mind and the undesirable things leave their hold for a while. The words that come forth from this rare personality are charged with his inner tranquility, so much so that men who hear them will also enjoy a serene stillness. It follows that air which passes close to ice will bring a refreshing coolness, as the air which passes near the fire will give warmth. So whatever the inner condition of a person, so his words will be charged with that atmosphere— be it anger, lust, or a sweet tranquility. Out of the abundance of his heart, a man speaks.

Everyone, literate and illiterate alike, is trapped in the powerful grip of these two most damaging traits. You have been asked to fully understand this, perhaps a thousand times, and you still do not understand the danger. Still, when the mind suggests something, you say, "Yes sir, whatever you say." Guru and God are very easily and quickly pushed aside. Very few people want to admit their mistakes, and with such conditions, salvation is very far away. To become a human being is most difficult; to realize God is not at all difficult. If only the soul would leave the senses and the mind, and come up above the body consciousness, it would achieve something great.

The mind is a lover of enjoyments, and in the Naam there is the *Maha Ras*—the most delectable Nectar one can ever taste. If only the mind would take one true sip, it would never again yearn for lower enjoyments. *This place is insipid, O friend* (mind); *Drink the Nectar of Naam.* We have also, *When that Nectar comes, this other taste is not to one's liking.* Now you are dragging the mind with you, to get inside. Then, you will have to persuade it to return! Beauty and attractive sounds are two principle factors in keeping one's attention outside, dragging it away from its natural, inner inclinations. The poisonous mind gets intoxicated while enjoying beautiful sights and sounds. Even a snake, on hearing the music of the vina, rests its head down and cannot move; it becomes helpless. If outer sounds can have such magnetism, what might be the attractive power of the inner spiritual music and beauty? All glory and beauty lie within you. Tulsi Sahib says, *When I went to Brahmand the world became insignificant; When I reached Par Brahm, Brahmand became like a washroom.*

So it is possible to gain control over the mind only in the company of a Satguru. He will help you to befriend it, and so make the path easier. Then it may start to listen to you, whereas it usually does not. Many find this difficulty in meditation, and say that their mind does not allow them to meditate. So Swami Ji is so beautifully advising one to: *With love, make it your companion.* Love is such a magnificent thing, that it can control even the worst-charactered person. No matter how much you may hate your pitiful situation, yet hate will only serve to increase the problem. You may throw all the filth out of a dirty house, yet the smell of that will spread and permeate not only the interior of the house but the surroundings too. The true solution is to start washing with the water of Love, and gradually the badness will be washed away forever. If you are good to your enemy, his enmity will be softened somewhat. Rise above the body, and if you would then care for a thousand things they will be given unto you. Guru Amardas says, *O mind, you desired a thousand things yet not one was fulfilled; Take my advice, and complete fulfillment will come.* One has seen this world and lived in it—now go up and enjoy *that* place.

> *Leave now all sensual indulgence*
> *And the way will be easier.*

If you do not stop enjoying the senses, you will not be able to leave the body. If there is filth stored up inside, you may cover it with the finest silks, yet you will not succeed in disguising the smell. You can pour the strongest perfume on it, yet the odor will penetrate through. If you cover a block of ice with a blanket, you will still get the effect of its coolness by sitting close by. *Except a man be born again, he cannot see the kingdom of God.* To be born again is not something new, but an old old thing which we have forgotten. Those who in the olden days used to take discipleship from a brahmin learned how to rise above body consciousness. And who was a true brahmin? He who knew the *Brahm* (Lord). A brahmin was one who gave experience of the Beyond. These days, only the custom remains. The same thing applies to the sacred thread given by the brahmin. It is made from three threads in one, and  means that for as long as one wears that thread one will live in truthfulness, desirelessness, and forgiveness. When all three virtues were established within one, one was born anew. The Holy Light which has been given to you people should be carefully guarded and practiced regularly.

At present you are at the mercy of the mind, for no one can say he is free, although at least you may not return to the world. When the mind tastes the Nectar of Naam, he will not wish to indulge in the lower enjoyments. Do this much, and you will have inner peace and happiness. There are other stages ahead wherein the soul falls again and again, even though she is not in this world.

Under the influence of the senses, it is very hard to reach the *gaggan* (the seat of the soul in the body) or rise above the body consciousness. If a man has even one strong desire, say that of lust, outwardly people may consider him to be a great soul, yet inwardly he is dancing to the tune of that desire. Outwardly he may be impressing people in many ways, but inwardly he is digging deeper that very pit into which he is fallen. Directly or indirectly he is drifting away from the Truth, and whatever he has learned has become null and void. So I humbly repeat that to become a human being is very difficult, whereas it is not difficult to realize the Lord. But the attention must persuade the mind to leave the senses and become proficient in the science of rising above into the Beyond. *When the senses are won, the five enemies will not attack.* The five enemies are lust, anger, greed, attachment and ego. Furthermore, *If the ten senses are controlled, the Light is manifest in that soul.* God's Light will fully manifest itself in that body wherein the five gross and five subtle senses are fully under control. Merely bowing down and making an outer show of respect to the Master will not help.

No matter to what religion you belong you will have to do this to succeed, for without it the Truth will not be opened up to you. It is not a subject to listen to or read about alone, it is a matter of doing.

Have you ever studied yourself to see if you have progressed at all? We usually find that we were better before, and now we have become worse, for this is the condition of the whole world today. A businessman gives great thought to the method of his business before he starts it, and every so often reviews the position of profit or loss, but we unheedingly throw away our precious lives, day after day, with never a care about how we stand spiritually. The aim was to gain freedom, but we are daily sinking into more slavery under the whip of our desires. If we live recklessly when our hair is black, at least when it turns to white we should give some thought to how we are living, and what it will avail us. Hindu or Muslim, Sikh or Christian—regardless of our religion we have to get out of the mind's clutches. But the same devilry continues! Merely learning a few words on the subject and then nodding the head as if one knows everything—is this Spirituality? We may be able to fool the world, but never the Lord. *To deceive people will avail nothing, particularly not God-realization.* The Lord is not an innocent child, to believe anything you wish; He sees the true condition of your life, inwardly and outwardly.

> *I have no other companion like you (mind);*
> *I am yours and you are mine.*

The soul offers the mind a token of friendship— "I have no other friend but you, for we have been companions for birth after birth—so listen to me today—I who have been a slave to you for so long"—with love and persuasion it tries to help the mind understand the situation.

*Now listen to your slave, and agree with me:*
*Rise above body consciousness and make your*
*home there.*

Whether it is said in very simple words or in a complicated fashion, the fact remains the same: the only way is to leave the senses behind and transcend into the Beyond. If you are really interested in Spirituality, you will be wise to fully accept this. You will also have to make your life pure and chaste. All Masters say the same, even those with a simple vocabulary: *What is there to realizing the Lord? Uproot it from here and plant it there!*

So ethical life is an important stepping stone to Spirituality. Truth is said to be above all, but Guru Nanak said that true living is yet above Truth, for without it one cannot recognize the Truth. No matter what your past has been—stop now! View the facts and start afresh. Stand still, and become tranquil—or you will not succeed.

Our Hazur used to say that people carry on eating the poison, and simultaneously groan and moan over its effects, but they will not stop eating more. Spiritual diaries have been prescribed after careful thought, and with deep purpose. Daily self-introspection must be kept up, and through this you will be able to see for yourself how far you are coming out of the senses' influence. With the Satguru's mercy one gets a little connection with the Light and Sound Principle, but if the life is not kept pure and chaste, the curtain of darkness will obscure the Light again. Some people say that when they come and meditate in the Ashram they get experience, whereas at home they do not. If your mind is pure you can sit anywhere at all; you will always have experience. In St. Luke, Christ says, *Take heed therefore that the Light which is in thee be not darkness.* You must be regular in your meditation to maintain that Light;

there are important reasons behind the keeping of diaries.

But what is our condition? *The same ungainly gait, which was there before and is even now.* We just know how to say, "Yes, yes" and nod our heads in a knowledgeable fashion. We know how to speak all right, but we do not *do* anything! We do not do enough bhajan and simran, and we do not care how incorrectly we live. O brothers, why do you come to a Master? Do you come just to bring him a bad name by not obeying his words? I have to speak of these things; how else can I make you understand how you are throwing your lives away?

It *is* difficult to obey. To give money is easy; it is also easy to bow down and make a show. To dance, sing, play religious music—all these things are simple matters; but to control the mind is exceptionally difficult. However, it must be done. Those who have taken initiation and do not medi-tate hardly ever show me their faces. When asked about this, they say, "But we attend Satsang." What is the use of this half-hearted effort? They do not keep a diary, and so there is no self-introspection. I always say, "Fold your hands to me, that is enough." Bowing down amounts to nothing if you are not obeying the Master's wishes. True prostration at the Guru's feet is really obeying his instructions implicitly. Make your life pure and chaste. Be a *humane* being—a man of use to other men. Do your bhajan and simran; release the soul from mind and senses. Bhajan and simran are food for the soul—do not give food to the body without first giving food to the soul. This type of obedience is truly bowing down in respect to your Guru.

It is most necessary to lead a pure and chaste life; not to go on remembering what we were, but to make sure of our future. To fall in sin is manly, but to remain there is devilish. One falls often, no doubt, but one becomes a good rider only after many a fall. But don't lie down and remain wherever you fall; that is bad. In the Koran it is written that God will not change any people who have no thought to change themselves. When there is a will, there is way. Keep your aim before you always, and work for it; then you will be sure of success. "O mind, listen once to me, your slave! Go above the body and make your home there!" To make a home in the Beyond means to learn to remain there for longer and longer periods, not for one or two minutes only. That place should gradually become more like one's home than this world.

> *As you were, so again become;*
> *Why suffer unhappiness and happiness here?*

Go back to whence you came and enjoy the real and lasting happiness there. There are unending miseries and joys in this world; none of them are real. The more you live above body consciousness, the more peace will reign in you. Even when you daily have to return, yet the coolness of spirit gained there will protect you from the heat of the world. And you can always go again at will. The world is suffering from illusion only. *The world is being consumed in illusion's invisible fire; As the inner fire of passion burns, so does the outer fire of illusion.* In sparsely scattered places you may find a complete Master sitting. One can enjoy the refreshing coolness only in their company.

> *Satguru revealed the secret unto me;*
> *Take the mind as companion, and return home.*

For as long as the mind remains within its own territory, you have to take it with you. If you want to start from the beginning alone, that is more difficult—almost impossible. Why? Because you have become the very image of mind, and cannot separate yourself from it.

*I, the soul, am in your power;*
*Without your help, I cannot contact the Shabd.*

Cooperation from the mind is necessary, for where does one contact the Shabd? Above the body consciousness, after leaving the senses. The soul cannot hear the Sound without rising above the physical, above the nine centers, reaching the tenth; and without the mind's help, the process is very long. This is an appeal to the mind so that it will agree to help—like a man inducing his friend to do some of his work for him.

*If you do not listen to me,*
*Then go into the cycle of eighty-four.*

If the mind does not listen and cooperate, then one has to continue on the wheel of births and deaths. So, it is to the mind's own advantage to be agreeable, if it wants to gain freedom from the coming and going in creation.

*Now show mercy unto me,*
*Hear my plea, search out that Sound.*

There is a Sound of Truth vibrating within—a song which is sung in every being. There is a great attraction in hearing this Sound, through which all other attractions will fade away, and the stage of senses will be left behind: one becomes free of them. *This mouse-mind has become heavy; by drinking the weight of God's Name.* The mind can be weighted down by the mercury-like quality of the Naam, rendering it impossible to run around loose or engage in its ever-constant oscillations. There is no other means of controlling the mind. The accounts of Lord Krishna's life state that he jumped into the River Jumna and controlled the hydra-headed serpent there with the sound of his flute. This many-headed serpent is the mind, which has a thousand ways of inflicting its poison, and without that Sound from the

Beyond, it cannot be controlled or overcome. Outer intellect and knowledge have no power over it, for though it may remain quiet for a short time, it will then run away again. If you cover a fire with ashes, it would seem there is no fire at all, yet a strong breeze will revive it and reveal the heat lying beneath. However if you throw water upon it, even a thousand tornadoes would fail to revive it.

Keep the company of those who are the Naam itself. *The Word was made flesh and dwelt among us.* In the atmosphere surrounding such personalities, there is a charging—a radiation—a rare tranquility. One Muslim prophet declared that the mind cannot be killed until it comes under the shadow of a Perfect Master. Even one thousand practices will be of little avail if you cannot leave the senses and get a contact with Naam, without which there is no salvation.

*Let you and me climb above—*
*We will reside on the hill Sumera.*

Sumera lies above the physical plane, and the soul says, "Come, let us go there—the days are hot here, and there we will enjoy a cool breeze—the whole world is being consumed in flames—come, let us rise above the heat of physical consciousness and enjoy the coolness—O mind, we will be happy there, for here we are both unhappy."

*When we reach there, you will be king,*
*And I will go ahead to Radha Soami.*

The mind becomes King of Triloki (the three regions— physical, astral and causal) and remains there, for mind is the instrument of the Negative Power, just as the soul is an entity of God, the Ocean of All Consciousness. So the mind comes into its own kingdom, blending in one with the Lord of the three stages, and the soul goes to its true home.

## II

*The mind replies thus to the soul:*
*"The taste of these I cannot leave."*

THE MIND says, "O soul, whatever you say is true, but I am powerless before these desires and cannot leave them, even though I want to." Can we not see our own condition in this? Many times the mind does agree and wants to join our aspirations, but it helplessly wanders away again into the outer attractions. *The steps are forward, but the mind goes backward.* It is too much identified with lower things, so all learning, writings, all outer knowledge is cast aside—nothing remains when a wave of passion seizes him—Guru, religion, sacred scriptures, all are as nought. So the mind says, "I do want to separate myself from these senses, but I cannot, so what shall I do?"

*"What shall I do, how can I obey?*
*At the senses' mercy, I cannot leave them."*

"The senses insist on dragging me everywhere—how can I get free? Tell me what to do." The senses are extremely powerful. Sometimes it is the sense of sight which will drag you, sometimes you hear something and all control is gone; the other senses also play their part. So one's mind is pulled around helplessly. Guru Arjan says, *The Guru has made me controller; I am mistress of the house.* This house is the physical form, and we can be queen in that house, for the Guru teaches such a marvelous method that enables us to gain control. Also, *Ten maidservants were given under my orders.* The ten senses become one's maidservants who obey orders. These days our condition is so degenerate that lust, anger, greed, attachment and ego are driving us farther and farther away from the Truth. Just look at the degradation in man! If a person could stand aside from it all and see the situation as it really is, one would be appalled and lament the folly of oneself and mankind as a whole.

Swami Ji also says, *Your home is above illusion, my loved ones; You have tied yourselves to this earthly house.* We were once indwellers of that true and everlasting place, but we got caught in the net of clay and water. Guru Nanak says, *You* (the Lord) *dwell in the true home; I am lost in this form of matter.* God resides in Truth, and we are deteriorating in this illusory existence. Spirituality is not merely waving a banner and shouting some slogan; neither does it lie in outer practice or in certain apparel and appearance. Spirituality means to withdraw from sense enjoyments and become connected to the Naam. You might do it today, or tomorrow, any time in this life, or not until some other life—but you must do this work yourself, no priest or minister can do it for you. Only a spiritual Master's attention can help you.

*"By force and exertion of will I lost everything;*
*Now I have no strength."*

The mind describes how he has often exerted his strength, almost wrestler-like, and said, "I will not do this!" But again and again he was tempted and overcome by the senses. We all make strong resolutions, but when it comes to keeping them we fall down. Swami Ji is quite openly revealing our own condition—these are our very own cries of anguish, and the promises we make to change tomorrow—that tomorrow which is in the Negative Power's hands, and never comes. Everyone is in the same boat and crying out the same cry; so look within yourselves and see what you are doing with your precious lives. Why not start the good work now? The mind is very wise, it is no insignificant thing. Like a magistrate, his thoughts are wise and he observes that with all his efforts there is still no freedom, only defeat. Some people are dragged in passion, some are roasted alive in the fire of attachment, some are caught in the nets of ego and pride, stiffly and proudly strutting their way through life. The whole world is in this terrible condition.

> *"I want to leave all enjoyments;*
> *Just seeing them I am helpless."*

There is so much attraction in the outer enjoyments that the mind ignores its wisdom and is rendered too helpless to fight. When a cat sees a mouse, it cannot resist it. So what happens? We say, "let us enjoy now and face whatever the consequences when they come." We are usually aware of our follies to some extent, but too late.

> *"The past I repent, and will always repent,*
> *But at the next chance, like a thief I repeat."*

We are sorrowful over our actions, but have no resistance and repeat our mistakes. It the lament of man over those things which have caught and kept him prisoner in the world. It may be he knows his condition; he reads, he thinks, he attends Satsang, he makes resolutions, but always falls back into the old habits again and again. This is why I have advised keeping a daily spiritual diary. It is a method of self-introspection which I have introduced after much deep thought on the subject. If you would only keep it... even send it to me blank! How many months would you go on sending it blank? The benefit of this is a moral upliftment—this is a very sweet way of explaining it.

With time, methods change. In olden days, clothes were washed by thrashing them against rocks, and nowadays we have got to the stage of dry cleaning, without the use of water. Masters have used many ways through the ages, trying to induce an awareness in men of their way of life. Those who are not following this Science correctly never keep diaries. The first thing the Negative Power does when he wants to keep control over a soul is to stop them doing bhajan and simran. The individual finds that there is always something to lure him away from his meditation. This is his first method, and secondly he slips that question into the mind: "Why go to the Guru or the Satsang? What is the use of it?" Satsang is the very place where a turning point can be effected and an awareness of wrongdoing and wrong living is achieved, so he will try to persuade us not to go there. If you have the strength to ignore him, he will then suggest that you just go and bow down and then leave. He will place all kinds of doubts in the mind, and instead of the fullest benefit from the Satsang, the person returns home with nothing but dissatisfaction or the bad effects of gossiping and backbiting from other wavering individuals. These are two very powerful weapons that the Negative Power is constantly wielding.

> *"How can I rise to the gaggan, my beloved?*
> *I am like an over-spirited horse."*

The mind says, "You want me to rise to the seat of the soul (*gaggan*), but how can I in this present condition? The sense enjoyments are always luring me on, and I gallop at full speed after them, like a spirited horse beyond control. I cannot sit still for a minute, so what to do?" The poor heart has laid bare its pathetic helplessness, and now Swami Ji reveals the solution:

> *"To you I now speak these words:*
> *Go to the Satguru, and plead to Him."*

Only through rising above the body and entering the gaggan lies the true happiness, but this is not in the mind's power, so he says we should go to the Satguru and plead to Him to take us out of here— "He has the love, and we are prisoners—He also has come as a prisoner, just for our sakes—He put on this bag of filth, this human form, just to release us. O Satguru, if you do not help us, then who can?" He who has left the house and is standing on the roof can catch hold of another's hand and drag him up. *The powerful Guru drags the soul out.* By giving a boost, the complete Master gives an experience of rising above body consciousness. We need this help, otherwise how would we rise above by ourselves? We get an inner contact and a taste of the Nectar of Naam which, by devoting more time in meditation, becomes the *Maha Ras*—Greater Nectar which withdraws one completely from the outer attractions.

So with Naam, the mind can be controlled. And to receive connection with Naam, one must go to the Satguru. A Muslim prophet says that this mind can never be killed unless one comes under the shadow of a *Pir* (Master). *The attention can be stilled in the company of a Sadhu* (Master); *Then the stillness of mind is realized.* Even the scriptures cannot be fully understood without the Master's company, for with stillness of mind all things are seen in true perception—unconfused. True understanding does not come when sitting at home and thinking. The Master's company is something like an ocean's breakwater, which when the waves dash against it, breaks the impact of their force so that they become less boisterous. In that very same water, one can swim without danger. The Master's company has a charging, a wonderful stillness. *In the company of the Saint, the Lord seems near.* This is the result of the radiation which permeates and surrounds the Master. So in Satsang we become aware of the Truth for a while, even at our first visit; but we again wander away. So the mind tells us the solution for these difficulties: "If you want to control me, take the Nectar of Naam. I cannot leave the enjoyments, for just by seeing some attraction I become helpless and a recklessness is born in me; heedless of everything, I say let me do it now and never mind the consequences; so let us go to the Satguru and plead with Him to take us out of this predicament."

*"Let us place ourselves at His feet, you and me;*
*Through that Satsang we will gain something."*

The mind is now willing to leave all its cleverness and appeal to the Satguru. *Satsang* is the name we give to the company of an awakened soul. *A Satguru makes a Satsang.* The company of learned people or the reading of books may be most interesting, but it is not a Satsang. There has to be one present who has risen above mind and senses and who has become truly awakened. A Muslim Saint says, *The whole world is asleep, and brother, you also are asleep with it.* How can a sleeping man awaken another who is also asleep?

At Satsang there is great charging, but you must be connected to it; it is no good just sitting there. Furthermore, your attention should be on the Master alone; even if you are thousands of miles from him physically, you can still enjoy Satsang. Naturally, there is more benefit in being completely attentive near his physical presence, for you will get a direct charging; but no matter where you are you will still have help, if you are receptive. Some people ask, what is the actual effect of Satsang? Well, if you tie a wild horse to a stake, he will naturally make a run for it, but when he reaches the end of the tether he will be brought up with a jerk. He may try to run away several times, but will always be pulled up by the tether. Satsang has some effect like this on the mind, and after repeating a few times the inclination to run away grows less, until it eventually learns to still itself. Satsang also cleanses the bad smells which come from the habits of lust, anger, greed, etc., that is, if the person is receptive. He becomes something different.

Why do Masters come and what is their work? They

release the soul from mind and senses and connect it with Naam. They come only for this purpose, though they go through many difficulties and work hard. People abuse them and call them atheists, but they are not concerned and carry on with the work. Eventually the mind realizes that to go to such a soul is the only remedy. Leaving body consciousness is the first step; if the soul does not go on further and achieve *Trigun-atit* (above the three regions), it will not get the permanent peace. Go to the Satguru and obey him. *The words of a complete Master, I tie on my heart.* Tie his words close to you—they should not enter from one ear and leave from the other—tie them securely in your heart.

> *"When the Satguru showers His mercy,*
> *Every moment He protects me."*

If you go to someone for protection with a sincere heart, putting all your hopes in him after all the disappointment and defeat, he has to accept and protect you on principle. He is not concerned that you may be a great sinner; he sees only that you are a soul at the mercy of the mind and senses. His work is to release this soul and release also the mind from the sense enjoyments, and to give the Nectar of Naam through which the life can be turned into success. He does not care if people consider him good or bad, or if one has faith in him or not, yet he will never leave those who are under his care. Christ said, *I shall never leave thee nor forsake thee until the end of the world.* Hazur used to say that when the Satguru gives initiation he does not rest until he has taken the disciple to the lap of Sat Naam or Sat Purush. You may leave him, and put your attention elsewhere, but he does not forsake you.

So brothers, obey my direction, do your meditation even if it be a little, and increase whatever experience you have been given. See into each action of your daily life, and keep a diary. Do not leave off your bhajan and simran. There is a remedy for mistakes, but there is no remedy for disobeying, and the road is long for such people. Those who have Naam will definitely reach God, but it will be a long journey for whosoever disobeys the instructions. You have to do it, whether in one birth, two, or four, so why not now? Remember that the disciple who always has his face turned toward the Guru, draws the Guru's attention. *If you keep someone in your heart, you will reside in theirs.* The tortoise lays her eggs in the sand and yet herself remains in the water; but her attention is always directed to the eggs. It does not matter if the disciple is in a different place than the Master, when the Master directs his attention the disciple should be receptive; that is all that is necessary. If there is receptivity in both hearts, then? Kabir Sahib says that even if the disciple is separated from the Guru by seven oceans, still they can be one through the attention. Turn your face, and direct your attention to him.

A man once wrote to me that the Satguru was closer to him than anything else, and whether it is early morning or night, he comes and sits beside him, talking to him and giving such amazing talks containing information with very deep meanings. The man said that he had written down twenty such talks from the inner Master. Now, surely the Guru must be something other than just a physical form! He does have a physical form, but he is not imprisoned therein. He comes as a doctor for those who are captured by mind, senses, and worldly attraction. Outwardly there may be no apparent difference between him and us, yet he is certainly not a prisoner as we are. If you think of him as merely a man, what will you receive? At the most, he will make a good man of you. If you think he has no higher spiritual powers, then how will he give you spiritual help?

Make a wave of receptivity from heart to heart—this is

the way to realize the Lord. Become even a little receptive and the Master in you will restrain you when you are in danger of going wrong. As a mother cares for her child, the Satguru cares a million times more. Even a gambler with the worst of habits will be loved and cared for by his mother; she will never allow him to starve. Having received the protection of a God-realized man, do you think he would ever forget you? Keep your face turned toward him, and even with the outer eyes observe how much help you get.

> *"I cannot rise of my own strength;*
> *Unless the Guru will release me from bondage."*

The mind has not the strength to rise above this jungle; he must have assistance from the greater power of the Guru—a complete Master, who will break all fetters. Life after life, one is a slave to the world, and after death one will again come to the world. *Heaven and hell, again and again birth.*

> *Hearing all this, the soul was overjoyed:*
> *"Let us quickly go and get our fetters cut."*

It is naturally a great day for the soul when mind at last is willing to cooperate, and once that awareness is there, without delay it wants to be at the feet of the Satguru.

It instinctively knows that He is the very life of all life who will release it from the miseries and strife. Whenever the mind has clear understanding and is inclined toward God, then quickly sit down for meditation—do not wait for tomorrow, do not wait even a few hours, or his mood will change and again he will cheat you out of the benefit. No matter what you are doing, when mind and soul are one, sit in meditation at once. Who knows what will happen in the next minute? Such an ideal mood is rare and valuable; there should be no delaying to take advantage.

THE MIND REPLIES TO THE SOUL

*Both entered into the protection of Satsang;*
*They drank again and again the overflowing Nectar*
*of Naam.*

When mind and soul sit together in harmony at the feet of a true Master, both drink the Water of Life. When the Master gives a sitting and the mind is willing to go with the soul, both taste the Nectar. *Drink a cup, and become intoxicated.* Guru Nanak says, *O Nanak, the intoxication of Naam inebriates day and night.* So this is the secret, if you to taste that Divine Nectar of the Naam: make the mind your friend and companion and get some work out of him, for he is a lover of enjoyment and in the Naam is great sweetness, tasting which, all other tastes become insipid.

This Science is not for any particular religion; it is purely the solution to a man-problem. Anyone, no matter to which religion they belong, may have the benefit of this solution which has been described so beautifully in this hymn. If you start today what has been recommended, you will be on the way to success and to achieving the true happiness which is everlasting. There is no need to regard your situation as hopeless—*There is hope for everybody.* No matter how bad or low or cruel a man is, yet there is hope for him, for the Satguru is a true Washerman, who purifies by washing away the dirt of the senses. Just do what he says—do not be a manmukh (mouthpiece of the mind), but become a *Gurumukh* (mouthpiece of the Guru).

By merely looking at a Master you will not get salvation; remember that. *Just by seeing the Guru, salvation does not come; While you do not love the Satguru's words.* Do whatever the Master says: follow his advice, obey him and become receptive to him, for the soul gains strength through receptivity. The work which may seem impossible just now will become easy. All sins are burned away in the company of a true Master, and from a true Master you can receive the precious gift of Naam. The Satguru is so powerful that not only the disciple gets benefit, but those who love the disciple will also gain his protection. This has been proven by historic spiritual records.

In my own life there is an instance of a cousin of mine who fell seriously ill and her father, my uncle, wrote and asked me if I would go and see her. He wrote that I should lose no time as her condition was extremely dangerous. In those days I was in Lahore, and had come under the grace and protection of Hazur Baba Sawan Singh Ji. As I received the letter, that very night I left Lahore by train and arrived the next day at my cousin's village, at about 1 or 2 p.m. I was then told what had happened the night before: At the time I was leaving Lahore, my sick cousin said to her father, "He has come, and there is an elderly man with him." She then described how I went away after telling the elderly man that this was the patient. She said to her father, "Don't let Bhapa Ji (elder brother) go." The father replied, "But he is not here." She said, "Yes, he came with this man, but now he is going." From that very moment her condition started to change for the better, and when I reached there she was much improved and asked me why I had left after coming to see her the night before. I explained that I had not come then, and that whosoever had to come had come. She recovered completely from her sickness, and I asked her one day, "If I show you that elderly man, will you recognize him?" She said, "Yes, of course." So when Hazur was in Rawalpindi for some two months' program I took her there. We were standing on the verandah of Lala Raja Ram Ji's house when I saw Hazur coming in the distance. I said, "Look there, who is that coming?" She cried, "Why, it is the same man who came with you that night to see me." So wherever there is affinity, that law of affinity will work. If your affinity has been developed, you will get protection; just see what great blessing can be received from the Satguru. It is another criterion of true Masters, and wherever the true Master is, you will find thousands of such instances. They do not make a show of miracles, but miracles in varying degrees are a frequent occurrence with each disciple. There must be reasons for the high praise of Masters which is found in the holy scriptures and records!—although this does not include of course the so-called acting, posing type of "master" of which the world has an abundance these days.

> *Both together rise above the gaggan*
> *And become intoxicated with Nectar of the Shabd.*

Go into And (the astral plane) and then Brahmand (the causal plane) and catch the higher Sound from there. Taste that Nectar, and then go even higher to catch a higher Sound and then taste that Nectar. In the huge domain of Maha Kal (the Greater Negative Power) there is Sound upon Sound vibrating. When you reach Maha Kal, the mind remains there, for he cannot go beyond that. From there, the soul goes on alone to its true home after personifying itself.

> *Radha Soami bestowed His mercy upon them;*
> *They were showered with diamonds, pearls and*
>     *rubies.*

The word *Radha Soami* has been used here to mean the Lord Himself. Sometimes it is used for the Guru, from which human pole the Lord speaks out. We should have respect for all names given to the Lord. When the Lord showers His mercy, the Satguru's compassionate eye falls upon the soul and both the soul and the mind start rising above. In that glance, there is upliftment beyond any price; you could not buy it with millions. And yet, the fortunate receive it free of charge. It is a matter of receptivity and devotion.

*Radha Soami showered such grace*
*Through which I conquered the bowl of negativity.*

The Lord, sitting at the human pole, makes it possible for the soul to overcome all negativeness. In the Gurbani it is asked, *What is the Negative Power?—I can kick it out or remove it altogether and replace it.* The records containing the words of the great Masters have an authoritative truth in them, for only the Masters (or anyone else on whom they may shower grace) see the true state of affairs. The Negative Power has no standing, unless with the approval of the Positive; but we are misguided, foolish people who sometimes allow ourselves to be drawn away from the true Guru—forgive me, but this happens. No matter what difficulties come, no matter what your condition may be, never leave hold of the Guru's hand—for your own sake.

You will have intoxication and upliftment in the company of him at whose human form the Lord Himself is working. It is a natural law that you will go to that stage which your Master has reached. This true intoxication can only be enjoyed in company with the Truth, not from books, etc.—though you may read your whole life through. There is a certain stillness in that company, and everything becomes clarified, for the waves of radiation issuing forth from that pole have a clarifying quality. Therefore all doubts regarding the Lord—what He is, what He is not—are removed. Just being near to a Master gives one a feeling that God is within one's reach. If one lives with full attention within the close surrounding of a Master, the Negative Power and illusion cannot affect you.

Swami Ji Maharaj has also said that the soul transcends that place where *Negative and illusion go on beating their breasts.* In other words, they cry out to see the soul escaping from their clutches. This escape can only happen with the grace of a *Samrath Purush*—a complete Master. Otherwise, who has the power to leave the senses' enjoyments, even though one thousand kinds of knowledgeable meditation be done?

Dadu Sahib has said that a true Sadhu is he who does not stretch out his hand to gold and women. One must rise above all enjoyments and not be ruled by greed and lust, for while one remains under their influence no real progress can be made. The quicker we withdraw, the quicker will be our progress; even daily promotion can be achieved. Not only will one see the Truth with the inner eye, but will discern easily and openly the true situation in outer life. Those who have already realized the Truth did not themselves drop straight from Heaven—so it is the hereditary right of each human being to realize himself and realize God.

Those who have already come to the feet of a true Master are greatly blessed indeed. There may be one, two, or more in the world; the more the better, naturally. History tells of occasions when there have been more than two at one time, and quite often two at once. Do not get into confusion: go to any Master, but just be sure that he is a true Master. What is the criterion for this? He must take you above the body consciousness for a while, open your inner eye, and give you an experience. Go to whoever gives *this* way up. You may call him by any name you like—Guru, Sadhu, Mahatma, Master, or anything else. When they asked Hazur what to call him, he said, "Call me brother, or think of me as a teacher, or equal to your father, but live according to my advice; and when you reach the higher regions and see there the glory of the Guru, you may say what is in your heart."

We often suffer from the mistake of sitting on the outside, discussing the opinions of others about the Master, but how can anyone have faith if they have not seen his true form?

Real faith comes when you leave your body and go into the higher realms of Light and see that Power working there, and see clearly also that same Power working in this world.

There is a village near Buland Shaher in U. P. and in that village a certain Satsangi had a farm. (This happened some years back.) This Satsangi had grown a very nice crop of watermelons, and eventually they were ready for gathering. The farmer and his workers had intended to gather them in one day, but due to the large crop the sunset hour approached before they could collect all the melons, so they planned to continue the next morning. When one worker suggested guarding the fruit in the night, the Satsangi said, "Do not worry, the Guru is overhead, so you may rest and be ready for the work tomorrow."

While they slept, a band of thieves came in the night to steal the fruit. They had started gathering the melons when one thief looked up and saw a Sikh coming toward him, brandishing a stick. He turned to call out to his confederates, but then he saw an amazing sight: each thief was being chased by a Sikh, and each Sikh had identically the same appearance! These Sikhs gave them all a good beating and drove them off the land. The next day when the Satsangi went into his fields he saw many watermelons gathered and left on the ground, and he could not understand why, if someone had gathered them, they had not taken them away.

After a week or so, that very band of thieves came to the Satsangi farmer and begged him for forgiveness. They told him all that had happened, and said that since that night each one of them had suffered so much with pain and high fever which would not leave them, that they had come to plead for his forgiveness. The farmer said, "I am nothing that I can forgive you, but my Guru is a complete Master."

At this they entreated him to take them to the Guru, at which he agreed and brought them here to Ashram.

So the purpose of this story is that we should always keep our face toward the Guru, that is all. That Guru-Power is not the physical body, but it resides in that physical form. Greatly blessed are those that have come to the feet of a true Master, and through his mercy have received the contact with Naam. This hymn came from one of the true Masters— how openly they describe the facts! It is most necessary to understand properly, and having understood, to then inherit that very thing. Even a single hymn is enough, if you live up to it.

*Sant Kirpal Singh Ji*
*(1894-1974)*

# 8

# Thief of Your Life's Breath

BHAJAN is imperative to right living, for the true meaning of bhajan is to go within and rejoin the Lord—nothing more nor less. It has ever been the aim of all true Masters to teach people this kind of bhajan: the inner bhajan through which, by contact with God within, the mind becomes intoxicated with His presence. The Music of the Spheres or *Akhand Kirtan* (perpetual melody) should be constantly audible to the devoted soul, thereby intoxicating it; for the soul is itself a part of that same Sound.

The Audible Life Stream has power to render this world's odious taints totally ineffective, and so we are urged to regularly attend Satsang—the only place where we can be in company with Truth. Our soul is not free from mind and senses; it is not fortunate enough to have as yet achieved oneness with the Truth; so it desperately needs the company of one who *is* at one with Truth. *Get dyed in the colorless Naam.* When the Masters dye the souls in the Sound of Naam, no other color can take effect; but for the unfortunate undyed, the world's influence continues to apply stain upon stain. The cause of all our distress can be traced to the fact that we have not been drenched in the true color of Naam.

From where does this color come? *He is the overflowing intoxicating color of Love, the company of the Saint infuses a real desire.* In the company of him in whom the Love of God, God's intoxicating color, is overflowing, one can absorb the radiation of this very nature. If then, through his mercy, we also get a contact or connection with the God in him, we will have that intoxication with us twenty-four hours a day. *The intoxication of Naam, O Nanak, inebriates night and day.* And if we study the matter, we find that all the grumbles of the world arise from lack of this contact.

When anyone would complain to Hazur about inability to still the mind, he would reply, "Your simran is not constant enough." And for the complaint of not being able to sit for long in meditation, the same reply was given. Our real difficulty is that the world's color has drowned us! If it could be bleached out then we would become clean and ready for a new fresh color to enliven us. A dirty cloth must first be washed clean before attempting to dye it. Our heart and intellect are stained with that color coming from the level of mind and senses. We are stained with the actions of life, and added to this are the stains of the past—birth upon birth. Even if you put aside past lives and consider this life alone... how many years have passed already? It might be that through the mercy of some Master you were fortunate to be in his company and enjoy the benefit of a little of that Naam color; but even so it is said that we must, *Do simran and serve the Satguru.* We are dyed in the worldly color through doing the world's simran, and it can only be washed out by doing the simran (remembrance) and dhyan (contemplation) of the Lord.

So you can say that the first step is simran—controlled thought—and it should be constant, without a break. This is the washing process, before the soul is ready to be drenched in the color of God. *One jap* (repetition), *one thought. Think of One, sigh for One, sing the praise of One. Through mind and body, with love repeat the Lord's Name.* With true service of mind and body, in love and devotion, one should increase one's remembrance of the Lord until there is nothing but constant sighing for Him. Then there is indication of awakening. We sigh for worldly things, but it is rare to find someone who sighs in remembrance of the Lord.

Simran is the first step. Logically, one will be drenched in the color of the one in whose name the simran is done. *If you keep someone in your heart, you will reside in theirs.* If the disciple remembers the Guru, the Guru will remember the disciple. And if there is remembrance on both sides, that creates receptivity, and the Guru and disciple become one. *Satguru protects the disciple with His life.* In such condition, the disciple becomes suffused in the Guru's color. In the clear heart, the true knowledge becomes apparent. Naturally, those who do Simran will be dyed in that color. When Masters feel so inclined, they reveal themselves somewhat and great wisdom comes forth—for *our* benefit, in whom the color of the Lord is not yet fast.

Realize that the soul is a conscious entity; it is ever-existent, all wisdom and perfect bliss. When the mind and senses are washed clean from their dirty color, and the soul which is attention gets connected to the greater attention, then without effort it will radiate bliss. It is said that those who do not do bhajan will never be free from misery: *Lethargy will constantly torment them.* They are always lazy. When does this procrastination come and when does it go? *For the negative work he is all attentiveness, while waiting on the Naam, he slumbers and slumbers.* To gratify the senses, he is wide awake and ready, even at midnight. But for bhajan... "not now, we will see tomorrow." This is mainly due to his regular association with outer enjoyments; he has inclination toward them. He has done little or no bhajan to speak of, has not drunk deep enough to enjoy its sweet nectar, and therefore feels disinclined. With lethargy, procrastination becomes the thief of time "not just now, wait awhile... we will do it tonight, no, tomorrow morning... let us just finish this work, and then..." The tragic result? If you put off the moment, the other moment which one imagines will be more opportune, will never come.

If one becomes lazy, then laziness will induce sleep. If your meditation is not fruitful, how will you know what is inside? Even when at initiation, through the mercy of the Master, something is seen within, yet a man will start thinking it is all imagination. This is how the mind hoodwinks us, with the result that the soul recedes into the enjoyments and scatters its attention. Though imperishable and unchangeable, it is under the mind's influence; through connection with the mind it came into creation, and has suffered the cycle of birth and death ever since. Imprisoned in the illusion, its attention dispersed in the world, it falls prey to passions, anger, etc., becoming more and more diffused. Through passion, the soul can fall very low. The seat of the soul is high, between the eyebrows. And the seat of passion? Well, everyone knows where that is.

*Where there is passion, Naam is not there; where there is Naam there is true desire. Both cannot stay together; the sun and the night are each in its own place.* Naam is the same as the ever-existent God, which is in each being and controls every soul in every form; but the link with Naam is made above the senses, behind and between the eyes, to where the soul withdraws at the time of death when it leaves the scene of life. This is termed the seat of the soul. If a soul is in the Naam's color, how can desires affect him? But when the attention is in the body, he becomes tormented by passions. Without the stabilizing force of Naam, the soul remains diffused in the world, subject to the constant agitation of the mind. Passion and anger have the same results. If an obstacle comes between us and our desire, whether apparent or concealed, then anger arises, followed by envy, criticism, backbiting, enmity, petty squabbling and other things—we drift from one bad habit to another. And all this is due to lack of substantial meditation.

Even if a little was done with deep sincerity, some intoxication would be enjoyed. *When this Nectar comes, other wine seems tasteless.* Having tasted the real Nectar of Life, one will leave a thousand tasks to sit and enjoy it. Every free minute will be put to use; one will readjust one's life to make more and more time for meditation. When people are asked why they do not meditate, their excuse is that there is never any time for this precious work, although the "true disciple" is always ready and willing to attend to the worldly pursuits. We are not faithful to our bhajan because we have not had enough inner experience of Naam.

*Those in passion and anger's torment are drowned to death in a river of greed.* Daily this greed increases: he who has a hundred dollars desires a thousand, and when he gets that he wants more. Added to this, people want praise without doing any good—they spend their lives in lies, cheating and cunningness—the life-span drifts away without an ounce of self-control.

Seeing this condition, the Master says, "Stop where you are! Look at your condition!" It is all through the lack of meditation, and the only cure is to join the soul back to the Lord. Even a little intoxication derived from steady daily practice will start to erase the taste for outer pleasures. These outer attractions are making it extremely difficult for the mind to withdraw and go inward. If we start to enjoy inner sweetness... *When that sweetness comes, this other flavor is not to the liking.* Naturally the sweeter taste will render others insipid.

The Master's work is to connect the soul with the perpetual Sound. He gives a connection with the Lord's very reflection—free, without charge. Having received this priceless gift of Nature, one should devote enough time to increase it, by daily practice. Then when one starts to really enjoy the Nectar, outer things will recede automatically without any effort. To gain control of one's being, to bring one's whole life under that perfect control, to help oneself to cut away from outer attractions, requires self-introspection. Start by consciously controlling a small fraction of your life. You will be able to succeed if you are also enjoying a little inner intoxication of Naam. All Masters say there is no success without meditation.

*Now that Kal* (negativeness) *has come, quickly sow the seeds of Naam; forget not yourself in illusion, now is the sowing season.* They tell us that the direct way out is not through karma (action, past or present) or dharma (religion or ritual correctness) for these are related at the level of senses only. While the soul is without connection with God and is not drenched in the color of Naam, it has to return to this world. In the Gurbani it is written, *To meet a Gurumukh, to have the company of a Sadhu, and the color of Naam; this is the true meeting, beloved, and whoever got these truly spoke Thy Name from his heart.* The treasure can only be received from one who has it. When a drunkard meets another drunkard, how they dance to the same tune! Similarly, when those who drink the Naam's Nectar meet, how high their souls fly together! Whatever company you choose to keep, you will become the same.

Those who see the Truth describe the same thing in different languages. Maulana Rumi has said that to be fortunate enough to have the company of a God-in-man for twenty minutes will give more benefit than dedicating one hundred years of full devotion to the Lord, sincerely and without show. This unique color cannot be made or manufactured; it can be received only from the direct source of supply. It is already within man, but covered with the filth of ages, and can only be ignited through the company of him who is in complete control of his attention—who is overflowing with intoxication. You may call it the alms of Naam.

Meditation is most necessary, for only by meditation will all things come of their own accord. There are those who steal the time away from their meditation—*The thieves of bhajan will be afflicted with misery. And we have, O Nanak, the whole world is unhappy.* What is the cure for this dreadful plight? *Only those are happy who are sustained by Naam.*

> *Man in physical form flitters,*
> *How can he sing the Lord's praise?*
> *Great are the senses' torments,*
> *Passion and anger torture him daily.*

These are the words of Guru Amardas. A hundred men if wise will say the same thing. Pitiful is the condition of those whose mind restlessly roams among nine doors (nine orifices of the human form), who are dragged around amid the vices of worldly life. The poor soul sometimes falls in passion or diffuses itself in anger. To learn the accurate and most definite way to reach God, one must keep the company of an enlightened person; and in his company one will be able to have true remembrance of the Lord. He can teach one how to hold this remembrance throughout every phase of life: working, walking, eating, sitting, etc.

> *This sphere of vices is insipid, discard it, friend;*
> *Drink the Nectar of Naam.*

Because of the senses, the whole world is drifting into vice of one form or another. If even a single sense is prominent, how damaging that can be! For instance, in moths the sense of sight is so strong that they burn themselves to death through the attraction of light to the eye. In fish, freely swimming in oceans and rivers, the sense of taste is so great that they allow themselves to be baited by various tidbits, are caught, and lose their lives. The poor fish, with the hook stuck in its throat, gives up its freedom after much torment of thrashing about in an effort to escape its captor. Consider the black bee, whose sense of smell drags it from flower to flower, until it is swallowed up by that certain blossom which closes tight at the minutest touch.

We have talked of sight, taste and smell. What of the remaining two senses, hearing and touch? The deer is an animal so fleet of foot that it is most difficult to catch. Even when jumping backwards, its stride can measure thirty or forty feet. How do they catch this will-o-the-wisp? Its weakness lies in its strong sense of hearing, and when a certain beat is sounded on the drum, the deer forgets everything, and comes close enough to place his head on the drum, and so the rest of his life is spent in captivity—imprisoned by man. Now take the elephant, whose strength is so obviously impressive that a man may feel terrified just to look at him. But during the mating season, the elephant's desire for the touch of the female is so dominant that he loses all control and runs amuck, even uprooting huge trees in his path. While he is in this state of passion, having lost all his better instincts, man can devise his capture. A huge pit is dug out and covered over with branches and grass. A female elephant is tied nearby as an attraction, and as he rushes toward her, he falls into the intervening pit. After starving him for many days, he is weak enough to be bound and taken away into slavery for the rest of his life, which may amount to one hundred years.

These are sample conditions of creatures who are slave to only one sense. What about him in whom all five senses are dominating? It may be a simple matter to discuss these things, but think of this difficult task! It would appear impossible to gain control of these five senses. So it is only by the grace of a true Master that one can be guided away from the dark edge of these powerful senses—for a while. *With indescribable strength the mighty Guru pulls the attention.* And inside is the ever-existent Lord, described as Naam.

*By repetition of Naam, the Light of millions of suns is apparent.* There is Light within, and the Song of the Lord, that everlasting Song, is playing. The Guru gives a connection with this—that is his greatness, the God in him. And when his precious gift is given, it must be increased. When the taste for it grows, the lesser tastes will fade away.

In the Bhagved (a Vedic scripture), it says, *Not with repetition or austerity, nor by rites nor prayer nor scripture, not by giving alms nor by pilgrimage...* There are countless other things mentioned, and finally it says, *Not even by control of the senses can the jiva realize Me as quickly as in the company of a realized person.* The company of the Master is gained through great good fortune, and only in his company will the mind cease its perpetuation and be perfectly still for a while.

Who is the Master? He is born in the same way as other men, taking on the human form, and we can daily see him eating, drinking, working in the world, and yet... *Sadh and the Lord, there is no fraction of difference, oh brother.* These are the words of Guru Arjan. So where does Mastership begin? He who transcends the nine doors and goes into the Beyond, in full control of his whole being— he can know what a Master is. The nine doors? The two physical eyes, two nostrils, mouth, two ears, and the genital and excretory orifices. He who can withdraw his attention and go out through the tenth door at the back of the eyes, is well on the way to becoming a realized soul. But where are *we?* Whoever has lived all his life at sense level and whose religious practices are on the same level, can hardly be expected to have knowledge of rising above all these things. He will definitely get rewarded for all his good actions, but he will come again and again into creation, as he considers he is the doer. These are the gold and iron chains described by Lord Krishna when speaking of good and bad actions.

Salvation comes only through the holy Naam itself. In the Ramayana it is likened to lighting a lamp in a hallway, whereupon the light will fall both inside and outside. This illustrates the effect of the repetition of Naam on one's inner and outer life. To repeat simran is the first step. The appearance to the devotee of the one whom the repetition is for, is another matter. *If you haven't loved the Guru completely, you are not really near the Naam.* The Lord within each one sees whichever of His children are yearning to meet Him, and makes the appropriate condition for them to come to the feet of one in whom He is manifested. It is a very rare privilege to meet a true Guru, and yet those who meet him do not love him completely. With outer show they touch his feet and sing his praises, but rarely do they obey his wishes.

All Masters tell the devotees to do their simran and bhajan. Hazur used to say, "You people give one tenth of your earnings, so you should also give one tenth of your time." One tenth of a day is two and a half hours. Some sit for merely five minutes, some for half an hour, and many not at all. Others sit when the occasion fits their mood. If the connection which is given at initiation is not increased, what happens? The attention remains outward and does not withdraw and invert. A person may sit hours on end and others may think he is a devoted meditator, but inside he sees nothing! The face he shows to the world is white, but in the court of the Lord it is black.

Oh brothers, awake! This is the time to understand what is what! The Masters come, lift up their hands, and shout to the world, "Oh brothers, do your meditation, for without it you cannot be free." It is said, *Take the Guru's teaching, for without devotion many clever ones have drowned.* Learning and high degrees are of no use in this sphere.

There was once a very learned man, who upon approaching a river one day, asked a boatman to row him across. The boatman agreed and while they were crossing the river, the learned man asked him, "Have you had any education?" The boatman replied that he had received no education at all. The learned man remarked, "Oh dear, you have wasted half of your life!" Halfway across the river the boat sprang a leak and began to sink. The boatman asked his companion, "Did you ever learn to swim?" The man replied that he had never learned swimming, and the boatman remarked, "All your reading and writing is wasted here," and swam to the shore.

Now I am not suggesting that no one should study at all. Education is good in its place. But if the soul does not learn to leave the body at will, and has not derived intoxication from being drenched in the color of Naam, no amount of speech or action will achieve success on the spiritual path. Remember this fact, for it is clear and simple. The Masters all explain the Truth in simple terms:

*The Masters in truth say, make your meditation.*

Listen! Open your ears and listen! He who has made his meditation has made everything. He whose meditation is not made will enjoy no meaning in his life's achievements. There is great purpose behind this emphasis on the importance of meditation. If your daily life is not under control, try to bring it in control, or, give more time to meditation and you will be able to gain control quicker. He who becomes the conscious co-worker of the Divine plan will find his righteous life is made. Whatever he does will be performed righteously; he will not be able to act otherwise. The reason behind your failure is that you have not truly loved your Master, but have merely made a show in various ways, physically or financially, or by lip-service. There is no one who sacrificed his mind to the Guru. Without giving up the mind, there is no success.

> *The mind was sold to the Satguru;*
> *This server's work was correct.*

Give the mind into his keeping. *This physical form is the Master's, this wealth is the Master's, this mind has been given too.* Those who can do this will receive the greatest gift. The receiver may be a Hindu, Muslim, Christian, etc., for all outer religions are merely labels; we are all simply human beings. A human being is a soul with a body, and the caste is the same as God's. We are all the Lord's children, but unfortunately are going along in forgetfulness. And when we come to the Master, what does he teach us?

> *This possessiveness has gone,*
> *Since I got the Master's company;*
> *There is no enemy, no stranger,*
> *All now are very dear to me.*

The change comes from within. We are human beings, but before that we are soul—the indweller of the physical body. Why is there so much dissention? When the people have right understanding, then peace will reign on earth. This is the only panacea for all ills; it always was and always will be. Whenever man forgets the truth—the unity already existent in all—then sorrow and misery descend. The most effective cure for all distressing conditions is to join the soul back to the Lord and realize in truth the unity that exists. *Naam is the panacea for all ills.* Naam is no mere outer expression or show; it is a term given to the all-knowing and ever-existent Lord. *Naam is the Sustainer of Khand and Brahmand.* It is the God-in-action Power which is controlling the whole of Creation (Khand and Brahmand) and to be connected to that Power means to meditate on the Naam.

> *Those who have meditated on the Naam, their toils*
> *shall end,*
> *And their faces shall flame with glory;*
> *Not only shall they have salvation, O Nanak,*
> *But many more shall find freedom with them.*

The most urgent work before us is being spoiled by slothfulness—all because the love for the Guru is not developed. Christ told his followers, *If ye love me, keep my commandments.* We are also told, *He who obeys the Guru's wishes knows what God is.* But do we obey? If we would obey implicitly for six months, we would see the magical change in our condition. You can get salvation in this very life! If the Giver is there, where is the pain in receiving?—but unfortunately, the one who was supposed to receive the priceless gift is deep in slothfulness, sleeping or drifting away in the clutches of the senses. Those who receive something decide to put it away and ignore it. How can you expect the worldly conditions to change if you are not changing?

I will give you an example from the life of Guru Nanak. A disciple named Bhai Ajitha once questioned the Guru, "Maharaj, you say that some have had but a fragrance of *sikhi* (true devotion to the Guru), and some live under the protective roof of a true disciple, but there are some who taste the Nectar from a true disciple. Please give me the darshan of these three types of followers."

Now listen carefully to this story: Guru Nanak took Ajitha to a certain house at night (houses in those days were made with inner courtyards). The owner said to his family, "There are some holy men outside, we must feed them." But they were very poor people, with very meager fare, and they collected a piece of bread from each one's share and with devotion offered it to Guru Nanak and returned to their places. Guru Nanak and Ajitha passed the night in singing praises of God, and in the morning the Guru sent Ajitha to tell the owner, "We are leaving now." The owner replied, "Brothers, you are going? Then go. Who asked you to come?"

As they walked on their way, Guru Nanak told Ajitha, "This man has had a little fragrance of discipleship. This type of person will listen, they will serve both financially and physically, etc., but they will remain where they are." You see, when someone gets a slight fragrance they are ready and willing to do anything, and yet when they leave that fragrance all their aspirations are forgotten. Ajitha then said, "Maharaj, I see this type of man every day; now please show me one who lives under the Master's protection." They went to a village and entered the house of a large family, who entertained and fed them with great love and devotion. When night came, they said, "Maharaj, have mercy on us. How can we control our mind? We are pitifully imprisoned in this world—show us the way to salvation." So the whole night was spent listening to the advice of Guru Nanak, until the sun rose at daybreak. When the Guru showed his intentions to depart, the family quickly cooked more food and packed it for their journey. As the Guru left, they pleaded for his grace and begged him to look after them and return soon to their home. So Guru Nanak explained to Ajitha that this was the type of people who live under a true Master's protection. How many people can you find who will spend the whole night talking about the Lord? Have you met anyone like that? Such people have hope of salvation. They may not go anywhere just now, but there is hope later.

Ajitha then said, "But what about those who have gained the Essence of Truth from a Master?" and Guru Nanak promised to show him such an example. Some days later they went to another house where lived a man, his wife, two sons and a daughter, who were imbued with the love of the Guru. They all received and entertained Guru Nanak with respect and devotion. To show true devotion to a Master is like showing it to God Himself. The wife immediately retired to the kitchen to prepare food. Her son came running to help her, but slipped on the floor, fell down and died. Of course she was distressed; but, thinking of the karmic laws, attributed it to give and take, and then thought of the Saint that had just come to her home. Resolving that the incident should not mar the occasion, she hid her son's body in a room under the covers of a bed, meaning to tell her husband only after the departure of the Saint.

Meanwhile, the husband had gone into the courtyard for something, accompanied by his younger son, who suddenly slipped, fell down and died. The father then had exactly the same thought as his wife, and hid his son's body in another room, after which he continued devotedly to help prepare the meal.

When the food was placed in front of him, Guru Nanak picked up the small daughter and placing her on his lap, asked her, "Where are your brothers?" She replied, "They are in the lap of the Guru. In life or death, we are all in his lap." Guru Nanak then picked up a morsel of food and put it in his mouth but could not swallow it. He said, "It will not go down my throat; they have bound me by their love and complete surrender to the Guru," and turning to the father said, "I want to meet your sons, so kindly call them." The husband and wife both became alarmed, for both were concealing the facts and did not know what to do. But the Guru insisted, so the husband called the names of his two sons. At once both boys came from the respective rooms where they had been lying. They told of their interesting sleep during which both were held in the lap of the Guru. Who can imagine the joy in the hearts of parents! Guru Nanak turned to Ajitha and remarked, "Now this is the type of person who enjoys the very Essence from the Guru's presence."

This last example was one of true living, the kind of life that we must learn to live. You can see for yourselves where you stand at present, and the only reason for that position is the fact that you do not know how to truly love the Master. Why would he who rises above the mind and senses try to keep you imprisoned here in them? It is the fervent wish of whoever has tasted the real Nectar that everyone should enjoy the bliss.

> *Meet the Master, my brothers, and take the True*
> *Naam into thy keeping;*
> *Tie this life's treasure to thee, here and hereafter.*

The treasure of the Masters has value in both worlds, so where does the Negative Power stand in this? The Negative Power comes in when we do not truly love, we do not obey, or we obey only as far as our mind agrees. This is what is called the power of negativeness. We even go so far as to give advice to the Master, at times. Hafiz of Shiraz made the startling statement that if your Guru tells you to drench your prayer-mat in wine, then do so! Why? Would the one who has the intoxication of Naam wish to trap you in the worldly intoxicants? We should try to carefully understand the Master's teachings and what lies behind them—not waste time in intellectual wrangling and reasoning. When an officer gives the orders to fire, the soldier must fire, and the responsibility of the decision rests upon the officer. So our duty is to obey, and die if necessary! As long as the condition of our mind does not develop to this kind of obedience, we will not get the full benefit that the Naam has to offer us. The Guru is not ignorant of the pathways to Spirituality.

You have got the connection, then daily increase it. And if you learn to obey without question, the color of this world will fade and you will be dyed deep in the color of Naam. Disobedience results in being consumed perpetually in the fire of senses, not only in this life, but hereafter also.

When someone remarked to Lord Vishnu that he must be very busy always preparing the hells, etc., for so many erring souls, he replied, "No, I do nothing—the souls bring their own fires and are consumed in them." We go through life strictly according to the inner condition of mind. The Masters show a straight road out, but the worldly people object to it, being convinced that he is doing nothing but obstructing the fulfillment of their desires. The Master comes to give the true understanding of life, but the people chase him away, protesting that he has come to rot their roots by flooding them with water. They do not or will not understand the deep meaning of Satsang, although in all religions it is stated that there is no salvation without Naam or Word.

It is already within you; you have but to be made aware of it. That person who is already all-awareness can awaken you. He who has no Light radiating within cannot show it to others. It is a work impossible to be accomplished by intellectuals or those learned in sacred scriptures, etc. Get the full benefit of meditation, and increase it day by day. The more you increase it, the nearer will you advance toward your goal. If you refuse, the day will come when you will be filled with regret for the lost opportunity. It is all a very simple matter of fact, and outer show of respect will achieve nothing. Learn to obey implicitly—this is the secret in a nutshell.

*Sant Kirpal Singh Ji*
*(1894-1974)*

# 9

# Chastity and Forgiveness

THE SUPREME IDEAL of human life is the realization of God. Religions were made to perpetuate the teachings of great souls who had attained enlightenment. They have left an account of their personal experiences for the guidance of posterity. They have all said that God is omnipresent. Whatever we see around us is undoubtedly His manifestation, but the question is how to see Him?

We find in the Jap Ji *The Lord's Word is all pervading. There is no place where His Word does not exist.* The Gurbani tells us: *We have seen the glimpse of God.*

One can experience God only by rising to His level of super-consciousness. Although the atmosphere is full of microbes, nothing is visible to the naked eye. Does that mean that there is nothing in the air? We can see thousands of tiny objects through a microscope. Now, there are two possibilities. Either whatever is present in the air is made to magnify so as to correspond to the visual level of our eyes, or our vision should become so subtle as to see these tiny germs clearly. So, it is impossible for us to see the highly subtle and indescribable Lord with our physical eyes. When we are able to develop super-consciousness and subtlety at His level, we can have some experience of Him. The question is one of developing the Third Eye. Who can open the inner eye? Only the Master's grace can do it. In the Gurbani we find, *Through the grace of a Godman, you will see the temple of the Lord within.*

The human body is the temple of God. In order to attain super-consciousness, one has to withdraw from all the physical attachments. So long as we remain identified with external objects, we cannot assume a subtle form. Tulsi Sahib says: *The Lord dwells within us, but we remain ignorant. Cursed is such a life.* Even after getting human life, if He is not manifest within, it is a great curse because we can accomplish this task only in human life. *O Tulsi, the whole world is suffering from cataract.*

Doctors do not give vision to cataract patients. They only remove the thin membrane covering the pupil of the eye. Similarly, the Lord is within us. He is our controlling power. The entire universe is His manifestation. He can be realized within, but not before our subtle eye is able to pierce through the darkness within.

Tulsi Sahib and Shams-i-Tabrez both have said the same thing: See the Lord with your own eyes and hear His Eternal Music with your own ears.

If we see through the darkness inside, we can experience the divine Light. Tulsi Sahib says that you will not be able to penetrate through the darkness without the help of a perfect Master. In this lies the greatness of a Master soul, who can dispel our darkness and give us the inner experience of divine Light. This is possible when our attention is withdrawn from outside and we rise above body-consciousness. This is not easy. Despite years of meditation, past sages and seers could not always get this experience (of divine Light). They used to practice Kumbhak (Hathic Yogic exercise) and after passing through the six ganglionic centers, got a little inner experience in the center of the two eyebrows. This practice takes hundreds of years.

Swami Ji has clearly stated: *Only the all powerful Master can pull the soul up; He alone can free us from the prison of oblivion.*

Who can rise above body consciousness? One who is unattached and is not engrossed in sensual pleasures can do it. Only such a person can easily tap inside. An ethical and chaste life is, therefore, very essential. Even if the Master by his own grace lifts someone, whose life is not pure, above body consciousness, the latter will not be able to withstand it. It is crystal clear that there are two main obstacles in the way: passionate desires and anger. To lead a chaste life is not enough. We have to overcome all desires. In anger the soul flows out. Self-indulgence and anger lead to various other vices. Unless these two enemies are disciplined first, others—greed, attachment and egotism—cannot be controlled. One who succeeds in conquering all these five enemies is free from suffering. The senses derive their power from the mind and the mind from the soul. If our attention is concentrated at the seat of the soul, the senses become powerless.

Saints show us the way back to God through Surat Shabd Yoga. Where is the seat of the soul in the body? At the time of death, the soul withdraws behind the two eyebrows after leaving the lower regions. Anyone who is able to withdraw his sensory currents at this point in his lifetime can open his inner eye. But, this can only be done through the grace of a perfect living Master. First, the Master helps us in withdrawing our attention from external worldly objects with which it is identified. In this body—the temple of God—dwell both we and our Controlling Power. The Master has great power to pull the soul above the plane of senses to the seat of the soul. He opens the inner eye. Thus, the spiritual aspirant has a first-hand experience and does not require any other evidence.

*Until I see the Truth with my own eyes, I cannot be fully convinced of what the Master says*, the Gurbani tells us very clearly. Unless the senses are controlled, the mind is stilled and the intellect too is equipoised, the soul cannot realize itself. Gyan Yoga will not be of much help. We only draw inferences to acquire knowledge. But, the true knowledge has to be experienced. Only an adept who has had a first-hand experience can give you a taste of it. Similarly, only one in whom the divine Light is manifest can show you Light. Intellectuals and religious preachers cannot do this work. True inner experience can be given only by the grace of a truly competent Master. By infusing his own life-impulse, he puts us on the spiritual path and then unites us with the Power of God. One who has subdued the senses qualifies for the divine grace.

Cravings and anger can be controlled by cultivating chastity and forgiveness. If you go into details, you will find that these are our main hurdles. If you were to listen to someone silently, you will find that he talks of his passionate desires, petty jealousies, factions, enmities, recriminations, etc. He will overrate some and underrate others. These vices must be dispensed with. Prophet Mohammed has said: *If you can control two sense-organs, namely, the one between the two lips and the other between the two thighs; I shall stand surety for you in the Lord's court.* We simply read and hear these words but never go deeper into their meaning. If these two virtues were cultivated, it would be a great blessing. In the absence of these virtues, meditation is hampered. This is the main object of my laying stress on keeping a diary. The first column in the diary is for *ahimsa* (non-violence) and forgiveness. Even if someone harms you, forgive him. Do not injure anybody's feelings. One who practices ahimsa will not tell a lie, cheat others or have ill-gotten gains. Now let us see what saints have said on the subject.

## CHASTITY AND FORGIVENESS

Chastity and forgiveness are the two basic and most noble virtues of all. If we acquire these virtues, we will be successful in our meditation. Christ says: *Suffer the little children to come unto me,... for of such is the Kingdom of God.* Children are endowed with these two qualities. They are totally indifferent to sex. They never mind if they are naked. If they go astray, we parents are to blame. If they fight each other, they soon reconcile their differences. Let us become like little children and we will be successful in our meditation. A competent Master, by virtue of the God-Power working in him, turns away your attention from outer pursuits, pulls it above the plane of senses and opens the inner eye. He gives to the spiritual aspirant some capital of inner experience, which is His grace, but it is our responsibility to preserve it.

Ibrahim Adham, King of Bukhara, once went to Sant Kabir. He served Kabir day and night. Mother Loi, one of Kabir's disciples, one day praised Ibrahim for his selfless service to the Master and felt that Ibrahim had become a deserving devotee for the spiritual gift. Kabir remarked that Ibrahim had not yet attained maturity. To prove this, Kabir asked her to throw rubbish on Ibrahim's head from the top of the house and then listen to what he had to say. She did so. At this, Ibrahim said that he would have dealt with the mischief-monger properly had he been in Bukhara. When Kabir came to know of Ibrahim's reaction, he said that the latter had not got over his pride of kingship and egotism and so he was not mature enough for initiation. After some time, Kabir told Loi that Ibrahim had become ripe for the gift of spirituality. As she had not noticed any appreciable change in Ibrahim, she wanted to know the criterion for this verdict. This time, Kabir asked her to throw the night-soil on Ibrahim. She did so. To her surprise, Ibrahim said, "O God, I am even worse than this." Remember, one whose heart is full of compassion for others, who wishes well after having been hurt and prays even for his enemies, is known as a *Mahatma*, a great soul.

Christ was asked as to what should be the code of conduct in life. On enquiring about the injunction of Moses in this regard, he was told: "An eye for an eye, and a tooth for a tooth." At this Christ remarked: "It was because your hearts were hardened that he gave you this injunction." When asked to express his own opinion, Christ said: *Love thy neighbor as thyself.* When further asked how enemies should be dealt with, he replied: *Love thine enemies.* Jealousy, malice, calumny, backbiting, falsehood and fraud can be overcome by love. Unless these vices are given up, there is no way out. Even good preachers and reformers are found wanting in chastity and forgiveness. They indulge in recrimination, falsehood, fraud, hypocrisy, etc. What is wanted is cultivation of forgiveness. If we develop childlike qualities, we can reach our Goal. Now let us listen to what Sant Kabir has to say about purity of life:

> *When chastity and forgiveness sprout in one's*
> *heart, the invisible Lord becomes visible.*
> *Without chastity one cannot reach Him; empty*
> *words are of no avail.*

Kabir says in very clear words that chastity and forgiveness are the two pre-requisites for God-realization. Without purity of life, all sermons or learning are of no use. Chastity means purity of thoughts, words and deeds. Chastity is life and self-indulgence is death. Forgiveness is difficult to practice. Outwardly we pretend to be humble, but inwardly we do not hesitate to harm others.

I remember an incident in my life. Long ago, my wife was relieved of her purse at a railway station. The police caught the thief and the purse was recovered from him. I was asked to lodge a report at the police station. I told the police it was unnecessary as the purse had been found. But on their insistence, I had to go to the police station, perhaps for the first time. I told the officer on duty that I was not interested in reporting the matter, but he would not agree and the report was ultimately lodged. Later, I had to go to the court as a witness. The police officer talked to me on this issue. He felt that justice must be done, but I contended that there were two aspects of the law, one justice and the other compassion or mercy. I emphasized that even after justice had been done, bitterness would remain. Whereas, through mercy he could be forgiven. Compassion leads to mercy which in turn leads to non-violence in thoughts, words and deeds. Anyway, when I appeared in the court, I requested the magistrate that if he could let the accused off on some ground, I would have no objection. The magistrate, after satisfying himself that there was no record of previous conviction against the accused, ordered his discharge with a warning. As a result, the accused and his relatives always remained grateful to me. What a tremendous effect forgiveness has! Justice could never produce this effect. Forgiveness is the greatest of all virtues. So is purity of thought. But alas, all our time is spent in tensions and petty squabbles. We find it difficult to pardon others. Remember, only a brave man can forgive others, not a weak person. Indirectly, we remain busy in condemning our opponents. Such persons can never realize God.

All learning and religious pursuits are of little significance unless the qualities of chastity and forgiveness are thoroughly understood and cultivated in life. Because of these two virtues in children, saints always have a great love for them. God does not dwell in the skies, but is within us. Unless proper background is developed, spiritual advancement is not possible. Kabir now explains in greater detail what chastity is:

*One who is chaste is the greatest of all and is a
storehouse of all virtues.*

Chastity is the main source of all virtues. It is rare to come
across a really chaste person. Nearness to such a pure soul
produces a soothing effect and even his reflection causes
awakening. It is not an exaggeration. By virtue of ethical
life, the body of a celibate is charged with the divine grace,
tranquility and fragrance. *Chastity is thus a great blessing.
Chastity brings all the treasures of the three worlds* (physical,
astral and causal).

You may ask as to what should married persons do. In
olden days (in India) people used to observe continence for
the first 25 years. Thereafter, having assimilated religious
scriptures, they would settle down as householders for
another 25 years. Having got one or two children, they
would leave their homes to enter *Vanaprastha Ashram* for
another period of 25 years, during which they would devote
themselves to achieve the ultimate goal of life—realization
of Self and God. After reaching the goal (in Vanaprastha
Ashram), they would become *Sanyasis*—those who
renounce the world completely and wander from place to
place to preach religion.

The real significance of marriage is to have a life-partner
who will stand by you under all circumstances—in pleasure
and pain, in riches and poverty. Both should cooperate in
striving to realize God. To go on producing children is not
our aim. *If a woman has to give birth, she should bear a
saint or a philanthropist or a great warrior. Otherwise, it is
better if she remains barren and does not waste the divine
Light.*

Our forefathers generally used to lead more disciplined
lives, but now there is little restraint. I have to say this

because of the deplorable condition in which we are. The world population is increasing at an alarming rate of ninety a minute.

We can well imagine the population problem after 20 or 30 years. So, it is all the more necessary for us to cultivate continence. St. Paul has said: *Husbands should love their wives as Christ loved the church.* Swami Ram Tirath has also emphasized: *Unless husbands and wives love each other as brothers and sisters, there is no hope for India.* Those who are awakened say so. The solution thus lies in leading a life of self-restraint. Even if a person is able to find a perfect saint who can give the disciple a first-hand spiritual experience, progress on the spiritual path is impossible unless we practice chastity and forgiveness. We should therefore forget the past and start leading a clean life from now on.

> *There is no dearth of scholars, religious and*
> *disciplined people, but we seldom come*
> *across a really chaste person.*

Kabir says that there are countless learned men, those who meditate and achieve concentration and those who are benevolent and disciplined, but a celibate is rarely found. I have come into contact with the heads of almost all religions, but only a few lead a life of celibacy. A celibate can reach his real Goal without making much effort. One who practices both forgiveness and chastity has nothing to worry about and will realize God. Let me give my grandfather's example. He was a clean-hearted man. He would not nurse any grievance against anyone. He became a widower at the age of 25. He never married again although he lived for more than 100 years. A day before his death, he told some people that he would be leaving the world the next day and if they wanted to convey any message to their dear ones in Heaven, they might let him know. Just before his end, some of his relations asked him to utter the name of God, but he said that "God is permeating throughout my body and I am going straight to Him." I am talking of chaste ones. Such people have an innate feeling about the presence of God.

The Gurbani pointedly tells us: *Those who have complete faith in God, they enjoy the quintessence of true knowledge.*

You may go on meditating all through your life, but unless you practice chastity and forgiveness, it will not bear any fruit. Anger causes excitement. Most of our ills are psychosomatic, being the result of emotional disturbances caused by hatred, animosity and worry. Saints always lay stress on the basic essentials of life, but alas, we do not pay heed to them.

> *Chastity is the ocean of happiness; none can*
> *    fathom its depth.*
> *Without the Word none can be called a Sadhu,*
> *    a disciplined soul;*
> *Without capital there cannot be a money-lender.*

Kabir says that chastity is the ocean of happiness. It is so deep that none can measure its depth. But only the Word-personified saints can realize it. The Word will become manifest where there is a life of continence. Nanak says: *One who loses semen, loses everything.* A person who practices celibacy and forgiveness can realize God and can truly be called a Sadhu. These two virtues are of prime importance and wherever these exist, other virtues come in of their own accord. Such a person by constant contact with the inner sound current, the Shabd, becomes a storehouse of all virtues.

One who has found a Master, but has not become his mouthpiece, a *Gurumukh*, has not yet freed himself from lusts of the flesh. After having found a Master, one must develop receptivity towards him. Who is a Gurumukh? One who has no wish of his own and lives in the will of the Master. Such a person is automatically relieved of all sorts of passions. As the Master is an embodiment of chastity, chastity radiates from him and penetrates into the disciple the moment he thinks of him. He is full of compassion and forgives all. Only a Gurumukh can escape from all kinds of indulgences since he abides in the Word of the Master. Christ told his disciples, *If ye love me, keep my commandments.* Hazur Sawan Singh Ji used to say: *We hesitate to commit an impious act in the presence of a child; don't we know that God within us is all-seeing?*

The Master is an embodiment of the Word and gives us a contact with it. By listening to the Eternal Music and seeing the divine Light, one gets inner peace.

Gurbani assures us: *Mind gets docile by communion with Naam.*

The Upanishads state that by attaining the Word, we attain all.

*So long as man has animal passions, he cannot be*
 *a Gurumukh.*
*When the Satguru resides within, the disciple*
 *is free from lusts.*

As you think, so you become. If your mind constantly dwells on a chaste person, you will unconsciously attract and imbibe chastity. Kabir says that one who becomes a Satguru incarnate will automatically rid himself of all desires. In the first place comes his sweet remembrance. The next is his manifestation within. One should, therefore, exercise great caution in adopting a Master. If he is really an adept in the science of soul you can achieve salvation. Otherwise, if you concentrate on the form of a so-called guru, you may at the most become like him.

You might have heard of Dadu Sahib? One day he was going bare-headed. Someone, knocking him on the head, inquired: "Where is Dadu's house?" He replied: "Go this way and you will find him inside the house." To his consternation, he found the same man (Dadu) sitting in the house. The visitor felt ashamed when he realized that he had insulted the saint. Dadu Sahib said it did not matter since even an earthenware pot of insignificant value is purchased after the buyer has made sure of its serviceability by knocking it all over.

> *A Master should be chosen after thoughtful*
> *consideration,*
> *Just as water should be taken after filtration.*

A perfect Master is a rarity. The world is full of so-called gurus, while there are only a few really competent Masters. Such Masters alone are described in the Vedas and other scriptures as sages, saints and great souls for they are Word-personified.

Christ says: *Word was made flesh and dwelt amongst us.* The Gurbani further tells us: *He who can give you a first-hand experience of the divine Light and celestial Sound is a true Master... Through association with a saint, the power of God becomes manifest within... A saint bestows the essence of esoteric science.*

Anyone can lecture, sermonize, or give a religious talk; but practical inner experience can be given only by an awakened soul.

> *Only an alert and wide awake person can practice*
> *chastity.*

# CHASTITY AND FORGIVENESS

*The thieves of sensual desires cannot rob such a*
*person.*

It is only an alert and conscious person who can cultivate chastity and can attain higher consciousness. By practicing chastity one gradually rises into cosmic consciousness. When consciousness dawns within, one is not troubled by the sensual thieves—we are being robbed by five deadly passions. In the absence of chastity and forgiveness, a thick wall of darkness comes over the soul and we are not our own. Christ has described this state as "death of the soul." What is the death of the soul? It is the bedimming of the Light-consciousness in us. Attachment to material comforts lowers our consciousness. Consciousness increases with increasing awareness. Where does this awareness come from? It comes by cultivating compassion and chastity. See how important these virtues are? But we do not pay attention to them. We have already been blessed with His grace and also with the capital of holy Naam. Is it not our duty then to safeguard our capital? We should keep his commandments instead of doing mere lip-service to him.

*One who is courteous to one's guests is a great soul;*
*one who offers them a seat is a saint. One who lacks these*
*courtesies is either a heretic or a pagan.* Now, all this is about our external conduct. One who is endowed with the two virtues of chastity and compassion would welcome even an enemy courteously. A mahatma (great soul) has this virtue. He welcomes anyone who calls on him even in the dead of night. Such a person remains cheerful even in the face of death. To observe celibacy in youth is a great thing. People usually postpone it for the old age.

*Those who do not meditate while young will not be*
*able to do so in old age.*

As in old age physical disabilities appear one by one, we cannot engage in meditation. One should therefore make a start while young. Saints have said that one who practices celibacy while young is a prophet. This is not child's play. We simply read these things and forget about them.

We do not forgive others. In the absence of forgiveness; anger, jealousy, hatred, back-biting, etc., emerge. Our hearts and minds are contaminated with all such thoughts. We talk of these things and do not hesitate to slander those with whom we are angry. My Master used to say, *All sensual appetites have some taste in them, but what taste comes from slandering others? If there is any, is it sweet, sour, saltish or insipid?* Still every family, society, and country is afflicted with this malady. A devotee, who is an embodiment of forgiveness, has nothing to fear. He will always greet others with love. If someone thinks ill of you, let him do that. In what way does it affect you? Instead, the former harms himself by being angry and jealous. If you retaliate, you will be afflicted likewise. One who considers that the Lord is omnipresent and is dedicated to Him, is not carried away by what others may speak of him. These are the shortcomings in our way to self-realization and God-realization.

*Forgiveness extinguishes the fire of anger.* Great souls go to the extent of welcoming those who find fault with them. Once a man went to Lord Buddha and started abusing him. When he was about to leave, Lord Buddha said: "Brother, listen to me: if the receiver refuses to accept the gift offered to him it remains with the giver. I refuse to accept the gift you have brought for me."

And Kabir says:

> *If one abuses and the other retaliates, there will*
> *be a shower of abuses.*

*But, with non-retaliation, the matter will end.*
*Where there is compassion, there is religion.*
*Where there is greed, there is sin.*
*Where there is anger, there is negation.*
*Where there is forgiveness, there is the Lord*
*    Himself.*

Compassion leads to forgiveness and greed leads to sin. Greed and attachment means desire for name or fame. For the fulfillment of one's desires, one becomes jealous of others. One neither becomes good nor bad by others' opinions. Those who indulge in slandering others, are unpaid apprentices of the C.I.D. of God. God and the Master are both within you. One who is true to the Master has nothing to fear, for his heart is pure and purity of heart gives added strength. One cannot realize God unless the mind is equipoised. Anger, jealousy, malice and ill-will, even in thought, fan the flames of invisible fire all around. Kabir says that at a place like this you will find nothing but Negative Power, but where there is forgiveness, there is God Himself. Forgiveness washes clear all inner defilements and leads to peace of mind. Otherwise, anger would provoke anger, and accusations counter-accusations, vitiating the entire atmosphere.

*All quarrels and strifes emanate from abuse.*

Kabir says that bad language is the root cause of all quarrels. You know how the great Mahabharata War started. Just by sarcastic words. One single sarcastic remark by Draupadi led to the destruction of Indian culture and civilization. Again in the Gurbani we find, *No power on earth can harm one who is protected by the Guru.*

If someone harbors in him thoughts of jealousy and hatred, they react doubly on him. This is the natural law. One noble thought gives rise to thousands of noble sentiments, and one evil thought to thousands of miseries. If you sow a single seed in the soil, the plant that sprouts will bear hundreds of similar seeds. Likewise, if you plant a mango seed, you will get hundreds of mangoes from it. One thought may produce a soothing effect, while the other may excite you. Every action, even a thought, has its reaction.

> *The words of a vicious person are like so many*
>     *arrows but saints alone can tolerate them.*
> *If lightning falls into the sea, what damage*
>         *would it do?*

Kabir says that malicious words are like poisoned darts. But a forgiver is like an ocean which is not affected even by lightning. So forgiveness is a great blessing. Kabir says that a man becomes tough by bearing external hardships. He who has prepared his ground can listen to the Music of the Spheres all the time.

> *The earth can tolerate digging and the forest cutting.*
> *Only a saint can bear harsh and malicious words.*

You may dig the land or cut a forest and they do not resent it. Similarly, only a saint is endowed with forgiveness and chastity. Ignorance of the law is no excuse. You can reap only what you sow.

Actions, good or bad, bear their own fruits. We must understand these principles and implement them in life. First, a perfect Master, capable of imparting the experience of inner Light, is hard to find. Even if you find one, you cannot reach the Goal without purity of life and forgiveness. If you follow and act on what I have just said, you will be liberated from the bondage of matter and mind. These virtues will bring to you higher consciousness and you will develop faith in the existence of God. After all, what is the purpose of worship? It is to develop firm faith in the existence of God. By self-introspection, you can see what your condition is. Learned people, moralists and theologians generally preach to others. What is their own plight? It is well said: "Wanted—reformers—not of others, but of themselves." We preach to others what we do not practice ourselves. The result is that all our exhortations produce little effect on others.

Be true to Him Who is dwelling within you. If you practice the two virtues—chastity and forgiveness—you will find that, without much effort, you will attain higher consciousness, complete awakening and perfect peace of mind. Thus, you will begin to radiate peace, harmony and tranquility to those around you.

*Sant Kirpal Singh Ji*
*(1894-1974*

# 10

# Change Your Habits Now

SATSANG is purely meant to discuss and explain the subject of contacting the Naam Power—it is not a place where the social and political matters are taken up. It is a place of righteousness, and we should regard and respect it as such. When we visit any religious temple, do we not enter with respectful humility? Where our attitude is not so, we surely expect to gain little from our attendance there. To talk of worldly affairs in sacred places is considered to be a sacrilege.

So your purpose in coming to Satsang is to imbibe the love of God, to sit in His sweet remembrance, to unite with Him. All things past and future, all irrelevant matters can be dealt with in your own place of residence. Come, but come with the very best of intentions. Bring the remembrance of the Lord with you, and take it with you when you leave. Do not listen to others' conversation and do not talk to anyone unless it be about the Truth. You will thereby gain full benefit from Satsang—otherwise the years will pass by without any real advancement.

Swami Ji Maharaj tells us, *Many days of attendance at Satsang have passed; Now give up your old habits.* So much time has been spent at Satsang without gaining the benefit. Only by having full attention focused will you receive. If the words enter through one ear and leave from the other, nothing will be retained. Furthermore, if you live up to what you hear, that will be a great achievement, otherwise your purpose in joining the Satsang will have failed. Swami Ji says, *O Man, let anybody attend the Satsang in the accurate way from today.* How to attend Satsang? When you leave home for Satsang forget all worldly matters and go in sweet remembrance of the Master; and so long as you attend the Satsang, you should not think of anything else except the Master and God. *If your body is in the Master's company, but your mind is elsewhere, Kabir says, how can you color an unbleached cloth?*

Even though you may not understand all that is said, yet if you sit with full attention you will profit by it. If your thoughts are somewhere else, not only will you lose, but other people will also be affected by the impure atmosphere you are creating, for thoughts are living and possess great power. Regard the Satsang as a place of purity; do not talk or think of anything but God, and whosoever attends will be blessed by the uplifting atmosphere. We do not go to Satsang to meet our friends or to socialize.

*The Master unites us in a true relationship, which can never be broken.* This relationship is with God Himself, who is manifested in the human form. It is such a relationship that can never be sundered, even after death, not to speak of during life. But we, with our poor understanding, assert ourselves with pride, ego, and low habits, desiring to be recognized. Consequently we succeed only in heaping more misery upon our heads. What is the use of attending Satsang for so long if you are not going to change the old unwanted habits? Dry land can become green again by giving it water, but of what use is land that is watered yet remains dead? Your attendance has become a mere routine—you cannot get salvation by rote—you will not get it; you will not get it.

Try to understand what the spiritual path means, and then live up to it; and the more it seeps into your heart, the happier you will be. *Let the words of the Guru abide in your heart, and you abide in Him.* This is the only way, the only hope. If you do not obey him, what can be done? For so many years I have pleaded with you. That which you receive here, you will not find anywhere else—but with all that you receive, yet you continue in your old ways of enmity, avarice, jealousy, etc.—you do not keep your spiritual diaries—whose fault is it that you are not progressing? Stop being childish and grow up. Those who do not wish to listen and obey should not enter upon this venture of the spiritual path. I am not saying any new thing. We are not all Saints—we have come here to become that, and you will become that if you fully understand and then live up to the teachings.

Everyone makes mistakes. I remember, I went on leave from my office once, and on returning found that two clerks had been dismissed. When I took their case to the Controller for appeal, he began to question the merit of it, but I asked him, "Is there any person without faults? You will not find anyone who has not done something wrong, and the punishment for mistakes should not be dismissal, for not only the man will suffer, but his wife and children also." They were reinstated in service. If these teachings are no new thing, then try to fully understand them now, and take them into your lives. If we could learn to obey and keep the diary, we would become gods and goddesses. Do not discuss or wrangle intellectually over the subject, but think carefully— have you not come here to keep the company of the Truth? Then why keep the company of others? This disease has ever been in evidence, and will continue, but the Masters come to prescribe the cure by making us realize the Truth. In Swami Ji's shabd, he laments over the situation:

*Many days of attendance at Satsang have passed;*
*Now give up your old habits.*

O Man, it is the time now to discard your old disreputable habits and adopt new ones. Habits are formed by repeatedly doing the same things, so we should first unravel all bad actions: lies, hypocrisy, cheating, criticism of others, enmity, avarice, malice, backbiting, and various others.If you do not intend to change these ways, what is the use of attending Satsang? *Your steps are forward, but your mind is retrogressing.* Satsang is the means of making us into something beautiful, but not by merely repeating God's Name. Change your habits now into good ones, for habit turns into nature with time. Cast away all negative thoughts, and instill positive ones in their place. If a person does wrong, forgive him, and he in turn should forgive your misdeeds.

In the Koran it written, *Even God has no thought for him who has no inclination to change.* How can we expect other people to show excellent examples? If we ourselves would change, the whole world would change with us. It is a message for all. One of the worst habits is that of criticizing others. All virtues exercised in righteous living are good, but that of *ahimsa parmo dharam* (non-violence of thought) is the highest. It can become a daily habit, for it lies inherent within us all; and although other thoughts are there, yet consciously or unconsciously it is working and will rise to the surface one day. That is why you are told frequently in Satsang that the past is past, forgive and forget, and do not make a foundation of bad thoughts or there will undoubtedly be reactions. You will be the loser, for again you will revolve on the cycle of births and deaths. So with love the Masters encourage their children to change their habits while there is still time. With great compassion for humanity, Swami Ji is telling us:

> *For how long will you try to deceive your Guru?*
> *Now recognize what He is.*

Hiding the true facts, you think, "What does the Guru know? What *we* want to do is correct." You get hold of an idea and place it above all else, considering everyone else to be wrong—even if your Guru tells you something different. How long will you keep this up? Make no mistake, he watches our every action, for the Guru-power is residing within our very being. But we foolishly think that he is not present to see us, so we can do anything and he will not know. He entreats us to try and realize what a Guru is. The Guru is not the physical form—he is not the human pole but is the all-omnipotent power of God which has manifested therein. It is accepted that God is everywhere and sees everything. Give full attention to learn what the Guru is, and then come to *know* it. He has love for everyone—for his own, for all others, even for those who are against him. His wish is to do good to all, and even though a knife were put to his neck he would not think ill of the wrongdoers. He is different and expresses this wealth of love and forgiveness because of the Guru-power in him. So he says we should stop all this deceit—if one thinks of one's Guru as a Guru, then obey him. After all, he does not give bad advice.

Sometimes it is possible that two idiots can be bound together in love breaking the chains of the creeds that are binding them, whereas intellectual people would snap the silken threads of love—without hesitation. *Gurumukh loses, and lets the world win.* He who loses out of love and humility, in actual fact wins the day, for he has saved what he has stored; otherwise in the fire of anger his precious store will be consumed to ashes. If there is no anger in a person, not even a wisp of smoke will be seen. Try to recognize your Guru, for Satsang is concerned with the Guru, not with a mere human being. When you go to Satsang, go in His remembrance for He is God in human form; be present there in His remembrance, and when you leave take that remembrance with you.

We should exploit those qualities which will assist us to join back to God, and discard all traits which are liable to lead you away from Him. It is not difficult to realize the Lord, but it is most difficult to become a man—a true human being. One hundred times and more we bow our heads and say "yes, yes, I will do it;" but in action we do just as we please. This indicates that as yet we do not truly understand the spiritual path. If you have not as yet changed your old habits, then do so at once. Make a start *now*. To have bad thoughts for others, to take sides in enmity, like a lawyer criticizing the lives of your fellow-beings—would you not expect the fire to flare up within you? The Guru sees all events with a different eye, for every man sees from his own level. If you have accepted someone as being superior to you, then obey him.

A teacher who has not reached the higher level can easily be the cause of further downfall. Those from higher levels always strive to reunite all humanity. You came to the Satsang to realize the Truth, to be free from your miseries. To fulfill this, whatever you learn must be adopted and reflected in your homes and daily living, that peace and happiness may blossom forth in you and in those who surround you. The Satsang is a place of special purity, and even your thoughts should be pure as long as you are here. No other thought save that of the Lord should enter your head, and whatever advice you hear, live up to it. If you obey, without exception you will change for the better; if not, you will suffer the consequences.

Guru is not just a man, and whoever looks upon him from that angle of vision is gravely mistaken. Kabir says, *He who considers the Guru a mere man will retrogress in the lower species, birth after birth.* The God in him is the Guru, though we respect his physical form because He is manifesting therein. Whatever he tells us, whether it appears to be correct or not, should be of the utmost importance and interest to us; otherwise, and with emphasis I repeat, that life will become complicated and nothing but misery will result. You can say that it is actually preparing the way for unhappiness. We attend Satsang to increase our joy, for those around us too; and when the soul is reunited with God it will reflect all His qualities. God in the Guru is all compassion, and without disclosing our sins he washes us clean—free from undesirable impurities. When the child becomes dirty with filth the mother does not throw him away but washes him with loving attention and draws him close to her breast. The soul of man is very dear and precious, so we loathe the sin but rather love the sinner. If all men refrained from wrongdoing there would be peace and happiness everywhere. If your aim is to become Masters, you will succeed only when you hear and then become that.

> *Do not think of the Guru as a man;*
> *He is the life of the Sat Purush (True Form).*

The question, who is a Guru, is not a new one—it has ever been asked through the ages. When it was put to Guru Nanak, he said, *Shabd is the Guru, and the surat is the disciple.* The ever-existent God or His expression, the Shabd, is the Guru and the attention is the disciple. When Kabir was asked the same question, he said, *My Guru is above the gaggan (heaven), and the disciple is in the body.* When our attention gets connected with Him, our coming and going is finished. *The greatest being ever born; He, you should know, is my Guru.* He is the Light itself, at whichever pole He is manifested, and only He can give the Light to others. By this the seeker can recognize the criterion in the true Guru. Christ said, *I am the Light of the world: he that followeth me shall not walk in darkness, but shall have the Light of life.* At whichever pole this wealth is found, you can be sure there is something else there too, worthy of your obedience.

He has not come for any particular person but loves everyone, and will wash anyone clean regardless of their condition. Those who are wise enough to obey him will find their progress flourishing. *Satguru's words—words are the Satguru.* The words he utters are he himself and those who bow down to his words will truly get salvation; but those who bow in hypocrisy and then do whatever they choose with the thought that the Guru does not know, make their lives miserable. That which is hidden in us is apparent in the Guru and wherever you find it blossoming forth in fullness, there you will get the experience. Anyone can talk on any subject, for and against, with a little training; but when a person receives something there is no question of doubt. The Power in the Guru—the very life of the Sat Purush—is forever, and will never die. When it worked through the pole named Jesus they called it the Christ Power, and it works at various human poles according to the age. Whoever is fortunate to be connected to this Power will find that it never leaves them.

> *Somehow or other, make your mind understand;*
> *Then put all your attention in Him.*

Making the mind understand is difficult for it tries to convince us that we are wrong in our search, but we must assure it that, having got the connection from where God is manifested, there is no need for doubts. Lectures, stories, bookish knowledge, acting and posing, all can be found in profusion—but who can give the Light? If someone can reveal the Light in the seeker, it is proof that he has got it. Having received from him, then obey him. If the mind dislikes obedience, then we must make it agreeable. When you frequently witness others receiving the Light, is this not proof enough? There would perhaps be cause for hesitation if you were told to fight or kill each other, but the Guru himself thinks good of even those who work against him. By acquiring such noble virtues we also will become Masters.

Iqbal says that when Hazrat Mussa (Moses) climbed the mountain to talk to God and to realize Him, did he not know that God Himself was in search of a man who desired only Him? Baba Jaimal Singh Ji left Punjab and went to search for Hazur in the Murree Hills—was there not any man in the whole of Punjab that was suitable? What I am stressing here is that you have to obey his commands. If you do not persuade your mind to accept the facts, thoughts will come that "am I less than he? I am as big as he is!" and many other illusory ideas, by means of which duality will increase.

> *Through love and mercy He speaks;*
> *He is Complete and Nameless.*

He creates love, for he is all love. He teaches how to love— the rays of love issue forth from him, wherever he goes. His words are uttered to increase the love within us, so obey him and change the old habits which have encrusted for life upon life. If you do not, then you will continue in the wheel of birth and death. If through obedience to the Master a love for God is created in us and we see Him in all beings, then where is the necessity to return to this earth? When his words are forgotten, the squabbling among ourselves increases. If you hurt someone or bring unhappiness into their life, their natural reaction will be to return the same treatment. Karmic reactions are a very powerful law, and you will be ruled by that law.

With so much love, Swami Ji makes us realize that our character must change. Masters are the very reflection of love, for the Positive Power works through love only. It can be observed that Saints work only with love, but Avatars also give punishment. The latter come when righteousness is at an ebb, to punish the wicked and reward the innocent, and to keep the world conditions in proper balance. The Saints tell us to err no more. *They at once give connection with God, to whomever approaches them.* Though the Lord is already within us, yet they make it possible for Him to appear, that we may see Him.

> *To give salvation to you, somehow or other.*
> *He took this physical form, the Guru;*

It naturally follows that man's teacher must be a man. If a monkey screeches, hundreds of monkeys will gather around him in answer to his call. Even if a bird twitters, others will collect. So the Guru comes in the human form to teach man the correct understanding of Truth. Excuse me, but the past Masters cannot come here and give this knowledge. Some intimation may be grasped from the scriptures, but those who have left the scene cannot give guidance as to their correct import. Even if a voice came from the skies to direct us, mankind would merely remark, "What has it to do with us?" On the other hand, if a man's Guru is a renouncer of worldly things, the disciple has doubt that his Master can understand his mundane troubles, for he feels that only one who has himself experienced the worldly ups and downs can really appreciate his condition. A true Master has achieved success in both the worldly and spiritual fields of life, and is thereby a living proof of what can be accomplished.

One's principles in life are highly important and one should never fall below one's supreme principle—and that is? The highest principle is Truth itself; and if you have love for Truth, then you must have love for all life. Soothe and erase away the mistakes of others with your love. Bloodstains cannot be washed with blood, but anything can be cleansed with the water of love.

*Give service unto Him and worship Him;*
*Think of Him as Guru Nanak.*
*He was Kabir; He was Sat Naam;*
*Recognize all Saints in Him.*

Develop into one who can serve the Master. What kind of service? True service means to obey his instructions implicitly; to live as he advocates in a clean, chaste, simple, and loving manner; to develop the Truth in yourself; to purify your thought. God dwells in every being, so love all life. Is this not what he teaches? You have got the human form through great good fortune, so make the best use of it and take advantage of every aid to reunite you with the Lord. Everyone makes mistakes, for all are not Saints as yet, but they should not be repeated. The same God-power worked through Kabir, Guru Nanak, and others at different times, just as a fused bulb is replaced by another. The teachings, however, remain the same.

You will remember that when they brought before Jesus the woman who had been found committing adultery, they asked him whether she should be stoned, according to the law of Moses; but Jesus told them, *He that is without sin among you, let him first cast a stone at her.* Can you put your hand on your heart and honestly say that you have never hurt anyone? Hazrat Mohammed Sahib says, *If you can control the two organs—one between the lips, and the other between the thighs—then I will stand before God in your support.* Jesus told the woman to "go, and sin no more." With love he forgave her and helped her to understand— after all, it was his work to make her into something.

Guru Power never dies; it is everlasting and continues forever. *Lo, I am with you always, even unto the end of the world.* These are the words of Christ, and not of Jesus, for they were uttered by the Christ-power or Guru-power in him. *The whole world is a house in which the Truth is residing.* Those who attend Satsang, in particular those who have got a true Master, should set an example in their love for one another, and their forgiving attitude. Christ also said, *By this shall all men know that ye are my disciples, if ye have love for one another.* Otherwise, where is the proof that you are on the spiritual path? The teachings are not bad, the Satsang is not bad, he who teaches is not bad—if anything is bad it is the mind, so make your mind understand correctly and everything will be set right. It is the only cure if you want advancement. If we have helped even one person by removing a little misery from his day, we have done a great service. With sweet words, with kind sympathy, share the unhappy burden resting upon our poor fellow beings or it spreads and grows as the days go by. From a man it travels to his family, his friends, and so on.

> *Only He can achieve your aim;*
> *Do not wander—be rid of your pride.*

What is our work in this world? To meet God—and for that we must first have the right understanding. *Our true friend is He who removes wrong understanding.* We have not come here to be property owners, socialites, or to have lofty ideas about ourselves, or to breed animosity among each other— we have come to imbibe the correct understanding about life. But sadly, we daily sow more seeds, and only we will reap the harvest thereof. And each type of seed will bear its own fruit. If you have sown enmity then try to smooth it out—do your best to wash it away with love, that it may not grow with time and take deep roots. *You came to the world to receive, and you got God's Name in the Master's home; Now give up your pride and control your mind.* We say that we are very important people, we are very intellectual, we give excellent lectures, we have great influence over others, etc.; but we should leave all this and take up the practice of Truth alone. Then only will the true happiness and joy well up from within us. We have come here to realize God, and only God can help us do so—who else is capable? *Do your work and do not entangle yourself in other affairs.* Think deeply, and if you find anything undesirable in you, weed it out; and with love help others to overcome their shortcomings also.

King Dhritarashtra, famous ruler from the Mahabharata epic, on a certain occasion insulted the powerful bow of Arjuna, and Arjuna immediately made to kill the king; but Lord Krishna stepped forward and demanded, "Arjuna, what are you doing?" Arjuna replied, "I have taken a solemn vow to kill anyone who insults my bow—it is my *dharma* (principle)." Krishna then asked, "What is the outcome of dharma—happiness or unhappiness?" Arjuna said, "Of course, it is happiness." Lord Krishna smiled and explained, "Just think, what will be the outcome of this action? Where is your dharma in this?" Masters have spoken thus through the ages. Christ advised, *Whatsoever ye would that men should do to you, do ye even so to them.* A butcher may think that to kill is good, but what is the outcome of his action? Can it be happiness? So when we act, we must weigh the outcome. While we cling to our old habits we will never succeed, without exception. True happiness will be ours when we join back to God, through the radiant company of the Master and through obedience to His words. He himself has taken this practical path, which is the shortest route to salvation.

> *This time is precious, do not fritter it away;*
> *Greater than He you will never meet.*

If you lose this golden opportunity, you have no idea when you will be given another. Give up pride, cunning, and other worldly habits, and cease wandering in vain from one attraction to another. You will never get another like the Guru you have got. Whoever you meet will attempt to separate you from the Lord rather than rejoin you back to Him. *Know a Satguru as one who comes to reunite.* He wishes to bring all children of God together and sit among them. Such personages are rare; and if you have found one, then obey Him—do whatever he says. If you refuse to obey, how will you hope to progress? The Master has no selfish motives; he is merely following the orders from above. This has nothing to do with any team or intrigue, nor is it a matter of creating policies. As everything is straightforward and above board, the question of policy does not arise; there is nothing underhanded or hidden; there are no ulterior motives behind the teachings. It is a very simple fact that only he whose soul has rejoined the Lord enjoys complete happiness. Human beings do have many weaknesses—you will find animosity and unrest amid peoples all over the world, and this is because each man is obeying his mind. If they were to obey someone who is above habits and failings, what an abundance of joy would there be throughout the nations.

> *It you leave your Guru now*
> *You will wander the four regions of illusion.*

If, having got the double blessing of the human form and the Satguru, you throw away the chance by disobeying him, what will happen? Those who live on another's earnings go under the law of give and take or illusion; if you offend or harm anyone, you reap the reaction of that and, under the same law you will be born there where the offended person is born, that the account may be accurately balanced. *Wherever your attention is, there will you reside.* Who knows when you will again get the human form? Fire consumes even green wood as well as the dry, and everyone must go sometime. If you spend your days losing everything but saving the invaluable treasure given to you, then your work here will be successful. True Masters do their work quietly, without a fuss and show. They lead a quiet life—not like the bulls in the ring, tossing their horns about. *Your earthly sojurn's purpose was distinguished; That was Amrit* (Water of Life), *given by the Guru.*

Jad Bharat was a king after whose name India was called Bharat. He was in search of God, and so he left his kingdom and went to live in the jungles, in order to realize Him. However, there he grew very fond of a certain deer which became tame and friendly—so what happened? After death, he was again reborn, but into the form of a deer. You should remember that what I'm saying is for your own benefit. A Guru wishes to see the whole world have joy in life, and when he sees faults and mistakes he tries to wash them away and ensure that they are not repeated.

> *Never will you get a Guru like Him;*
> *Acknowledge, oh acknowledge this at last.*

It is easily understood why gurudom has a poor reputation nowadays, for the gurus are mostly political at heart, with self-centered motives for holding power over people and making money, etc. Instead of sincere sympathy for the plight of mankind, lies and cheating are used to gain the confidence of the followers. And sadly, people are more easily pleased and satisfied with suchlike performance than with what a genuine Master has to offer. Truth is truth—a lie is a lie. Black cannot be white, no matter how much it is washed. The true Master is met through great destiny behind the disciple. *Without great good fortune, you cannot meet a Satguru.* If you have been fortunate to meet a Satguru, just obey him and you will succeed. What is worth more than having our soul reaching the Lord's lap, never to be separated from Him? Now that so many years have passed, give up your old habits at last.

*Reading scriptures, singing the hymns,*
*Why so much pride in this?*

Are you proud because you can sing better than others, or because you can thrash out the written words? Or perhaps you are the best lecturer around? What real achievement is this—singing and reading and being proud because you know more than other people? It is written that King Ravan was a learned yogi who was familiar with the four Vedas and the six Shastras. Today, in what manner do we remember him? In effigy, we give him a donkey's head. Why? Because he lost whatever knowledge and progress he had gained. So to be academically proficient is no spiritual accomplishment. *To be clever, to read, to write—that is an easy thing.* It is not difficult to be clever or cunning, to bring together the earth and sky with eloquent words. *To control desire, to leave the body, to control the mind—these are difficult.* Keep the Truth before you. *You go on praising your Guru, but will not allow Him to reside in your heart.* He will have salvation who will bow down to his Guru's commands: *The whole world sees the Satguru, but salvation does not come with just a glimpse. Without love for His words, you will not get it.* These words are always uttered with no distinction of individuals—they apply to rich or poor, high or low, for Saints speak freely, even about themselves if necessary. Pride and ego do not let us progress—when we make mistakes we will not admit them. In our hearts we have the thought, "There is none greater than me." Self-respect and praise are both food for the mind. Caught up in this failing, we at times push the Guru aside, saying, "What does the Guru know?" A mother always considers her child's betterment, and so the Guru has concern for the progress of his disciples. Is it likely that the mother will cast out the child if he misbehaves toward her? The fact is that we do not even try to recognize what the Guru is. Give up the ego, or it will be your downfall.

CHANGE YOUR HABITS NOW

*This pride has spoiled you.*
*This same pride even now does you great harm.*

We may have been given human birth many times, but pride and ego killed us again and again, ruining all our good work and causing us to return to the same scene time and again. In the past it was our ruination, and it is winning the present also. Do not obey your mind—obey the words of the Guru, which will bring you great joy, whereas obedience to the mind will give you unending distress—the mind ever gave birth to trouble. Wash anger away with love, just as your Guru does. He never leaves his duty, though mankind may make good or bad remarks about him. He does not live on the earnings of others—does not accept anything for himself— has no desires. If anyone brings money to the Satsang, it is used for the Satsang. Up to today I live on my pension and have managed to live within its means. If the advice is good, you should appreciate it and be grateful—if through the advice your distress is increased, it's a different matter.

*Oh beloved children, I have unfolded it to you;*
*Think not that thy habits are good.*
*Hurry and leave all deceit;*
*Increase your devotional attitude.*

Your carelessness will result in the loss of everything most valuable if you do not change your habits. In the heart there is one thing, on the tongue is another, and our actions denote something different again. Leave such deceit as soon as possible—leave all cunning ways and develop sincere humility. If you do this, the Guru himself will embrace you. An attitude of devotion will take its own place within your being. You are greatly mistaken if you think you can gain his pleasure by merely saying you love and serve him when your heart denies it.

*It after this the mind does not agree,*
*Then you will see the result yourself.*

If you refuse to understand, then nothing can be done. You will just have to continue paying up for your mistakes. Even the Saints are defeated at this point and say, "If you will not listen, what can we do?"

*On your head, the Negative Power's orders;*
*That's why the mind does not obey.*

The hand of the Negative Power on your head will not allow the mind to obey you. He will go on increasing the duality to make it more and more difficult and confusing. The Negative will not help you to overcome this duality—only the Positive can do that. It is a marked difference between the Powers.

*One thing I have discovered, my brother;*
*You are dishonorable.*

In the end, what can one do if no one wishes to listen and obey? Honor is a noble virtue—what kind of man is this, that has no virtue in him?

*Constantly keep the Guru's company;*
*Perhaps one day the mind will agree.*

With the co-operation of the mind, go on perservering. If we see the Guru through a dark curtain, it does not mean that the Guru has turned black! Slowly, slowly, slowly—do not leave the Guru, but go on trying to understand, then definitely there will be hope of the curtain being drawn aside forever. To be constant and then unfaithful, sometimes this and sometimes that—this does not remedy anything. A rolling stone gathers no moss. That which has to be developed is the "inner man." If the Guru is true, and

I have told you how to discover this, then stick to him, listen to his words, and do your best to understand. You will make the grade if you ignore your mind. The mind may stand in between, but the soul knows what Guru is and what God is.

> *Radha Soami has unravelled it;*
> *Why should man be in doubt?*

God manifested on a human pole was termed as Radha Soami by Swami Shiv Dayal Singh Ji (who is usually called Swami Ji). It is surprising that mankind does not accept the true facts of life, when God Himself is explaining them through the Godman.

*Sawan Singh Ji Maharaj*
*(1858-1948)*

# 11

# Gurubhakti: A Lesson in Love

THIS DAY we have gathered together in the loving memory of the Godman, Hazur Sawan Singh Ji Maharaj, who revived the age-old perennial science which we had forgotten. The object of the celebrating the birth anniversary of a Master-soul is to make a fresh appraisal of his teachings; and by following his footsteps, we keep his memory alive. Ordinarily, we are expected to live daily, nay hourly, in the loving presence of the Master and be ever thankful to him for the indelible footprints left by him on the sands of time. That, of course, is an individual affair. But we must, once a year at least, hold a memorial service on the occasion of his advent into the world for the spiritual uplift of man. Whatever time we spend together in this congregational service to the memory of the Godman will be amply rewarded and should, therefore, be considered a great blessing.

What then are the lessons we can take from such a dedicated life of selfless service as that of Hazur? For it is by knowing them that we can strive to follow them as best we can and advance on the path of Self-realization and God-realization. It is to his great credit that he revived the most ancient science of Para Vidya (the knowledge of the Beyond, the great unknown cause that lies beyond the senses, the mind and the intellect). In the modern age, the teachings originated with Kabir and Nanak, and the torch of light was carried on by the successive nine Gurus and then Tulsi Sahib, Swami Ji Maharaj, and afterwards by Jaimal Singh Ji and Hazur Sawan Singh Ji Maharaj by whose grace the sacred teachings are being imparted even now to the spiritually hungry souls. Fortunate indeed are those blessed souls who had the privilege to be initiated by him. We must, therefore, make the best use of the short life-span allotted to us. The greatest purpose of the human birth is that it offers us an opportunity, rare as it is, to experience our own "Self" and God. None can help us to unite with God but one who is already united with Him. In the Gurbani it says: *Some Godman may link us with the Power-of-God.*

That divine power is, of course, within each one of us for we live, move and have our very being in Him. Further in the Gurbani it says: *My Lord consort pervades in all beings, but blessed is one in whom He is manifest.*

It is this God-manifested being or the Godman who can guide us Godward. The question here is: Why can we not unite with God by our own unaided efforts? It is because the soul is under the powerful sway of mind, which in its turn is being controlled by the senses, and these senses are running riot with the sense-objects. We are thus totally identified with mind and matter, and have no independent existence of our own. So it is the God-in-man who can link us with God. In other words, one who has established a contact with God can show us the way to effect this contact for ourselves. Thus, God in the garb of man is the Guru of all. When Guru Nanak was questioned on this subject, he replied: *Verily, it is the holy Word, Shabd, or the Sound that is the Master; and the soul in man, permeating through and through the physical body, is the disciple.* Now what is meant by Shabd? The absolute God is Ashabd (Wordless); but when He comes into expression, He is known as Shabd (Word). The Gurbani tells us: *With one Word, the whole creation came into being.* Again Gurbani says: *It is from Shabd that the whole creation comes into being and ultimately gets absorbed into it, and it is through Shabd that regeneration takes place.*

This manifested Power-of-God which is the substratum of the entire creation is called Shabd. This Shabd then is the Jagat-Guru or the Master-power. This very question was put to Kabir, "O Kabir, who is the Master and where does the disciple reside? How did the two get together in an indissoluble Union?" He replied: "My Master is in the Beyond, while the disciple is in the body. Both of them got together by means of Shabd and now there is no fear of separation between the two." So the Master of all the world is the Shabd-power or the holy Word. Guru Gobind Singh has put it succinctly: *He who is one and the same in the beginning and the end is the manifested Power-of-God, the Shabd, and that is the real Master.*

Thus the physical body in which the Shabd-power is manifestly working is worthy of all our adoration, for that power alone can draw the soul to Himself. The Master is not the physical body but the divine Power which is enlivening his body. And the Gurbani clearly tell us: *God speaks through a human frame, as without it how can He speak to us?*

The physical body is not the Master but blessed is that body in which that Power is manifest for spiritual guidance. This Power-of-God as manifested on the human plane helps in liberating all human souls entombed in the meshes of mind and matter. Swami Ji says: *The great Power-of-God in the Guru helps in disengaging the souls from the shackles of the body and in raising them upwards.*

The living Master is competent enough to unite with God such souls as seek his guidance. The prime job of a Master-soul is to unite all the children of God under his saving protection. Gurbani says: *Free from birth and death under the compulsive force of Karma comes the redeemer of souls;*

*with a touch of his life-breath he alchemizes the human soul and connects it with the holy Word.*

Such great souls come into the world for the spiritual welfare of humanity. They are commissioned from above for this job. Now perhaps you may understand what is meant by a living Master. He is in fact God manifest on earth or the *Word-made-flesh* to dwell among us as Christ puts it. The Gurbani tells us, *Dwelling in the Guru, He distributes the holy Word.*

Man alone can be the teacher of man. It is with the help of some human instrument that God works for mankind. God does, from time to time, descend in a human garb for the uplift of the people stuck fast in the mire of the world and all that is worldly. A Saint has a two-fold mission: to awaken people from a long-drawn dream of the material world and to reveal to them the saving life-lines within. Like a radiant pole-star, he guides the erring humanity. When it rains, every place, high or low, equally gets the blessing of the life giving showers. Hazur's name was Sawan, and significantly enough like Sawan-rains, he blessed the people with spiritual showers; and everyone—Hindu, Muslim, Sikh or Christian—benefitted from his teachings.

Now we revert to our original question: Whom should one love in the world? If we look critically, we find that love is an innate quality in man and everyone is devoted to one thing or another: may be service to one's family, community, nation or religion, or it may be to the development of some art or craft or any other such thing. And yet there are some who love themselves above all else, and self-indulgence is with them the be-all and end-all of life. Once there was in our country a ruler named Mohammad Shah Rangila. He was given over to bouts of drinking. When Delhi was in the throes of a wholesale massacre, the people petitioned the king to intervene. The king was so busy drinking that he had neither the time nor the heart to attend to this appeal for mercy and exclaimed: "Let these papers of no importance be drowned in the wine." Similarly, it is said of Nero, a Roman emperor, that he fiddled while Rome was burning. There is no dearth of such people in the world. He who worships his family is far better than the one who worships himself and lives for self-gratification only. So, also he who loves and serves his society, religion or country is still better progressively. But all these varying types of love and devotion are more or less characterized by a sense of ego and smack of pride; and as such, more often than not, the result is a clash between family and family, class and class, or country and country. We have had what are euphemistically called crusades or holy wars fought in the blessed name of religion, but born out of misguided religious zeal and, to speak plainly, out of sheer religious ignorance, bigotry and intolerance. But on the contrary, the love of God far transcends all these petty adorations as it consists in total self-abnegation and selfless sacrifice because of the knowledge that God resides in all hearts; and He is the substratum of the entire creation. God is an unchangeable permanence and everlasting. But we have not yet seen Him, and without seeing Him how can we love Him and inculcate devotion for Him? So we have, of necessity, to bestow our loving devotion on the human pole where the Power-of-God is manifest. Guru Amardas Ji says: *If you want to worship God, worship the Satguru who is God personified or the Word made flesh.*

He then grants contact with the holy Naam and helps us in crossing over into the Beyond. The worship of Satguru is really the worship of God. The easiest way of developing the worship of God is to develop *Gurubhakti* (love of the Master). In Gurbani we have: *The loving devotion to the Master is above everything else, and I love His holy feet with all my strength.*

Now what is *Bhakti* (loving devotion)? It is the love of God. God is love and love is God. The way back to God is also through love. Love knows naught but service and sacrifice. What is it that distinguishes love? He who loves, desires to sacrifice his all for the sake of the beloved; and after having sacrificed all, does not look for any reward in return. God Himself speaks thus in the Gurbani: *If you desire to join Me in the game of love, Come unto Me with your head on your palm as an offering. If you want to tread the path of love, never for a moment hesitate to offer your life.*

This is the type of sacrifice that love demands, and in doing so never think that you have done any favor. You should rather feel grateful that you have won love so easily.

Amir Khusro was a great devotee of his Master. One day he exclaimed with delight that he had received happy tidings from his beloved. "What is it?" the people asked. "My beloved has ordered that I be decapitated tomorrow in the open market," he said. "Has your beloved given you any assurance to see you and cast his loving glance on you?" enquired the people. "None whatsoever," was the reply.

This is what love demands from the lover and complete submission to the will of the beloved without any rhyme or reason. Love is just a one-way traffic so far as the lover is concerned. It knows no bargaining. All it connotes is implicit obedience. *Not my will, but thine*, cries the true lover. A Persian poet has defined love thus: "What is Love? It is to be a bondsman of the beloved, and to go wandering and offering one's heart."

Love then means to dedicate yourself—body and soul— to someone and to wander the earth over in his search.

A real devotee dedicates his very life to the service of his Master and dissolves his will in that of His. It is a life of complete surrender with no mental reservations. Sarmad, a great Gurbhakta, said: *I have given away my heart, my life and my very soul; Having passed on all my burdens I know no greater gain than this.*

All the ills of the world originate with mental activity. We are stuck fast in the heart-focus from where the rays of the mind start and passing from the sense organs envelop the sense objects; and we get attached to the world around us. How little do we realize the great motor-power of the soul behind, enlivening the mind and the intellect. If we could divest ourselves of these adjuncts and dedicate our very life to the service of a Godman, we would at once become a freed soul ready to go Godward. Can there be any greater gain than to escape from all the trials and turmoils of the earthly life? This is what we gain by practicing the presence of the personified God in our midst. He is a living embodiment of the God-into-expression Power and helps us to reveal and develop it the same way as he has done.

Swami Ji says: *Contemplate thou on the form of the Master; Besides it, there is no other way of escape from bondage.*

The term *Dhyan* (contemplation) is derived from the root *dhi* which means to fix the attention on the living Master. I may illustrate my point by taking the analogy of a newly wedded girl coming back to her parents' home. However busy she may appear to be in household chores, all the time she thinks of her husband. In exactly the same way, the attention of the disciple should always be grounded in the Master—the Word-made-flesh. Guru is Godman, i.e., man plus God. Those who get attached to man only remain entangled in the body, while those who see the God manifest in the man, the link with Him is revealed to the disciple. He learns quickly how to rise above the body. As you think so you become. It is He who loves us first, and our love is simply reciprocal. Mother loves the newly born child first and the child loves the mother in return. Our love is but a kind of reaction of the love of the Master who has drawn us to him. Gurbani says: *"The Master loves the disciple with all his life."*

This is known as Gurubhakti. When you think of the Master with all your heart and soul, you cannot but obey Him implicitly. Christ said: *If you love me, keep my commandments.*

Love calls for direct and immediate obedience and not merely lip service. In this respect there is a general weakness in all of us and we fail miserably. We must learn to understand Him and be able to do what He bids us to do, even though at moments what He says may not appear sound to us. He speaks from a higher level and sees things from afar to which we have yet no access. So if all the time we think of Him, no matter while we are engaged in worldly pursuits, we will gradually imbibe his spirit. Our outer entanglements shall not then bind us. In this way we will get cut off from outer attachments, the more his divine power will enter into us and transform us into his likeness. Christ has said: *I am the vine, ye are the branches: He that abideth in me, and I in him, the same bringeth forth much fruit: for without me, ye can do nothing.* All this may be likened to a grafting process. When we engraft the twig of one tree in the body of another tree, then the fruit of the second tree will be of the quality and taste of the tree from which it got the graft. Similarly, if the disciple reasonably develops his receptivity by constant devotion, loving faith and implicit obedience, he will, when asked, give you the same reply to a question as you would get from the Master Himself. When two hearts work in unison they operate with the same vibrations, as in telepathy. Such a disciple naturally gets from the Master

His own impulses. So Gurubhakti is the *sine qua non* on the path of the Masters. Swami Ji has rightly said: *Those who engage in the practice of listening to the Sound Current without Gurubhakti or devotion to the Master are but fools.*

The essence of Gurubhakti is that our thoughts and feelings be detached from all else and be centered at one focal point, the eye-focus. Our Hazur used to illustrate this sublime truth thus: *Suppose there is a pipe with many holes or small openings in it from which the water is trickling drop by drop. If we were to close down all these holes save one, then the water will gush forth from the one hole left open in a strong current and to a great height. Exactly in the same way if we cut off all our worldly connections, then the sensory currents will get collected at one point and then shoot forth from the tenth opening at the eye-focus.* Hazur used to say that the Guru does not need our devotion; but if we adore him and offer our unstinted love to him, it is helpful for our inner spiritual progress. The principle of "as you think so you become" works here. Swami Ji says: *The holy Word or the Shabd is revealed just by the grace of the Guru, and then the long and strong arm of the Master pulls the spirit-currents out from the body below.*

Now you will understand the basic need of Gurubhakti. It does not mean dancing around the Guru or shouting this way or that. If you do not care to listen to what the Guru says or to understand and follow his behests, it is not Gurubhakti at all. Such persons cannot get any spiritual benefit even if they live with the Master for ages upon ages. On the contrary, those who turn their back upon the world and are wholly engrossed in the love of the Master and make loving devotion as their ruling passion, they easily and quickly get transformed into the likeness of the Master. Just take a worldly example of a person full of lust and see how he lovingly dotes upon the form of his beloved and in her presence feels inebriated. Guru Ramdas says: *I feel highly elated with joy by looking at the physical form of my beloved Satguru.*

If one could, from afar, just get a glimpse of the glorious turban of Hazur while standing in the midst of thousands of persons, a thrill of joy would run through from head to toe. Maulana Rumi says: *Even if I were to behold the face of my beloved, hundreds of times with hundreds of eyes, I would still like to see him again and again for each time one gets a novel experience from such a blessed sight.* He goes on to say: *Just as a drunkard feels restlessly agitated by looking at a vintage splashing in a goblet of wine, similarly by looking into the cups of the deeply set eyes of the Master, the souls of the devotees soar high in ecstasy divine.*

Those who have attained the climax of love like this for the Master, they feel divinity surging in the fibres of their being. It was a matter of common experience to see people standing statue-like for hours on end with their eyes intently fixed on the radiant face of Hazur. The sweet and loving remembrance of the Master, the contemplation of His form and careful attention to His discourses are some of the tried methods for the purification of the mind. If the Master is full of piety, you will automatically become pious. After all, what is there in Him which attracts us so much? He is charged with the spiritual glow and the divine glory which attracts one and all alike. An Urdu poet says: *Where there is no beauty, love cannot evolve; and a nightingale finds no delight in flowers painted on the walls.*

It is the glory of the living God in him which attracts others. The radioactive rays emanating from his person sink deeply into the hearts of the devotees. So long as there is no inner charm, no one can charm the people around him. Swami Ji warns: *A soul entombed in the body cannot possibly do Gurubhakti; when even the gods themselves are ignorant of His greatness, how can the incomprehensible Satguru be comprehended? He may be known as much as He may, in His grace, reveal Himself.*

Guru Nanak was considered by the worldly people as one who perverted the intellect of others. He was not allowed to enter the town of Qasur (now in Pakistan) lest he should misguide the people. But there were others who recognized in him a living God in the garb of man. So it all depends on how much he may choose to reveal himself to each individual. Similarly, Hazur was looked upon by many as a very pious old man, whereas those who had had the good fortune to go near him would see something higher in him. And still fewer who had developed some inner receptivity and devotion found a veritable Godman. Hazur used to explain the matter: *A highly qualified teacher attending to boys in a primary class would reveal as much of his knowledge as it may be possible for the novices to grasp. But the same teacher when teaching middle classes would impart higher knowledge to his students befitting their capacity to learn; and when he will go to the higher secondary, he will show more of his learning; till in a college, he will be at his best.* In other words, as a student advances from class to class and his understanding ripens with the passage of time and experience, he imbibes more and more of his teacher's learning; and the teacher too, tries to impart greater knowledge which may be commensurate with the capacity to understand and assimilate. The time factor then is important in any type of development. The more a person attends upon his Guru and diligently follows his instructions, the more he develops his receptivity; and in the same proportion, the Guru reveals to him more and more spiritual experience. It all depends on *Upasna* which means proximity to the spiritual preceptor. If you sit near the Master with heart and soul attuned, you are sure to be benefited a lot by his divine radiation; and that in turn will develop your inner receptivity or power of assimilation. The easiest, the shortest, and the simplest way to get greater benefit is to lose yourself completely in the holy presence of a Sant Satguru. Swami Ji says: *O Soul, be fully absorbed in Satsang at least this day.*

What then is "full or complete absorption"? is the question. It means that while in the company of a Saint, listening to him one should forget not only the place where he is sitting, but become wholly oblivious of the very surroundings in which he is and dissolve his very being, losing all consciousness except of the holy presence of the Master. This blanking of one's self is called "absorption." The more one empties himself of his worldliness and pettiness, the more he will be filled by the divine grace emanating from the divine presence before him. This is the secret of a successful Satsang. Excuse me, when I say that it is seldom that we get a Satsang or company of a truly perfect Master for such highly advanced souls—souls one with the Lord—are very rare indeed. They are not easily available and recognizable; and if by some mighty good luck we do come across a Godman, we do not know how to derive the fullest benefit from his company or Satsang. The way to make the most of such a rare opportunity and derive the maximum benefit is that one should try to come to the place of Satsang as early as possible and sit silently in a prayerful mood, blanking the mind of all the worldly thoughts in the august presence of the Master, inwardly absorbing his words of wisdom. If by sitting close to fire we feel warmth and the proximity of a glacier gives a cold shiver, there is no reason why one should not be affected by the divine aura of a Master-saint whose radiation has an unimaginably long range.

The devotion to and the love of the Master are synonymous terms. Love is all comprehensive and it knows only service and sacrifice. Guru Gobind Singh while speaking of his own descent on the earth plane says : *Having merged in the Lord, I did not like to come down again into this mundane world, but was prevailed upon by God to do so—for the spiritual welfare of humanity.*

When loving devotion is at its highest, nothing remains of the individual self for it becomes universalized and all pervading. Hafiz says: *My heart is so filled with the love of the Lord, that I cannot think of myself apart from Him.*

We have, therefore, to rid ourselves of the personal ego for it stands between us and God. Gurbani says: *The true Lord is attained by Gurubhakti.* This is the way that He comes to dwell in us, absorbing the mind in Him. The main object of all spiritual practices and disciplines is that we should develop Gurubhakti or devotion to the Guru which, of course, grows out of love. This is why all saints and sages laid stress on cultivating love. Guru Gobind Singh says: *What does it profit to close the eyes, and sit stork-like with folded wings, And to take dips in the seas of the world, gaining nothing here and hereafter, And while traveling in sense-pleasures, waste time in useless disputations. Verily I tell thee, listen all if ye may, they alone get to the Lord who know how to love.*

Similarly, John in his first Epistle says : *He that loveth not knoweth not God, for God is love.* Again, in the holy Koran, we have: *A loving man cannot do without a beloved.*

It is in fact the beloved that teaches the lover the art of love and enables him to progress steadily on the path of love. As God is love so is the human soul a particle of divine love. The essence of love is at the core of all creation and more so in man. Man is he who has in him feelings of loving sympathy. What is it that characterizes a sage or a saint?

*He is a cup bubbling over with the love of God,*
*His proximity quickens in us the life of love.*

As light comes from light and life from life, so does love come from love. Love does not grow in fields nor can it be had from a shop, but we may catch its infection from the love-laden eyes of a lover of God. There are some people who are fondly in love with the pleasures of the world and care not for the next. Then there are others who are carried away by hopes of a paradisal bliss. But those who love the Lord share the things that really matter far better than either of them. Love ignites in us the flame of Living Light or the Light of Life. That type of love is:

> *Meeting the God-intoxicated soul I enquired*
> *about the nature of divine love,*
> *The only reply was that in its fullness it could not*
> *be described.*
> *The flaming love of the Lord cannot be kept under*
> *a bushel,*
> *One may not open one's mouth but tearful eyes*
> *belie and shed tears involuntarily.*
> *A heart devoid of love is a charnel-house,*
> *An iron monger's bellows which breathes without*
> *the breath of life.*

Kabir says: *Humility, simplicity, devotion and courtesy are great virtues, But he alone is great who observes decorum with all.* Decorum or propriety is the core of true living which ranks almost as high as truth itself. We must love all, respect all and be courteous to all, which we seldom do. We generally play double-faced like Janus and apply double standards in all our dealings. Our head and heart do not work in unison nor do our acts and words exhibit the same pattern. Guru

Nanak says: *Humility tinged with sweetness is the essence of all virtues.*

It is from the abundance of heart that the tongue speaks; and unless there is sweetness in the folds of our mind, we cannot speak sweetly. All the sages, therefore, speak of love as the only way of salvation. Guru Nanak pointedly tells us; *Beauty, lineage, prowess, learning and riches are of no avail, Endowed with all these but devoid of love of the Lord, one is as good as dead.*

How can we get the wealth of love? It comes to the elect of the Lord and he showers it in abundance on whomsoever He pleases. The worldly wise entombed in mind and matter can hardly aspire to it and do not get it. Once princess Zaibul-Nisa went to Sarmad and requested him for the rare boon of God's love. Sarmad said: *O Sarmad, the burning passion of the Lord is not granted to the avaricious, Nor the moth's love for the flame, to flies that hover round filth. It takes ages to get revelation of the Lord in one's mind; O Sarmad, this wealth is not doled out to all and sundry.*

Now the question is: Whom should we love? As love is the law of life, we cannot do without loving one thing or the other. We bestow all our love on the world and all that is of the world, wife and children, riches and possessions. But all these objects of the world betray us at one stage or another and leave us rueful sooner or later. We must love something which may be eternal so that our love is not falsified. The former is not love in the strict sense of the word but blind infatuation commonly known as attachment. Why not then find something worthy of our love and which can befriend us both here and hereafter? In this context, I place before you a small hymn of Kabir so that we may understand the subject better.

*We must love one who will not leave nor forsake us till the end.*

He alone is worthy to be loved who will stand by us in all the vicissitudes of life on the earth plane and also lead us into the Beyond before the judgement seat of God. In the Gurbani we find this statement: *O Nanak, snap all ephemeral ties of worldly relations and find the company of a true saint; the former shall break away in this very life, while the latter shall abide with thee even after death.*

The friends and relations in the world, howsoever near and dear they may be, do not stand by through thick and thin. Some of them leave off in poverty and indigence, some in prolonged illness and disease, and some in adverse circumstances and misfortune. At the most, a few may help you to the funeral pyre and that is all. The friendship of a saint is everlasting. He abides forever and forever and even stands by to help you before the judgement seat of God. Thus Kabir says: *When in affluence, all flock around thee and feed thy vanity, With the turn in fortune, all fly away and none comes near.*

Even the most sincere stand by helplessly when you are at death's door and gasping for breath. When they see you fighting and losing the battle against death and helplessly struggling for life, all that they can do is to pray to God to relieve you from the tortuous agony of the last moments. What else can they possibly do? Again in the Gurbani we are told: *Serve the true Master and develop the holy Word. The Master receives at death those who have done their best to follow Him.*

We should, therefore, be the doer of the Word and practice it day and night. It is the "comforter" of which Christ spoke. It helps us in diverse ways when we are helpless in death's trap or in treacherous situations. It materializes in the likeness of the Master to advise and encourage us, no matter where we may be, on the snowy mountain-tops, in the burning desert sands, down in the ocean depths or high up in the sky. And again, when one is in the last moments of one's life it appears in the radiant form of the Master to escort the soul into the Beyond, leads the spirit gradually from plane to plane, as and when He thinks fit, until He conducts you safely to the Abode of God. My Master used to say that a Satguru while revealing the holy Word, at the time of initiation, actually reveals His true form *(Shabd Swarup)*, which always remains with the initiated soul till both merge in Sat Naam, the primal manifestation of God, Who then helps the soul to Agam (the incomprehensible), Alakh (the ineffable) and Anaam (the Nameless, without form and attributes). It is because of this momentous and signal service and sacrifice of an eternal nature that we are advised to cultivate love for one who loves us eternally and befriends us both here and hereafter. Maulana Rumi, speaking of this love, tells us:

> *Love is different from sensuality in men,*
> *For senses feed upon the objects of senses,*
> *And thrive upon the food we take.*

Thus we see that love is something sublime and sacred and should not be confused with lust which is the outcome of base desires and sensual appetites. It is love of the soul for the Oversoul, or of the created being for the Creator. How then can we come by love is the next question.

> *Love neither grows in the field nor is sold in the*
> *    market,*
> *Even the high and the mighty who aspire for love*
> *    have to pay for it with their head.*

Love is the zest of life, for we live by the love of the Lord. Guru Amardas has said: *Accursed is the man whose heart is bereft of love.*

Love the Light of Life in which we live. What does it avail to have a human birth if we know not what love is and make the most of it? We must taste the blessings of love and be really blessed. That is the whole purpose of human existence. But what do we do? All the time we are busily engaged in doing things on the plane of duality and are lost not only to God but also to our own true self, forgetful of our essentially divine nature. Is there no remedy then? The reply is: Yes, there is a remedy: *The love for a Godman inspires love for God.*

If you love one who is truth-personified, He will surely pass on His infection to you. This is the way to be inspired with the love of the divine. Live in the divinely awakened and you will live in the divinity. Hence the supreme need for cultivating love, the life-principle, that will abide with you forever and ever. *Without love, the mercurial nature of man finds no rest.*

Tossed in the seas of sense-pleasures, we have lost our moorings and are drifting rudderless along the stream of time. Until we find some safe anchorage, a haven of peace, we are ever a prey to chance winds and storms of life as it is. Every day we see strife and struggle everywhere, clashes in households, men set against men, tribe against tribe, and country against country. Why all this confusion? Because of the lack of loving understanding, of loving toleration for the views of others. In spite of our man-made artificial barriers — national, linguistic, religious and political — are we not members of one great family of man? So long as we do not rise above these petty, racial and clannish prides and prejudices, which have bogged and clouded our vision, we cannot gain access to the bright sunshine of loving unity and have peace within and without. And this will be possible only when we rest our soul in the causeless cause. St. Augustine tells us: *Thou hast created my soul, O God, after Thee and it is restless until it rests in Thee.*

During my second world tour I had an opportunity of meeting national, religious and political leaders in various countries and I placed before them the principle of "live and let others live," and it had a chastening effect on them. I told them that God had put under their care and protection millions of His children; and if they could not, for one reason or another, take proper and adequate interest in them, they should pass over a part of their burden to others. This line of thought appealed to them and at one or two places where relations had almost reached the breaking point, better counsels prevailed by divine grace.

Love works as a great healing balm in the affairs of the world. In our households, if we could make use of a sweet tongue, we would have paradise on earth. A sword-cut may get well in a few days, but the wound caused by a sharp tongue festers all the while like a running sore. The more one ruminates on the bitter words, the more do they rankle in the mind. The great epic of the Mahabharata war was the outcome of just a few bitter words uttered inadvertently by Draupai. When the Kauros visited the queen's palace, at one place the glittering surface of the courtyard looked like ripples of water. Naturally, they pulled up their garments. Watching them, Draupadi facetiously remarked that the children of a blind father could not but see things blindly. The result was a great homicidal war in which the most ancient culture and civilization of India came virtually to an end. This weakness for fault-finding and sarcasm has unfortunately become a common feature of the present day society. We are keenly alive to a mote in others' eyes, but cannot see a beam in our own eyes. We try to be clever in making allusions and speaking in oblique terms. This in fact is a very nasty habit for it deeply hurts others' feelings.

I would suggest you all—old and new initiates—to maintain introspection diaries, and at the close of each day make a note of all your failings during the day from the path of rectitude, viz.; truthfulness, purity, straight-forwardness, non-injury, selfless service and the like. In this way you will know your faults easily and try to eradicate them one by one. It will also enable you unwittingly to cultivate corresponding virtues on all levels—in thought, word and deed. *Ahimsa parma dharma* or non-injury is the highest of virtues. If you have love in your heart for all, you will not then try to deceive any person, for in doing so you will in the first instance be deceiving yourself. Far from this you will try to be of service to others. *Service*, you know, comes before self and becomes sanctified by being selfless. All these are aids in purifying the mind; and the more the mind gets purified, the more it is fitted to receive the light of truth and the more you will be able to radiate it in your acts and deeds. I have always insisted on keeping such a diary. In the Gurbani it says: *A seer of Truth can lead you to Truth, And from death can take you to life eternal.*

This then is the purpose of the prayer that the ancients were never tired of repeating time and again: *O God, lead me from darkness to light, from untruth to truth, and from death to immortality.* And now we have seen how we can make this time-hallowed and time-honored prayer fruitful. Gurbani says: *He who links you with the Power of God, take Him verily to be God.*

For who else but God can lead you to God? This is a profound truth; and you can verify it for yourself when by mighty good fortune you find a Godman, or a Godman picks you up, for we all are engaged in the game of blindman's buff:

*Satguru Himself is doubtlessly the immaculate One,*
   *Despite the human garb in which He appears.*

Again:

*Godman is but Godlike in spite of the human cloak*
   *He wears.*

In crystal clear words, Maulana Rumi declares: *When you approach a Godman, you approach God, and when you move away from Him you are farther from God.* Why? Because Godman is a deputy of God Himself on the earth plane. When we sit near a living Master with a vacant mind, we are filled with His divine vibrations which penetrate through the very pores of our body. This is the sign of His greatness and goodness. It is very rarely that we get a real Satsang, i.e., by a really God-intoxicated person. If we do get an opportunity, we hardly take full advantage of it. Unless we go to Satsang with faith and receptivity, we do not feel the effect of the radioactive rays that emanate from His person. When even a stone lying in water gets the cooling effect of water, there is no reason why a person, howsoever ignorant he may be, should not get intoxicated in the presence of a divine being. He will surely breathe the exhilarating fragrance of the Satguru provided his mind is blank (free from worldly preoccupations). A living Master is Word-made-flesh, and the atmosphere around Him is highly charged with spiritual vibrations with the result that one begins to feel their effect and experience blissful calm within. Once one tastes this, one grows indifferent to all the pleasures of the world.

After all, there must be some specific spiritual gain in the company of a saint that all the scriptures of the world have spoken so highly of the value of Satsang and its necessity for progress on the spiritual path. But a Guru must be a perfect Guru and not a half prophet laying claim to the whole truth. It is not a matter of acting or posing but one of revelation of the life-principle within. The bitter experience of fake masters compel the people to disown even the greatness of real teachers, and they prefer scriptures to direct experience. Once bitten twice shy. But without the aid of a really perfect Master, there is no way out for a soul to escape from the shackles of mind and matter in order to enter into spiritual realms beyond, to regain the kingdom of God now, and to enjoy life eternal. Love of, and obedience to, such a Master unlocks the portals of heaven; and the soul is led by the ever-loving spouse and Radiant Guru Dev safely from plane to plane and becomes eternally united with the Satguru (Sat Naam or Sat Purush, the True One) .

> *As the water of a river in spite of the enclosing*
> *banks remains water,*
> *So does the Power of God manifest at a human*
> *pole as Truth itself.*

Guru and Satguru are but synonymous terms being just two phases of the Reality. Outwardly, He is a Guru for imparting spiritual instructions to the disciples, but inwardly He is a Satguru for in Him is working manifestly the power of *Sat* or Truth. He is in brief *Word-made-flesh* and dwells among us for revealing to man the lifelines within each individual: Guru Nanak says,

> *O Lalo, I speak nothing on my own,*
> *I open mouth only at His bidding.*

A Guru is one who has become the mouthpiece of God. The devotion to the Guru then is the first stage in spirituality and it consists in implicit acceptance of His commandments. *If you love me follow my commandments,* was the exhortation of Christ to his followers. When you come across a real Guru forget everything else and listen attentively to what he says; and even if you do not fully understand his language, it does not matter much. His radiation will of itself have a soothing effect on you. His magnetic rays have an unimaginably long range. If you sit quietly and listen, it will be to your benefit. Try to live up to what you hear; your life will take a change for the better. The sage Lukman used to say: *When you go to a saint, sit quietly before him and listen attentively to what he says on his own.* But do we do so? We keep talking either with others or keep interrupting the saint by useless questions, with the result that we return empty handed.

Today we are celebrating the birth anniversary of Hazur (Sawan Singh Ji Maharaj). It would, therefore, be a fitting tribute to his memory if you resolve to make your life a continuous saga of love and service—love of the Lord and service of His creation. As you have not yet come face to face with God, then for the time being try to develop love for one in whom the Power of God is working for the good of humanity. The first step in this direction is to do what He directs you to do: *There is no difference between the Satguru and His words.*

We must learn to believe and have faith in what He says. Now that we are sitting in the sweet remembrance of Hazur, it will be a great day for us, if we resolve to turn over a new leaf in our lives. For this purpose we must maintain a spiritual diary. It will enable us to introspect. At present we are unable to see the foibles lying hidden in the depths of our minds. But when you try to plumb the unconscious, you will gradually be able to see them on the surface, at first in trickles and then in torrents.

*O Mind, learn to love the Lord and love Him yet more.*

This is what Kabir has said. In the same vein we have the words of Jesus: *Love the Lord thy God with all thy heart, with all thy mind, with all thy soul and with all thy strength.* And again: *Love thy neighbor as thyself.*

Asked as to what should be the Christian attitude towards wrong doers, he declared: *Love your enemies, bless them that curse you, do good to them that hate you, and pray for them that despitefully use you and persecute you; that you may be the children of your Father-in-heaven. Be ye therefore perfect even as your Father which is in heaven is perfect.*

This then constitutes the love in the teachings of all the great sages from time immemorial, and it shall eternally remain the same. They all exhort us to mold our life on these lines. Courtesy does not cost you anything. All the time we are malevolently concerned with what others say and do. The world would be much better if we could stop involving ourselves in the sayings and doings of others. Again, we do not confine our mistakes to ourselves, but all the time busily sprinkle folly among our neighbors with the result that we get from them a hundredfold in return. What good does it bring after all?

On a day like this, I repeat with all the emphasis at my command that Hazur was a veritable ocean of love; and we should and must, if we love him, learn afresh our lesson in love, by following in his footsteps by diligently working at the spiritual practices that he gave out for our uplift. By withdrawing himself from the physical plane he has not forsaken us; for his godly power in its full radiance still sustains within and he is, more keenly than ever before, waiting at the focus of our being to help and guide us.

# GURUBHAKTI: A LESSON IN LOVE

God is not sitting on some throne in heaven. He is enthroned in the heart of each one of us. We must, therefore, learn to love and serve our fellow beings in distress and suffering. God Himself has declared: I love him who loves my created beings. This is the great lesson that Hazur taught us in the first instance and if we put it into practice in our everyday life, his grace shall most surely descend and help us in our spiritual progress. Let us see what Kabir says:

*Poor Kabir, from his life-long experience cannot*
*help reflecting again and again,*
*Self-effacement is the only way that will take you to*
*God and to your eternal home in heaven.*

Kabir says that the only way to salvation lies through love. It is by love that you rise above self and become selfless. Without transcendence of the self (the ego) in us, the light of God does not dawn. When you are charged with love, love of God-in-man, you cross over from stage of duality to oneness. How can we get to the fount of divine love? Love can be imbibed from the love-laden heart of some God-inspired soul. In a few words, Kabir has provided us with the Master-key that unlocks the doors of heaven: find out a Godman and learn from him the secret of love. Try to understand what he says and then diligently practice his teachings. He commands you to be chaste and clean in thought, word and deed; and to cultivate love for all that exists by the love of God. As God is not separate from His creation, you will see the spirit of God enlivening the entire universe. You will not then feel isolated from the world. Your little self, now cramped within the human mind, will expand, become universalized, and embrace the totality of all beings. This is the secret of success on God's path. There is no other short-cut to it. Try to be true to your own Self and then you will not be untrue to anyone. Alongside do Bhajan and Simran (sit in sweet remembrance of the Lord with rapt attention), make it a point to give daily nourishment to the soul as you do to the body. This is the love of which Kabir has given us a description in a few words. Mere lip-service and acrobatic feats will not do.

I would explain my point by means of a parable of two gardeners. A king had a fine orchard which was entrusted to the care of two gardeners. One of them was hard-working and would silently go about his job tending to the trees and flowers with due care and attention, keeping them in proper trim. The other was lazy but had a glib tongue and strong lungs. Whenever the king would visit the garden, the former would just pick up a few flowers and humbly present them to his royal master, while the other who did nothing would jump about and dance before the master and sing of the master's virtues, deportment and clothes. Now whom would the king like? You can give the answer yourself. Certainly, the one who applied himself to his work diligently and honestly without making any fuss. Similarly, the all-knowing Master looks to your innermost intentions, the sincerity of purpose in you, and honesty of efforts you make in following His commandments, and bestows on you the gift of His spiritual wealth according to your merits.

Kabir concludes his hymn with the following memorable words:

> *He who gives precedence to the Guru over every-*
> *thing else and religiously follows his teachings,*
> *O Kabir, such a person has nothing to fear in all the*
> *three regions.*

There are three mind zones or mental regions in which the embodied soul moves up and down in the giant wheel of life, propelled by the compulsive karmic force: the physical, the subtle and the causal, with no easy way of escape therefrom. Kabir tells us of a way-out through the kindly grace of some Master-soul that can lead a jiva unscathed from these into the Beyond, the purely spiritual realm—Sach Khand or Muqam-i-Haq of the Muslims or the Garden of Eden (New Jerusalem) of the Christians. The Master is the greatest gift of God to mankind.

Hazur used to tell us that we refrain from any evil act in the presence of a child of even five years. But, strange as it may seem, we have not even as much regard for the King of Kings—the all-knowing Master who knows even the innermost latencies of our mind. We shamelessly indulge in things which no sane person would do in the false belief that no one is looking at us. We must at all times remember that the Master in his subtle form is ever with us and watching all our deeds. Be careful to avoid misdeeds and misdeameanors at all costs. And last but not the least we should in no wise transgress the limitations imposed by him and pledge on this blessed day positively to follow his instructions with a rededicated zeal. Please make a careful note of all these things so that you may live in peace and be really blessed.

*Sant Kirpal Singh Ji*
*(1894-1974)*

# 12

# To Gain His Pleasure

ANY PLACE where one can enjoy the intoxication of God has its own value, be it temple, church, mosque, or any other religious edifice. However, it stands to reason that the very best place to seek God and enjoy His presence is wherever His reflection can be seen. The stone-constructed places of worship were all made in the remembrance of God, but it is not possible to see the reflection of the Lord in any of them. That can only be found in the human form—a certain human form wherein God has manifested Himself. Such a personality is just like God walking on earth. Those accomplished in religious lore, tied up in rituals and customs, will usually advise against seeking God in the human form; but the earnest investigator should consider carefully just what benefit can be derived from a living Guru.

If we take the temple or the mosque for an example, we find the former dome-shaped, like the human head, and the latter forehead-shaped, both after the model of man-body, and with great respect are the prayers done therein. These are given the highest importance, while the true temple or mosque of the man-body is ignored; we never go in there. The Truth lies forgotten within us, and we are left with outer things as consolation. To make a model of the man-body is very easy, but we are constantly adding cover upon cover over the true Light of God within our being; and to stop doing this is extremely difficult indeed.

My Master used to give an example of the true wife who,

disregarding the good or bad remarks that the world may have for her character, will keep her attention constantly upon her husband alone, knowing that she is true to herself and to him. So we should go toward God with that single goal in mind, and never worry about what is said by others. Travel with unceasing attention in the Lord, for you are His and He is yours.

The target was always one and the same, for all religions, but what happened? Hafiz Sahib explains that *We were on our way to meet the Lord, but in between our attention was arrested.* Religious and customary rites have taken our attention from the true purpose of our journey; and as long as the mystery of life is not unraveled, we may spend our whole life searching among outer things, but the Truth will never be revealed. Who are we, and what connection do we have with the physical form? In what way are we related to God? Before these questions can be answered, that eye must be opened through which, by actually seeing, the Truth will be revealed. A Muslim Maulvi Sahib exhorts us:

> *Why do you scatter your attention in intellectual*
> *pursuits?*
> *Whatever path you walk, become submerged*
> *therein;*
> *Deaf and mute to all else.*
> *With full concentration proceed toward your goal;*
> *Take a headlong plunge!*
> *Weighing and doubting will only stop your progress.*

Further on he says, *I am in Him.* This happens only at that grand meeting when two become one—when He alone is there, He whose reflection we are. When the curtain of separation is drawn aside, there will be no parting and no meeting. There will be no yearning. Christ told us that *I and my Father are one.* Guru Arjan says *Father and Son have the same color.* When the soul reaches this awakened condition, the wandering, searching, and sorrowful separation will cease. A true Guru is not separate from God; therein lies his greatness. By losing himself he has become the very image of God, and he who loses himself in the Guru becomes the same as the Guru—a *Gurumukh* (or mouthpiece of the Guru). St. Paul mentioned this stage by saying... *yet not I, but Christ liveth in me.* Our Muslim prophet continues:

> *The place inside is so filled with my Beloved.*
> *That there is no room for me; only He is there.*
> *In You, am I; look in my eyes and see the oneness.*
> *If you do not see, am I to be blamed?*

Even the thought "I am not there" does not occur. Within the eyes of an illumined soul pulsates the power to drag you like a magnet, into the Beyond. This was the original reason for doing *arti* (a Hindu rite, with lighted candles).

At one Satsang, I was sitting beside Hazur—he sometimes made me sit beside him, just as a father would—and I said that there was an age in the past when the Guru would wash his big toe in water and give this to the disciples to drink, for there was great charging in it. During the time of the tenth Guru of the Sikhs, he gave *amrit* (nectar) made from sweetened water, on drinking which they were infused with life, again due to the charging. Then in the days of Tulsi Sahib and Swami Ji Maharaj, it became customary for *arti* to be done, sitting in front of the Guru, eyes level with eyes; but that age also passed. In the time of Hazur, my Master, the custom was to touch the Guru's feet. Now that is finished and it remains only to look into the eyes of the Master and be absorbed into his radiance, as eyes are the windows of the soul. The purpose of all these gestures was for the disciples to derive the benefit of the charging from the Guru's radiation; but when the Gurus leave, just the empty action remains.

The highest of the senses is the eyes. Nose, ears, mouth, etc., are on a lower level. When the two eyes meet at the practical point above the nose, they become single and the inner path is opened, through which we become familiar with the Beyond. When the *four* eyes meet and become one, there is no separateness and no question of duality. From eye to eye the treasure is given. From eye to eye one gets an intoxication, and the physical body becomes insignificant— as nought. Even the thought of it does not remain. Criticism, ridicule and unpleasant worldly affairs ride harmlessly over one's head. This is the knowledge of oneness.

Hafiz Sahib has said that the words uttered by the Saints are for those who are ready to receive them. This is their last connection with the world, for their hearts have become pure, and they have the right understanding. They are ready therefore to realize the Lord. The immature will continue with the outer practices, for their time has not yet come. Though Truth is in each being, yet it must be rekindled by the Guru through the eyes, for the charging involved in the process cannot be done through form and formularies. This charging is an intoxication never forgotten by the person throughout his whole life. There are those who think that the Guru's succession can be accomplished on legal papers, but how is that possible or even feasible?

There is only one thing to understand—how to remove the separating curtain between "me" and "You." *Get the true bhakti from the Guru; then only can He invade the mind.* When you have completely surrendered yourself to the Guru, no questions or doubts remain. Everything becomes serene, calm, quiet, and the awakenedness springs forth. Life comes from life—there is no other way of realizing the Truth. Those who see the Truth in all its Reality say, "This is a very curious image, this human form!" They are not the human form, but are something else. Bhai Nandlal Ji, who was a very devoted disciple of Guru Gobind Singh Ji, says, *For one hair of my beloved Satguru, I will sacrifice both worlds (this and the next).* Only he who can see even some small reflection of the Truth can make such a statement.

For Muslims, a living Master is considered to be heresy, and when Amir Khusro was initiated by his Guru the people criticized him, calling him a heathen. Khusro was unshaken and remarked, "Yes, I am a devotee of a living form, but what has this to do with the world and its opinions?" When you become someone's, become his very image. To incur the pleasure of a complete Master is to incur the pleasure of God. Swami Ji Maharaj says, *If the Guru is pleased, then God is pleased.* But the Guru should be a Guru and not just so called. Of what value is the pleasure of he who is under the influence of his mind and senses? People often get a bitter experience and then blame the whole of Gurudom, but those who are fortunate to have their inner eye developed even a little, see an inner reflection of the Truth. *Even one enlivening glance from You, O Guru, is enough to infuse me with Life.* If he turns his eyes from us, both our worldly and spiritual existences will finish. Once this happens, it is most difficult to regain his attention, for no one knows what action will be pleasing to him.

Perfect Masters do not allow vanity, self-importance and self-praising to remain in their followers, but gradually weed them out. Bulleh Shah, who belonged to a high caste, took Initiation from Sai Inayat Shah Sahib. One day, the Master sent some of his followers to Bulleh Shah's home, telling them to sing and dance outside his house. They did this, calling out, "Oh, Bulleh Shah, we are your *gurubhais* (brothers under the same Master), so come out and meet us."

Now, singing and dancing in the streets is considered to be unseemly behavior, that of very low-caste people; and when Bulleh Shah was told that his brother disciples had come, he said, "No, I do not know them—they are nothing to do with me."

When the disciples returned to the Master, he told them, "It does not matter, from today I will not water that plant." Remember that the Guru gives nourishment to the disciples through his attention, even if they are thousands of miles away. *A Satguru looks after his disciple with his own life impulse.* Only a few days ago a disciple in the West wrote to me: "When I sit for meditation, and even for some time afterward, there is a sweet fragrance." I explained that this was a direct result of the thought-waves which are received when one is receptive to the Master. Receptivity is very necessary. If a radio set is not tuned properly, there will be no sound. It is most difficult to please a Guru: he is above offerings of money, property and worldly goods. You cannot have his pleasure by demand either. His pleasure may be gained through respectful attention, obedience to his wishes, devotion, and selfless service to humanity. If the disciple does not wish to live like this, then what can be achieved without the Guru's mercy? I remember once in Lahore, my Master called me and said, "Kirpal Singh, I have planted the saplings; you have to give them water." I replied, "Hazur, however much water you send through this hose-pipe will be given." To be careless about our attitude and actions in respect to our Guru is very dangerous.

Bulleh Shah's inner enjoyment was stopped from that moment, and by the Guru's orders he was also not allowed to enter the Master's court. In those days, Shah Inayat permitted his followers to express the holy hymns in song and dance before him, and appeared to show his pleasure at such occasions. There was a certain prostitute who was very talented in her execution of the holy songs, and she would attend him regularly each week. For Bulleh Shah, it was as if both worlds, inner and outer, had sunken into deep and silent gloom—such was his condition without the glance and thought transference of his Master. So in desperation, and greatly anxious to regain his Master's favor, he went to the prostitute and begged her to give him any amount of work, in return for which, he requested her to teach him how to sing; with the hope of giving the Master some enjoyment. For instance, if a Master approves of selfless service and helping the poor, then his disciples should do that; for to become his true loved ones, they should develop the Master's own habits within themselves. Merely pretending to do his will has no effect, for he knows and sees everything.

So Bulleh Shah studied the art of singing and dancing for nine months; and one evening he said to his teacher, "Tonight, let me go and sing for the Master instead of you." She agreed, giving him her clothes to wear; and with quickening heart he hurried off to the Master's house. His songs even now are heart-rending to the reader, filled with great sadness as he describes his separation from the Master. He who knows everything can recognize a person by what he is, not by what he is wearing; and when Bulleh Shah sang with so much pain and feeling the Master could not help himself, and, rushing from his seat, wrapped Bulleh Shah in his arms. Now many who were watching this began to wonder that such a great Master would embrace a prostitute; so Shah Inayat said, "Listen, brother Bulleh, take off this finery, that the people's doubts may be removed."

How can you recapture the Master's pleasure when he is displeased with you? And then, when he restores this blessing, what do you gain? This hymn of Guru will disclose some knowledge on the subject:

*I fall at his feet to gain his favor.*
*Oh, meet a Satguru who is God Himself!*
*There is no one else like him.*

If the Guru is pleased, then so is God, for God has manifested Himself in the Guru. Satguru is the very image of the Truth, the ruling Power, for his will governs everything and there is no one comparable to him in this world or the next.

*I have searched all Brahmand;*
*But not found one like my Guru.*

A person can only speak of whatever level he has reached. The worldly will think on a worldly level, but they who have reached Brahmand and beyond say that even in Brahmand there is no one to equal the Guru. He is Truth itself, and he is also the pole at which the Truth is manifested.

When two hearts take joy in the same thing, most decidedly they will love each other. If one likes to serve the poor and do meditation, the other should do the same; and without any effort love will grow between them. Maulana Rumi has said, *He who approaches you; approaches God; and he who departs from you; goes away from God.* Uttering empty words will be futile, for saying one thing and doing something else may hoodwink the world; but no one can deceive the Guru. My Master used to say that the Guru Power is all-awareness and if a soul is not fit he will not be given the inner road. There should be nothing left of the mind or senses. Guru Arjan, whose hymn I am now taking, was tested very severely by his Guru. The Masters test the disciples again and again to see how much loving devotion he has, and to what extent he still remains under the influence of mind. He who sacrifices everything for the sake of his Guru has achieved all.

During the strife-worn days of Guru Gobind Singh,

a certain man named Nabi Khan Ali Khan was killed, and someone went to inform his wife of her husband's death. On hearing the news, her first words were, "Is my Guru all right?" For a true disciple, the Master is more beloved than any other relationship, for it is one of the soul with God. Naturally the child who heeds his father's slightest wish will enjoy his pleasure. Whoever insists on his own ideas and does not want to obey, doubtless he will also get the Master's love; but the inner key will not be entrusted to him.

I will now tell you how Guru Arjan won his Master's pleasure. It happened that one of the relatives of Guru Ramdas Ji (Guru Arjan's Master) was getting married in Lahore, but the Guru himself was in Amritsar at the time. So he sent for his eldest son, Prithi Chand, and told him to go to Lahore and spend about fifteen days there, over the wedding. When these highly enlightened personalities come, they are always surrounded by people who either want their money, or wish to be their successors. In reply to his father's orders Prithi Chand protested, "If I go there, who will look after everything here?" He was afraid that his father would give the succession to Guru Arjan, who was most beloved of the Master, and so he refused to obey. The other son of Guru Ramdas was Maha Dev who was usually in a spiritually intoxicated state, so the Guru sent for Arjan Sahib and told him to attend the wedding instead of Prithi Chand; and then instructed him, "Do not return here until I send for you."

Guru Arjan took the Master's orders without question and left for Lahore. A person of lesser spiritual strength would have ignored the orders and declared that out of love for the Master they had to return, but for Guru Arjan his Master's orders were of supreme importance, making a barrier between the Master and himself which he would never think of surpassing. Remember, he who obeys orders will achieve success in his goal. Many days passed and there was no word, so Guru Arjan wrote these words and sent them to the Master:

*My mind is desiring Thy darshan;*
*Like the rainbird in anguish,*
*The thirst remains unquenched—there is no peace;*
*I am living like that without the Beloved's darshan.*

He sent these words to his Master by a man, but the man gave the note to the Master's son Prithi Chand, and therefore it never reached the Master's hands. What a dying man does not do in desperation! He wrote another letter. From Lahore to Amritsar is only thirty miles, but he could not go there because of his Master's orders. Remember, he who breaks the wall of the Guru's orders will never realize the inner knowledge. He may get a little inner experience and help, but he will never become perfect. So in the second letter he wrote:

*Glory be to that place where You reside;*
*Your face is so beautiful,*
*Seeing this, the inner Sound easily vibrates.*

This letter also got into Prithi Chand's hands and again there was no reply. He then sent a third letter, which he marked with a number "3." In this he wrote:

*The separation of minutes was likened to an age;*
*O Beloved, when will that time be when I may see*
*    You?*
*I cannot sleep; and the nights cannot pass without*
*    one who is my Lord.*

When this letter arrived, fortunately Prithi Chand was not there at the time and the Guru Sahib received it. Though the Masters know everything, they do not disclose what they know, but allow things to come out openly of their own accord on the material level. Forgive me, but we frequently consider our Guru to be less than a man. The Guru Sahib called Prithi Chand and asked him about the two previous letters, but Prithi Chand replied, "Maharaj, do you think that I am a thief?" The Master gave him a hard look, and turning to another man said, "Go and look in the pockets of his clothes." He then sent for Guru Arjan Sahib, and when he arrived, told him, "You wrote me three letters, and whoever will complete that poem will be my successor." When a test comes, a simple thing becomes difficult. I remember that I also sometimes wrote poems to my Master—through separation the thoughts would come, and the poems were written. Some rivals started copying me, but always there is a difference between wine and water. Guru Arjan wrote the fourth stanza thus:

> *With great destiny I met Him;*
> *The Ever-Permanent Lord was found in the house;*
> *I desire only to serve, and never be separated for a*
> *    moment;*
> *I am Thy servant, O Lord.*

This shows the kind of respect the disciple should have for his Master. I once wrote to my Master and requested him to give me the ability to love, but only that kind of love which does not transcend the limits of respect. The Master was in Dalhousie when he received it, and after reading the letter he placed it on his heart and said with such humility, "I really appreciate such-like love." A devoted one's poem is written to gain his Master's pleasure. Guru Arjan was one of those rare devotees who truly achieved this, and at the end of this hymn he indicates what is gained by it.

Just as we cannot say what God is, so it is impossible to describe the Guru. He has a physical form, but he is not the physical form; if he were, what could he give us? If the whole earth became thin paper and the seas turned into ink and all the trees were made into pens, were we to cover the paper with praises to the Lord we would never succeed in describing His glory. I used to study in a Christian school, and always had an inquisitive nature. I knew that we said "Shri Guru Nanak Dev Ji Maharaj," for in India we attach many respectful terms to the names of Masters and certain respected people, and had noticed that the Christians called their great Saint merely Jesus. So I went to a Christian bishop and questioned him: "Why do you not put a prefix to Christ's name, when even the most insignificant common man is at least referred to as Mr. Somebody?" The bishop said, and I can still distinctly remember his reply, "We consider Christ the son of God, and as we cannot glorify God, so we cannot extol Christ. If we start prefixing His name, we will make him smaller, not greater."

Another Master says, *You are the Emperor above all; how can You be praised?* Without doubt, there is none equal to the Guru. He who starts seeing another as equal to his Master, HIS SOUL BECOMES AN ADULTERESS. Truly, the Light is in everyone, but not manifested as in the Guru. When two great souls meet and see the God in each other, that is something different again—something qualified. I remember one incident in Lahore in a house called Pari Mahal (Fairy Palace), where at the time Maharishi Shivbrat Lal Ji was staying on a short visit to Lahore. He was the successor to Rai Saligram Ji, who was one of the chief disciples of Swami Ji. When my Master was told of his presence in Lahore, he went to see him, and I accompanied the Master. It was a very strange sight that I saw. My Master, who was always the very depth of humility, was trying to touch his feet; but he wanted to touch Hazur's feet.

*His sweetness is above all others;*
*Above the sweetness of mother and father.*

For a child who plays in his mother's lap, she is the sweetest of all beings to him. The true devotee who plays in his Master's lap will place that relationship above all others.

> *Sisters, brothers and all my friends are very close*
> *to me;*
> *But there is none like You in this world.*

To the child who plays in his father's lap with no other thought than to try and please him, the father will give whatever he wants. When all other relationships are broken and the Guru is the only one in existence, then you have succeeded in your work. On this path, mere words have no value: you must obey his every command. Make your life pure and chaste; do service unto others; be careful of evil words. Love everyone, as God is in every being. When you serve others, you are serving Him.

> *By Thy orders, Sawan (the rainy season) came;*
> *And I ploughed the furrow of Truth.*

The rain comes in the form of the Guru, like a refreshing coolness upon the parched earth. My Hazur's name was Sawan. Like a rain of mercy, they come by God's orders; and we should take full benefit by clearing up the land of our whole being with Satsang, where all the dirt and filth is thrown out. We scatter our thoughts abroad, but at Satsang we can withdraw toward the Truth. All Masters encourage this. Christ says, *For where two or three are gathered together in my name, there am I in the midst of them.* There will be strong charging there, even if they are thousands of miles from the Master's physical form. Guru Gobind Singh says, *Where five disciples sit together, there God will be.* How can any good come from a gathering filled with criticisms and disagreements?

This Satsang was started with my Guru's orders, so

throw away your laziness and lethargy, and become pure. In Satsang the flow of mercy is pouring into you, so get the fullest benefit from it. Weed out all imperfections, one by one; that is why I have told you to keep a diary. When the soil is weeded, it is ready for the seed to be sown, then the true growth can begin. If small pebbles and rocks are not removed, the seed may sprout but will not bear fruit.

> *In great aspiration, the seed of Naam was sown;*
> *I pray each second for mercy that it may bear fruit.*

This seed of Naam, once sown, cannot be set aside by any power. That seed will bear fruit sooner or later. But without the water of Satsang, how can the seed be expected to sprout green and fresh in all its beauty? Once sown, it will not die; but in unprepared soil it will not fructify. He who does not do his meditation in this life will have to come again. As this seed cannot sprout in any other form, he will be given the concession of not retrogressing below the human birth. But why not complete your mission now? He who is unlearned in life cannot become learned merely by going through that change which is called death. No one should be under the misunderstanding that, having received the connection with the Holy Naam, he has got salvation. He *will* get salvation, but in how many lives?

> *When I met the Guru, I knew he was the only one;*
> *My heart can never accept another.*

Once the disciple has recognized his Guru, he can only understand his Guru's teachings and none other. Hanuman (Lord Rama's greatest devotee) was once asked what day it was, and he replied, "O Ram." On being asked what month it was, he said, "O Ram." He was so immersed in the sweet remembrance of his Beloved that he could think of nothing else. Wherever he looked, he saw Ram; and every person he spoke to was Ram. It is really worth having a Guru if you are receptive like this.

> *All the transitory objects have dropped away,*
> *Since I got the company of a Saint.*

At the feet of a true Guru there are no factions, political fights, or religious wranglings. The Master simply places a man-problem before you. He tells us that when he met his Guru, there was nothing else in life. He is one, and yet he is not one—this also is a mystery. *He who knows and becomes one with Him, becomes the Doer and the Giver.* We are devotees of the Light; it matters not in which pole it is expressed: all are one and the same. He whose eye is open can see the beautiful play of God's expression.

> *Each man has been allotted the task;*
> *But success depends on Thy will.*

The Satsang is started by His orders, and He makes the work a success. Hazur used to tell us that when Baba Jaimal Singh Ji gave him orders to start the spiritual work, Hazur went to Baba Garib Das and Chacha Pratap Singh Ji, who both told him, "If we give initiation the soul might not get salvation; but if you give it, that soul will surely have salvation." When my Master gave me orders to do the work, I asked him to whom I should go for such assurance; and then added that I would do the work as ordered, but that he should give the protection. Hazur assured me that it would be so. With His support, I started the Satsang; it is not mine but His, and He will take everyone across. Whatever blessing He extends is being given out. All credit goes to Him.

When I went to the west, many people were helped and I told them that the credit for the blessing went to my Master. Forgive me, but so many seekers for Truth have spent their whole lives struggling to find it—and did not receive even a glimpse of Light. Here, everyone gets Light. It is another matter if after receiving the gift they refuse to keep up the practice and thereby lose it; but at initiation, almost all get something, do they not? Those who obey instructions increase their progress daily—one hundred percent. Who is there to place his hand on his heart and declare such assurance? Ashtavakra gave this knowledge to King Janak, and even today people are still repeating his name. How great is the mercy of the Master who gives such an invaluable boon! The age has changed, and so have conditions. If today this experience was not given so easily, no one would come on this path.

In the West many sects have sprung up which deal with suggestion, hypnotism, mesmerism, and other doctrines, which are not Spirituality. Spirituality is purely a matter of self-analysis, knowing oneself and knowing God—the demonstration of which is given at the time of initiation. Many are doubtful of this science in the beginning; but I tell them to see with their own eyes, for there is no greater proof. In the past, the subject was very vague, for Masters agreed to give the experience only after long years of study, when one was fully prepared. Today, it can be seen immediately what Spirituality is. What a magnificent blessing!

> *Brothers, this is the Guru's court,*
> *He is doling out this gift!*
> *Eat, drink and be merry;*

You should eat, drink and enjoy for you are getting this gift free—there are no charges. Even if you spend all life in penance, you will not get this thing that way. Only one man was to be found in King Janak's age who was God-realized; that was Ashtavakra. Today, can you find thousands? In the past there were few, and even now there are few; but the world is not without them. Make the most of the good fortune, for blessed are they who have received this rare gift.

> *I have become the lord of this physical form,*
> *And have tied up the five devils.*

Masters have no ego; they always acknowledge in humility that everything is achieved with the Guru's grace. Why shouldn't he gain full control over his mind and senses, who has all love for his Guru alone. He says he has become lord of the house, and he has captured the five thieves, viz., lust, anger, greed, attachment and ego. Who can make such a statement? Only with the Guru's strength can anyone declare so boldly.

> *O Satguru, when I came to Thy feet*
> *These five strange aliens came under my control;*
> *He was pleased, and I was blessed with His grace;*
> *Now they cannot revolt or raise their heads.*

The five senses of action and knowledge are foreign to our nature; they must be overpowered and placed under our orders, instead of vice versa. When that happens, they have no courage to stand and defy us, and they will not disobey. Can anyone affirm such a staggering achievement? People say that Saints and Mahatmas do not assert themselves, but they do speak directly. If they did not give the information of what to get and how to get it, where would we begin to seek for the Truth? They tell us that there is such a wonderful nectar inside that will intoxicate the soul. They themselves are intoxicated; their mind and senses are completely controlled. Their eyes are open but they do not see; their ears are open but they do not hear, if they choose not to. They are the controllers of all the senses. With whose power is this achieved? With the grace of their respective Gurus! When one gets the Naam's inner nectar, all worldly intoxicants seem ridiculous; and when the seed of Naam sprouts, all outer things become meaningless. All glory and beauty lies within you. You will forget outer things with their false attraction. The five devils will come under perfect control, and will have no courage to jeer at you; there is so much nectar within that even they become intoxicated!

> *O Satguru, again and again I glorify Thee;*
> *With each breath I think of Thee!*

There was a certain intoxicated lover of Bheek Sahib, who constantly repeated "O Bheek, O Bheek" for he saw God clearly in his Guru. His contemporaries condemned him as an atheist, and passed judgment for his execution; but they could not execute him without the king's authorization, so they brought him before the king. It is possible that this king was Akbar the Great, who was renowned for his keen sense of justice. When the king looked at the accused man, he said, "I feel he is an intoxicated holy man," and he asked him, "Who is your God?" The man replied, "Bheek." The king then asked, "What is your religion?" and he said, "Bheek." At this, the king ordered that he should be released. His accusers protested that he would run away, but the king said, "It does not matter." He then looked keenly at the holy man and told him, "For a long time we have been without rain; and if it does not come soon, there will be famine in the land. So could you please ask your Bheek to send the rain?" The man replied, "Oh yes, I will ask him to send the rain." Only complete faith in the Guru could display such calm confidence. He who has not experienced the true inner connection with his Guru will not have such strong faith, for faith is built on knowledge. When the holy man turned to leave, the king asked him when he would return, and he answered, "On the third day I will return." The very next day, there was such a heavy downpour of rain that the whole countryside was flooded, and on the third day the holy man returned to the king's palace. The king smiled at him and said, "Your Guru was very gracious to us in sending the much-needed rain. I am giving you these precious gifts—please place them before your Bheek Sahib as my thankful offering." The devotee got very indignant, saying, "These perishable things for my Guru? Most decidedly not!" Such people care nothing for the world and its possessions.

> *You have brought Life to this derelict house (body);*
> *I could sacrifice myself in gratitude.*

Gratitude is a very rare virtue. Because of friends and relatives, we even risk our Guru's displeasure, and this is due to lack of gratitude and faith. We sometimes consider the Guru to be less able than an ordinary man. With this type of outlook, what can we hope to achieve in progress? The worldly things are more beloved: Guru and God are accepted casually for whatever can be derived through them materially. The attitude is one of tolerant duty, with respects paid in a condescending manner. Man always thinks he is the greatest of all, but if he really *became* great he would not be in this blind egoistic state.

> *I am in perpetual dhyan (contemplation) with my*
> *    Beloved;*
> *The fruit comes to him whose attention pierces*
> *    through the veil.*

If you completely surrender unto Him, then nature itself will be at your beck and call, all your desires will be fulfilled. Guru Amardas Ji says, *O mind, you once desired a thousand things, but did not get one. Now see, that each thought will be fulfilled.*

> *All the work has been resolved, and the mind's*
> *    hunger satisfied,*
> *What else can I desire from You but You?*

*All else is misery upon misery.*
*Give the Naam, which renders all fulfilled*
*And takes away the hunger of the mind;*
*I have abandoned everything and am a true*
        *servant of the Lord.*

He who surrenders to the Lord lives without worries, doing the work sincerely and truthfully, and leaving all else to the Guru.

*That Naam—giver of all happiness—has been*
        *tied to me.*

Naam is the Sustainer of all things. He who has Naam has got everything. During one of my visits to America, an intimate meeting was arranged with a group of scientists. One man asked many questions and obviously strongly doubted the subject of Spirituality. After some discussion, I asked him if science had succeeded in creating even one ounce of consciousness. He said, "No." I then explained to him that the pursuit of science must necessarily remain in the domain of matter, whereas all the teachings and knowledge of the Saints lie in the domain of consciousness. There were a number of disciples present at this meeting, and they were of the opinion that this gentleman would not turn up on the morrow, which was chosen for the initiation program. But he was the first to arrive, and he got the most experience. So this is a path of awareness—the path of perfect Masters, and you may accept it as their mercy, or due to their greatness, that they have made such a difficult achievement into a child's play. Were it not for this fact, the seeker would require a great background of past lives and then many years of study in preparation for this path. So Guru Arjan advises us to eat, drink and enjoy what we have got for this is the precious time and the rain may not fall forever.

## TO GAIN HIS PLEASURE

*I am the most content of all;*
*The Guru has established the Shabd within me.*

He is encouraging us to have some longing for a thing of
which we have no conception of the value. All the wealth
is lying in the disciple's Father's home—and for whom is
it but his own child? The most obedient child will naturally
receive the most. Whatever the Guru has got, he considers
not his own; and the more he gives freely, the greater the
flow. Eat, drink, and enjoy to the fullest, while you have the
opportunity.

*Satguru, the Lord, placed his hand on my head*
*and manifested God within me.*

His greatness is proven when he actually shows the way, even
without the physical gesture of placing the hand on the head.
By his grace alone do we rise above body consciousness and
see the Light within: He is the Giver—comparable to none
other.

*I have opened a true dharamshala**
*And have gathered the true seekers there.*

A blind man cannot seek one with sight, but one who can
see can gather the blind together. Christ told us of the sheep
he had to find and take care of. Man is helpless with merely
his own efforts to assist him. Sincere seekers will find that
all will be arranged and made possible without them doing
anything. Even before I arrived in America, there were people who knew nothing about me who were seeing the Master's
form and also Baba Sawan Singh Ji within. When they saw
me physically they told me that they had been seeing me
within for months, and some for a year or more. Brothers, it
is all His work, not mine.

---

*In India, a common place of rest for travelers, erected in the name of righteousness.

During my first world tour, on the way back to India, I agreed to pay an unarranged impromptu visit to Germany. Someone who was accompanying me remarked, "But how will those people recognize you, for they have never seen you? In other countries at least the program was prepared. Even if they recognize you by your clothes, how will you know them?" I replied, "He who is sending me there will make all the arrangements—why should I worry? He will Himself arrange all to receive me." When the plane landed in Germany there was a small crowd awaiting me, and each person had a rose in his hand. I said, "You see, there is my reception." They came running toward us, asking about the luggage and telling us that the cars were ready and waiting. So He Himself does His own work. The commission comes from the Lord and He works through whomsoever He chooses, be it one or thousands.

> *I wash His feet and fan Him;*
> *Again and again I express my thankfulness for*
> *finding Him.*

A true Guru never says he is a Guru, but in all humility will serve whoever goes to him, for he comes to serve humanity and to give something to the world. When he comes, the entire world gets the benefit of his Light.

> *I got Naam, dan* (alms) *and ashnan* (bath).

The Guru gives us the Naam, which you should know is the Sustainer of the entire Creation. Contact with Naam, the Nectar of the Lord, creates true love in us; and as love knows only giving, the disciple himself becomes a giver. He is born to serve and give himself to the world. While he has the physical form he will give, give, and give. When the physical form is no longer there, who can ask from him and who will come to take? He starts to give everything: physically, materially, and eventually he gives the mind. Having become the controller of the mind, he serves humanity with unending joy.

> *Nanak with the Naam rises in continual*
> *heights of glory;*
> *Peace be unto all the world, under Thy will,*
> *O Lord!*

The Master serves all humanity with his good will: physically, mentally, and even outwardly in all manner of ways, making use of whatever outer knowledge he has acquired in his lifetime, to help the people to understand the Truth.

The bath that the Guru gives in the holy waters of Naam will purify the mind and senses from all evil. These three things—Naam, *dan* and *ashnan*—are gained by sitting at his feet. Unfortunately, people think that by *ashnan* (bath) is meant an outer bath to clean the body. Though it behooves man to keep the temple of the Lord clean, the inner cleanliness is vitally more important—and that is the work of Naam.

One of the clearest criteria that can be observed in a true Master is that he is always sacrificing himself for the sake of others. He knows how to give and give only, not to take. He a giver, not a beggar. If the Guru starts taking, then what will we give? He has no thought of business, but gives this priceless jewel as a free gift of Nature. In many countries they take up collections to pay the lecturers and the expenses of arrangements, etc. When I was traveling in America I gave free talks without charges, collection, or need of buying tickets. One day while I was giving a talk on "God and Man," a man stood up; he was a Russian and offered five thousand dollars to me. I told him, "Look here, I have not come to collect dollars. What I have gained at the feet of my Master is a free gift of Nature, and must therefore be given freely." The people were at first surprised, and then overjoyed at this. Through this very principle the praises of true Masters are being sung all over the world. I am receiving invitations from America, Europe, the Far East, Australasia, the Middle East and Africa, and they state they have heard of the gift which is being given to all. Dear brothers, who am I to give It?—The Giver is giving It, with His grace, and with the grace of all the great past Masters, for whom, forgive me, we have not enough respect, I am sorry to say.

> *All are being freed, O Nanak,*
> *On the boat of Truth.*
> *Day and night there is awakening in the world;*
> *All listen with open ears to praises sung in Thy*
>     *Name.*

When the Master comes the world begins to awake, and hearing his words they wonder, "What is this new thing which is entering our very being?" During my tours abroad, many talks were given in churches. They rarely allow outsiders to speak in the church, yet they welcomed me for they said that these teachings are as given in the Bible. One minister went as far as to say, "I have been in charge of a Presbyterian Church for forty years; but today for the first time I have understood what the Bible is telling me." He came and bowed to me in front of everyone with tears in his eyes. I want to point out that all glory and praise be to those past Masters who have given us these teachings.

> *Now orders have come from the Gracious One*
> *Through which all pain and misery will vanish.*
> *They are at peace,*
> *For through the Naam they gained true humility.*

Initiation into the Holy Naam is a panacea for all ills, and the repetition of Naam brings peace and true humility. He who sees the Truth in all its glory will be full of humility. St. Augustine says there are three ways of realizing God: the first is humility, the second humility, and the third humility. In the courts of the Masters, humility reigns supreme, for true humbleness is the adornment of a true Saint. They are Ruler and Controller of this great power; and yet they never show pride or vanity, giving small indications of what they are and yet saying, "It is His grace."

> *The Amrit is drizzling down;*
> *His words are those of the Lord Himself.*

Remember, that water collects on the lower levels. When the cup of humility is ready, then the inner Amrit will fill it to the brim. Some people say doubtfully, "How can you say these things are true?" The Masters explain that whatever words come from the true Master's mouth are words from God Himself.

> *In full faith I rely on You;*
> *You Yourself will do everything for me.*

All is the Lord's work—what is it to me if the world blossoms or perishes? My work is but to be a tool in your hand, to do what You will. With Your mercy alone is the world gaining any benefit. With Your wealth the world is prosperous. A time like this may never come again—we are encouraged to eat, drink, and enjoy the blessings pouring out from the Lord.

> *Your devotees have but one desire,*
> *and that is You.*

A true Gurumukh will have desire for God alone—so much so that "he" should become "Thee" and "Thee" should become "me," and no one should say there is any difference.

Hafiz Sahib says, *I should become You and You should become me; I am the body and You should be the Life; that no one may say that I am one thing and You are something else.* There is some slight difference in the wording, but both Masters have given exactly the same meaning.

> *O Giver of peace, reveal Thyself to me;*
> *Clasp me to Thy breast;*
> *Allow that I may never be separated even*
> *    for a second.*

It is the true disciple's constant wish that he may never be separated from his Guru. It is a great blessing to have a living Master, and even greater blessing to be near him. The bath taken from his glance of mercy is a flow of Truth which cleanses deep through the being. The devoted disciple sheds tears at the very memory of this. He who sees him outside and inside both gets some consolation during separation; however, he also cries out of love, for there is nothing more beloved for him than his Master. The yearning of the heart pours out of the eyes, and there are no words to describe this condition.

> *I searched in the world, above the world,*
> *    below the world;*
> *But could not find one like You.*

How can there be another like the Satguru? Only a Satguru can be the same as a Satguru. Do you know the story of Sukhdev, son of Maharishi Ved Vyas? When Sukhdev wanted a perfect Guru, his father told him that King Janak was the enlightened soul of that age. After that, Sukhdev went to King Janak's kingdom several times but always returned without having seen the king, for he had the doubt in his heart that this king enjoys the pleasures of palace life with all his queens, etc.; how can he possibly give any enlightenment?

Now Narad Muni, a powerful devotee of Lord Shiva, saw that this man was losing all his progress with each doubt he had about King Janak, the great soul. To save what little he had left, Narad Muni turned himself into a very old man, filled a basket full of mud, and began to pour the mud into a fast-flowing river, just as Sukhdev was passing by on his way once again to King Janak's kingdom. He saw the old man and asked him what he was doing. The old man replied, "I am building a dam." Sukhdev laughed and said, "Have you no sense, you fool? Can you build a dam by just pouring mud into fast-flowing water? First put some foundation of wood or rocks, and then put the mud." The old man, replied, "I might be a fool, but I have only wasted one day. The biggest fool is Sukhdev who has finished nine of his merits of progress, and the tenth and last he is about to destroy by again doubting a perfect Master."

This encounter with Narad Muni shocked Sukhdev to his senses, and he went straight to King Janak's palace. He stood near the stables and sent a man to tell the king that "Sukhdev has arrived." The king said, "Tell him to wait there until I call him." In strict obedience to the Master's orders, Sukhdev stood on the same spot, first for a whole day, and then all the next day. Sometime on the third day he was called into the palace. Having stood obediently in one place for so long, he had become covered in horses' dung up to his waist, for the grooms had been shoveling it into the corner where he stood. So he took a bath and changed his clothes, and then presented himself to the king. As he came near the king, he saw that he was reclining on a couch, with one foot resting on a red-hot iron plate. The other leg was being massaged with cool sandalwood paste by some of beautiful queens. It was very revealing to Sukhdev; and as he gazed in amazement, a man came running into the court and cried, "Your majesty, the city is on fire!" The king said,

"It is God's will," and did not move an inch. After some time another man entered the court and said, "Your majesty, the palace is on fire now; and the flames are coming toward this room." The king replied, "It is God's will."

When Sukhdev saw the flames and felt the heat, he picked up his stick and small bundle of belongings and prepared to rush out; but the king caught hold of him, saying, "You are a fine kind of world-renouncer! My whole city has burned away, the flames have consumed my palace, and I merely said it was all God's will; but you in your panic are trying to save a stick and a bundle of clothes!" He then talked to Sukhdev for a long time, telling him, "You are a brahmin and full of ego about it. You are also very proud of being the son of Ved Vyas." Doctors operate to remove morbid matter, and in this way King Janak was removing the doubts and faults in the mind of Sukhdev. When Sukhdev Swami returned home after his initiation, his father asked him, "What is the Guru like?" Sukhdev replied, "In brightness he is like the sun, although the sun has got heat and he has not. He has got the coolness of the moon, though the moon has shadows on it and my Guru has no shadow." A Guru is a Guru. The stories of the great Masters are for people whose eyes are open. Otherwise... for instance, Guru Nanak was not permitted to enter the city of Kasur because the people, blinded by lack of understanding, declared he was an atheist and a bad influence. Wherever the Truth works in full power, the Negative Power will also work in full force against it. He does not want his prisoners to escape his clutches, but regardless, the Satguru goes on distributing the wealth without concern.

When I was small, about twelve or thirteen, I remember clearly that one day I read the life of Ramanuja (I was very fond of reading biographies). Now when Ramanuja was initiated by his Guru he immediately went and stood on a platform and collected a huge crowd around him. He shouted to them, "Today I have been initiated by my Guru and I am going to tell you all about it." Some of the people were shocked and warned him, "Are you mad? You will go straight to hell for disobeying your Guru!" I was deeply impressed by his answer. He said, "I alone will go to hell, but so many of you will get salvation!" Reading this, I vowed that, "If ever I get any spiritual wealth, I will give and give without hesitation." My Master saw that I was a spendthrift, and that's why he gave me the work. It is all his grace. One of the initiates, an English lady, once met a Christian friar and she asked him, "Have you ever seen the inner Light?" He replied, "Yes, after nineteen years of hard penance on Mount Sinai, on one occasion I saw some cloudy Light, but very dim." She said, "Why, I see bright Light daily."

What value can we place on such a treasure as Naam? We do not seem to know how to respect it even. We get this precious thing and, having no value for it, do not keep it carefully. It is gained too easily and freely. The Western people have more respect for it. My first Western tour was four or five months only, and in this short time there was a grand awakening all over the Western Hemisphere. There was a genuine surge of seeking for Truth, and when they got it, there was more respect for what they had been given. In India we take it for granted. Christ said, *Take heed therefore that the Light which is in you be not darkness.* Introspect your deeds daily, with the help of the spiritual diary—and do not allow anything to cause you to forgo your meditation. If you live like this, there will never be darkness within. Tragically, we do not care—we have no time for the most important work. If you had to die today, what would you do? Do not live in the illusion of thinking or believing that after death you will get something. If you have not made spiritual progress in this life, you will not be a spiritual person merely by going through the death-change. Believe in the salvation of Life. Do, and see for yourself. If you do nothing, then how can your condition be helped?

> *Each place is permeated with You;*
> *O Nanak, only true bhakti will make this apparent.*

The name of Prahlad is well-known in the history of true devotees. He was ordered to wrap his arms around a red-hot iron column, to test his faith in what he believed. Even the large crowd present at the time murmured, "O God," as he approached the column. But what did God do, to preserve the faith of young Prince Prahlad? The prince saw a small ant running up the fiery column, and with joy in his heart he leaned forward and clasped his arms around it. The column immediately split open and out of it stepped the Avatar, Narsing. I am illustrating that God is everywhere, but only those whose eye is open can see His glory in all things. True devotees have got His sustaining protection; standing in the midst of thousands, they can be pillars of strength and faith. In the West, many intellectual people came to hear my talks, and not for one moment did I ever stop and wonder how they would receive my words; with great power I would emphasize the teachings. It is all His grace, and He Himself prepares everything. The trouble is that we forget that He is the Doer, and not "I," and we do not keep our face turned toward Him. Rather we go on finding fault with Him, and are full of doubts. Like this, how will we grasp the help offered to us?

*Sant Kirpal Singh Ji*
*(1894-1974)*

*Sant Kirpal Singh Ji*
*(1894-1974)*

# 13

# Protector and Protection

THE FESTIVAL of Raksha is observed by our Hindu brothers, and the true meaning of Raksha Bandan is to have good intentions toward someone and be a protection for them in every way—to protect them from difficulties, unhappiness, calamities, etc., or to save them from the force of such occurrences as cannot be prevented. The custom has been upheld in India for many generations; and at the time of wars, for instance, sisters would tie a small token on the wrists of their soldier brothers, and whisper the prayer, "May God protect you!" It is a common custom, still continued nowadays; but unfortunately with time it has deteriorated from its true meaning, and we find that when the sister now ties the token, she feeds him some sweetmeat and then expects some money in return, and so the true reason for the custom is lost.

What is Raksha or protection, and who can give it whole-heartedly? When a child is born it has no awareness of anything, but its mother protects it from birth until it is fully grown. The father is the bread-earner, but the mother is the protector. First, for nine or ten months she carries the baby in her womb, giving it all her love and attention; then when it arrives in the world she starts to take care of its every need. She keeps him clean, for he is constantly dirtying himself. If he gets wet and there are no more dry clothes, though it be the depth of winter she will keep him warm on her breast and cover him with her own clothes, oblivious to the danger of catching cold herself. When the child gradually begins to have some awareness of his surroundings, he starts to realize a little of the love of his mother toward him, for the mother first loves the child, not vice versa. The child's love comes in response, and when he learns to love he is reluctant to leave his mother's lap. She spends her life in worrying about the child—his health, his food, his education, good character, and his future. Everything concerning him is dear to her heart until he stands on his feet and gets established in life. Even then her worrying does not cease. You will find that most mothers are like this, the whole world over.

However, this worldly life is not the true living—we have to be born again, not physically, but into a new and different world. Christ said that unless a man be born again he cannot enter the kingdom of God, and only after getting this physical form can we get rebirth into the Beyond. Just as the mother is the physical protector, it is even more necessary to have a protector through the second or spiritual birth and on through the spiritual life until one has grown in awareness and is able to stand upright spiritually. With conditions as they are today, even man's closest ties offer little protection. A brother is not a true brother; father is not for his son and the son will do nothing for his father. Even the mother has started cursing her child, who in turn has lost all respect for its mother. It is such a terrible and degraded condition that mankind has sunk into—I feel like weeping. Anyway, one might have the sympathies of a righteous person, but for how long can he protect one? For as long as he stays in this world—not beyond that, and in the process of rebirth he will be of no avail whatsoever. So who can protect us in the new world? He who dwells there. The true Raksha Bandan happens when you have a protector for your soul, who can take care of you in this world and the next, and without whom nothing can be achieved, with all due respect and gratitude to our physical and material protectors.

The mother hen sits on her eggs with full concentration, so that the chicks will form. When they are fully formed, she conveys to them that they are ready for the world which is waiting for them with open arms; the sun which is brightly shining, the grass is green and fresh, and there is plenty of food to eat. But the chick is in darkness, and cannot realize there is any other state. The mother then has to resort to tapping on the shell with her beak, and upon hearing this he instinctively feels encouraged to do the same from inside and in a short time he is putting his head into a new atmosphere filled with light and life. Only then does he understand the promise conveyed by his mother.

If we want to be born into the new world, we need the help of someone who will not only take us there, but who will protect us to the end of the journey. Do you think this is work for our mother, father, sister or any friend? No, it is impossible. The whole world is unable to assist you. There is an account of an incident during the life of my Master, Baba Sawan Singh Ji, of a woman disciple whose only son was arrested on a false charge of murder, and was given the penalty of death by hanging. The sessions judge presiding over the case was also a disciple, and before the final verdict was concluded, Baba Sawan Singh Ji requested him to help the accused, and said, "I know he is innocent and falsely implicated"; but the judge disregarded the Master's words and gave the death sentence. A few days later, I was present when this same judge came to pay his respects to Hazur; and when the Master passed very close to him, without even looking in his direction, he said casually to another person, "I have no need of a judge—I can ask the Lord to do my work." Just then, the mother approached the Master and started crying. "He has been sentenced to death," she said. Baba Sawan Singh Ji replied, "Don't worry—you just put in an appeal." It was not the type of case that had the slightest chance through appealing, but on the Master's advice the mother did appeal; and when they re-examined the case, certain facts came to light and eventually the son was released. So one can see that even when there is no hope in any direction, a true protector can give the maximum help. Frankly, what is a human being's life but a series of interruptions? At each step there is a barrier—what one wants does not happen. Some people are dying, some are sick, some are in difficulties of various kinds. There are thousands in poverty, and in appallingly afflicted conditions. The whole of mankind is lamenting its unhappiness every step of the way. Who is there to give consolation in this world, and guidance in the next?

Guru Nanak has said on the subject, *O Nanak, break off all connections with the imperfect, and search for a perfect Master; they will abandon you even while you live, but he will never leave you even after death.* Maulana Rumi has also said that one should grasp the coat-tails of a man who knows the secrets of this world and the Beyond. The protection of such a personage cannot be described, but the individuals who experience it hold the knowledge close in their hearts. His single thought is very powerful, for God is Super-consciousness. He is a part of the Creator—a drop of the Ocean of All Light. Remember, with one thought God created the world—from One, many came into creation. If we, the soul, become the mouthpiece of the Oversoul, then how powerful will we be! Our soul, though it is the same as the Oversoul, is surrounded by the mind and the senses, and is enclosed in the carcass of the physical form. The Masters come like motherly hens to foster the children, which is very necessary, for unless they sit at some Master's feet and absorb his words they cannot be reborn—remember that— though in the beginning it may be by mere words that the facts of life are conveyed, of a new world more beautiful than this, viz.: And, Brahmand, Par Brahmand, and Sat Lok or Sach Khand. O Soul, you are the dweller of *that* land — why have you allowed yourself to be captivated here?

On hearing the words of the Masters we slowly start thinking and want to know what else there is. When the Master gives the soul a connection with the Beyond, it hears it, and responds. *There is no way without the Shabd to leave this pot of clay.* With repetition or Simran, you can achieve single-pointed concentration, and with concentrated attention — Dhyan — you will come to a standstill; but Shabd is the only power to take you up into the Beyond. The Master is that consciousness which has become the mouthpiece of the All-consciousness and his single penetrating glance can lift the consciousness of not only one but hundreds at one sitting, if necessary. To be connected to such a personage is the true Raksha Bandan; otherwise, it is merely a worldly custom.

What are a Guru's responsibilities, and what does he do? When one gives real thought to this, one's soul shivers to realize the extent of his protection. People do not understand that the Guru's responsibilities are vast. They are overjoyed with the prospects of becoming Masters themselves; forgive me for saying this. Each one's desire is to be a Guru, Sadhu or Sant, and spellbound with these thoughts he forgets his duty toward himself and what he has to become in reality, thereby spending his precious time in leisure and wasting away whatever he has got. But the Master, with each breath, goes on saving the disciples all the time. Whenever he initiates, he sows a seed for a new life, like the seed enters the mother's womb and then develops. *Howsoever God's words come, he brings them into outer knowledge.* He is a perfect being — the mouthpiece of God, the conscious co-worker — who sees that it is God sitting within him who is doing everything. This kind of Master sows the seed of attention and gives a way up into the Beyond, which is a new experience.

In India some time ago, the Masters who gave Initiation into the Beyond were termed *Brahmins*—the supreme caste—but today only the caste remains, and initiation is but a mantra; mere words, that is all. The raksha or protection is a question mark. You are in the *custody* of a true Master from the day he gives initiation. He becomes the very breath of the disciple. Baba Sawan Singh Ji used to say that from the day the Master gives the blessing of Naam, the Guru becomes the indweller, along with the soul. From that very moment, he starts forming the child, with love and protection, until ultimately he takes him into the lap of the Oversoul. Until that time, he does not leave him for one minute. This advancement may take one, two, or three lifetimes. Masters have mentioned up to four, but if we become receptive it can happen in one lifetime.

God is working in the Master, and if you think of him in this way, then whatever you desire will be given. In physique he looks the same as other men, but he is not man alone; he became a man to dispense the treasure of God to the souls. *He is not in birth and death. The benefactor came for the souls, to give the treasure of devotion and join them back to God.* Like a father gives the germinal seed of life, the Guru bestows the Life Force—the incomparable gift. There are many kinds of gifts, but the gift of Naam is above all others; and having given it, the Master then develops it within you, because he wants you to reach the same stage as himself. He wants you to enjoy the bliss that he enjoys. The Master goes on protecting and giving, whether the disciple knows it or not; for he is like a small child which never realizes how much worry and trouble it is to its mother. The child may turn out to have a bad character, and perhaps become a gambler; but the mother will continue to concern herself with his needs, that he may not starve and so on.

A child thinks that he knows his mother very well, but what child understands about a mother's heart? We also think that we know our Master, but we can know only as much as he wishes to reveal to us. We can see only as much as our eye is developed. To convince us of the Truth, he will approach us in various ways: as a brother, or a friend, and will sometimes appear to be inferior in knowledge or intellect. He acts in whatever way will help the disciple to gain confidence in his Master. In this depth of humility, his greatness is revealed. Thus, this great personage gives rebirth to the soul, and gradually makes us as great as he is. Truly, it is a profound blessing to have a living Master, who has come to give new life.

You may ask, "Is all this the truth?" but you can prove it through your own experiences; and in the many letters I receive daily there are numerous accounts of the Master's protection. For example, a car was traveling along the road and it overturned into a very steep slope. The disciples in the car remembered the Master, and the car righted itself onto all four wheels again. Disciples who have faith in their Master can go through many dangerous experiences and will be astonished how they are saved and protected. These things are daily occurrences. Become receptive and obey his orders implicitly, even though at times he may show anger and displeasure, for he has taken this task upon himself, and has to make you into something. A sculptor will pick up a rock lying on the roadside and chisel it to make eyes, nose, etc.; and finally it becomes a work of art, a valuable thing. The Master will make the disciple into something priceless, and those who are receptive will progress quicker, regardless of how long they have been traveling along this path. What good would it be if the stone started fighting with the sculptor, saying "I do not want a nose chiseled—I do not want my face like this"? He has to make something of it and he does so with great love.

Sometimes, due to the fate karmas, many difficulties cross the student's path, and who is there to console and give strength to bear them? A single word from a perfect Master goes to the depth of the heart, that it can stand upright and bear the burden. I remember when Pakistan was formed—you know the condition at that time—whole families died, friends were killed, many people starved, even rich people were destitute and hungry for a slice of bread. Naturally they tried to console each other, but the misery and hurt was so deep that they were inconsolable. However, when they came to Hazur he would say, "It is all right, don't despair—God will give you more," and he would lift his hand in love and blessing. His words were like soothing balm on their raw wounds. The truth is that there is great power in this Attention; and when one is helpless and feels that there is no hope, one will get full protection and assistance by turning one's face toward the Master.

For example, if a child has to undergo some minor operation by the doctor, he will feel more assured and protected if his mother holds him in her lap, where her tender concern and love will help to take his attention from what is happening. There are many disciples who, while going through serious operations, have seen their Master as the surgeon performing the operation. It is a question of love and faith in the Guru. Some have seen the Master standing near them with loving and concentrated gaze; they lost their fear and forgot the operation completely. These are not stories from invention, but true facts which have happened and are still happening.

It is very necessary to have a living Master. On this

subject, Guru Ramdas, the fourth Guru of the Sikhs, says:

*She who has given birth will look after the*
*child with all her strength;*
*He may be in the house or outside, but she is*
*concerned for his every morsel.*

As the mother takes care of the baby selflessly with all her strength, in all his needs, even going without herself if necessary, so does the true Guru take care of the disciple through all the tribulations of life. If the disciple's eye is open enough, he will see for himself how he is being protected; and even if he does not see he will still receive the protection. If the child gets dirty, the mother does not spurn him, but washes him clean and lovingly embraces him to her breast. We are covered with the filth of ages of worldly living, and the Guru with all love and concern teaches us how to refrain from soiling ourselves.

*Many times she will reprove,*
*But always press you to her heart in love.*

Guard the invaluable gift from the Master with your very life, for it will remain with you in this world and the next. It is not a trivial thing to meet a Guru, but with deep sorrow I observe that many people do not have respect for their Master. A child can never forget his mother and all she has done for him; if anyone does forget their mother's love, it is a great sin. To forget all the blessings the Guru has bestowed is unforgiveable. Kabir says, *This sigh will never leave my heart; that I can do nothing in return for all that the Guru has done for me.* Forgive me, but the task of the Guru is not an easy one. To make something of the disciple, to put him on his feet, to give him new life, to reach him to his true home—this is the Guru's work. Giving lectures or fine talks is not the Guru's work. His talks are merely to help them be aware that they are in deep forgetfulness, but the Master's duty is a matter of custody.

> *O Lord, we are the children of God,*
> *But in ignorance.*

The Master unfolds our understanding, first as a teacher and then by taking on all the headaches, like bringing up a child from infancy, worrying about everything we do, just like a mother. When the child is fully grown, the mother knows that when he is hungry he will himself come for food; but if by chance he does not come, she again goes looking for him everywhere. If the disciple does not listen, the Master will offer alternative ways to help his progress; but if he is clever and keen to learn, he will understand much from but a single gesture, and so learns accurately and advances rapidly. When the disciple does not learn from Satsang, books and messages, the Master uses many other ways to encourage him. There is the indirect method. Baba Sawan Singh Ji would sometimes rebuke a man when the actual wrongdoer was another, standing nearby. He would say, "This is not right; it should not happen again," and the person being addressed would wonder in his heart, "What have I done, that he is saying this?" not realizing that the words were indirectly meant for someone else. The ways of Masters are often misunderstood through lack of spiritual growth. At times the disciples would perpetrate wrong deeds (it is very easy to fall); but when they came to Hazur he would show special love and say, "It is good you have come." This special attention was given particularly to save them from themselves, but many would foolishly think, "If we sin, our Guru is very happy with us!" This is our intellect misguiding us. Fortunately for us, the Master's purpose is always the same: to save the child, that he may stand erect. The road is very long, but he gives his time to each individual; after all, he has great love for each and everyone—what can he do?

If, after all these means are applied, the disciple still does not understand and progress, he uses yet other means to keep him on the straight path. Forgive me, but when he pulls the rope, the soul writhes in torment. When the child does not obey and wastes his life, the Master shakes him hard; and though he might be a hopeless case, the unceasing love of the Master will infuse a breeze of enthusiasm into his heart eventually. If you go on sitting at his feet, you will come nearer to realization. That is why it is advised, *Don't leave the Satsang—whatever has gone wrong will right itself.*

Why is your condition today so appalling? Because of the mind and the senses overpowering the soul, and too much living for outer enjoyment. There are grievances in your hearts against others: you cut each other's throats and squeeze the blood out. In this condition, what is the saving factor? Go to the Satsang regularly: one day you will think a thing is right, another day you will think a thing is wrong; but do not cease to attend and your condition will right itself. The more a child is obedient to the Guru's every wish, the quicker will be salvation.

A certain Mahatma by the name of Panap Das has said that a man should have three blessings: first God's, second the Guru's, and third your own soul's. God's blessing you have already got; He has given you the human form and to come across a perfect Master is His very special blessing. The Guru's blessing you received when he gave you rebirth by taking you above the senses and rejoining you to the Sound Current within, which will take you back to the source of all Life. But what about the third blessing which is your own? What is that? Having received the experience and connection with the Truth from the Master, then whatever he advises, you should do. Give whatever is the time requirement necessary to your inner progress. This is your own blessing on yourself. When the child learns with interest, he benefits from the teacher's pleasure also.

These days, most teachers are just paid; but when I used to study as a child, they were people dedicated to humanity in children. If a child was promising, the teacher would wave aside the question of fees and call him to his own home for extra tuition. We often went to our teacher's home. He did not have any water laid on there, so we used to bring it in buckets and do other work around the house, purely out of love for him. He loved us and taught us with love.

There are Satsangis and near Satsangis. By near Satsangi I mean one who has come in closer touch with the Guru. This teaching is the same for all children; but those who become receptive come closer to the Master, they get a special protection. Though his protection is extended to everyone—all are fed and eat the same bread—yet the child who is more hungry will receive more food. O Lord, we are your ignorant children. The Guru teaches us and makes us open up into awareness. Today you may do one thing, tomorrow something else; you are unstable and always wanting new things, from which you go on desiring other new things. The Master always gives permission for what you want, and remains with you in all you do, but gradually continues turning you toward the Truth that your interest in It becomes more and more powerful. When he has your interest well established he will make a new life for you and take you into a new world. Now, tell me, is there anyone who would not like to have such a Guru?

When the world turns its back, the Guru is standing beside you. Through desert and forest, over seas and mountains, in this world and the next, he is with you. In the other world the Guru is called *Guru Dev* (the Radiant Face of the Master) which appears within the Light. A man's face cannot appear inside, only the God-power. When the Guru Dev comes, the disciple will know that he has become a true disciple. If you would all keep daily diaries and honestly note in them all happenings, you would see what a grand treasure you would accumulate; but we listen to the Master's advice and then forget it. We even forget the subject of the Satsang after a few minutes. How can we expect success? Christ said, *If ye love me, keep my commandments.*

> *Satguru's words—*
> *Words ARE Satguru.*

The words of a Master are the Master himself, and those who respect his words will most certainly get salvation. Generally we respect him only when we see him, and when not in his presence we do what the mind tells us; but remember, he sees our every action. Our Hazur used to say that when a man comes to the Master, he sees him just like a clear glass bottle, and knows whether it is pickle or preserve. But no one knows what goes on behind his bland expression; he is completely unfathomable and will not show what he sees in a person, but will try and wash him clean. Some think he knows nothing, but he gives them his protection always. Those children who are in a dangerous condition get extra care—though very often they think they have succeeded in hoodwinking the Master. What foolishness this is!

> *Glory, glory to the Guru—Satguru the teacher,*
> *By whose various teachings we gained great*
> *wisdom.*

The Guru awakens us from our unconscious state, gives physical and intellectual food that we may have good living and right understanding, and protects us in all phases of life. Our Guru is the Blessed One who has bestowed all this wealth upon us; whoever has such a Master is blessed also. I want to emphasize that if after getting this priceless gift, no consideration is given to it—that is the greatest of all misfortunes. There are certain birds which when migrating fly many hundreds of miles, but their thoughts are with their children for they have left their eggs behind. The Master might be anywhere, but his thought and protection are constantly with his children, wherever they may be.

*The Satguru protects the disciple with his life.*

Breath for breath, he remembers you. Without the Master's remembrance, love for him cannot be born in the disciple. He sends out rays of love, and the disciple experiences a strong pull toward his Master. This is also a gift. Now the question arises, should one always be near to the Guru physically? To be always close to the physical presence of the Master takes extremely good karmic background, and only happens with great destiny. Should the followers leave their homes and cast aside their duties? A true Guru will never recommend this; why should he? If he was only on the physical level, then he might advise this; but he tells us that he has another form other than the physical and can travel thousands of miles from where his physical form remains. A true Master stresses that it is not necessary to be always close to his physical form. There is no doubt that if one is receptive by being near him, one will be enriched with greater wealth; but it sometimes happens that those near him become critical of outer happenings around him, with the result that they do not gain anything. You can live far or near, but your face should be ever turned toward him; that is the point. Kabir said that even if the seven seas are between the disciple and Guru, the disciple's attention should be directed toward his Master. The speed of attention is very fast. One can judge from the force of electricity; the pranas or life current have faster speed than electric current, and the attention is faster than pranas. With a radio set, one has to just tune it to a certain point and one can hear the sound immediately. Even if the disciple does not set his attention on the Master, the radiation goes on emitting, and the effect of this is the making of him. If he becomes receptive, then the Master appears before him.

There are disciples in various parts of the world—North America, South America, Africa, England, Germany, France, etc—and who is protecting them? It is not the physical form that travels around, but the higher power, the God-power; you can call it the Guru-power, and it is also called the Christ-power too. This power is protecting the disciples, many of whom have seen clearly the form of the Master—the Master-power—in their daily lives. The power that works in the human pole *is* the Guru; and if messages can be transmitted and received through radio, then why not become a human pole connected to the Guru through the Guru-power? There should be no obstruction in the way, like worldly affairs, children, one's own physical form or wandering thoughts. Another thing is: purity is very necessary in living and in being free from ill or impure thoughts. A radio will not work properly if it is jammed up with dirt and dust.

We frequently hear accounts of how the Master has protected his children. At death, he appears before the child, who in full consciousness happily states, "The Master has come." When a child learns to rise above the body consciousness at will, the Master is there to protect and guide him, talks to him and takes him upward from stage to stage. If Gurudom is looked down upon today, it is purely through incompetency and material motives. They themselves are doomed, but the tragedy is, so are the thousands who follow them. However, there is always hope; and if any have a sincere longing for the Truth, God will see that they are in torment to realize Him and make it possible for them to meet a true Master. *How is it possible for the servants to be well fed, if the master is starving and naked?* If at the time of initiation, the man you are following does not give you anything—it may be little or more, according to one's background—and open your inner eye, then it means that he is not competent. He should give you something, and that is the criterion of a true Master. Even if he gives a little at the beginning, then there is hope for much more; and whatever he gives, protect it with your life. After you have got contact with the God-into-Expression Power, where will you go from there? To the Formless and Nameless—the Source, from where the expression is coming. The word "religion" is derived from the Latin *religio*, through *re* and *ligare*, which mean and "back" and "bind"—so we have, "to bind back to the Source or God." This is the actual meaning of the word, but we are satisfied with sticking a label on ourselves and performing customary rites and rituals, which are merely the elementary steps to prepare the ground for higher things. No matter what you do, your life will not bear fruit until you meet someone to give you rebirth and connect your soul back to the God-power.

Only recently I received the urgent news that a certain disciple was dangerously ill. I wrote and told the people to advise the patient to concentrate within. They wrote back and said that my instructions had been conveyed to the patient by telephone, and within hours she had started improving, and is now on the way to recovery. This was just through a word on the telephone, so you can see that the thousands of miles between cannot stop the protection of the Master-power. However, that physical form in which the God-power has manifested is also pure, though it is not a question of praise for the physical; it is worthy of respect because God is manifested therein.

I will tell you of another instance. There was a man in America, named Walter Kirel. When I initiated him, he had a very good experience; but after some time he fell ill. When a man is in a helpless condition, he gets restless and worried. He wrote and told me that the doctors were pressing him to eat meat and drink wine. Each time he wrote I tried to make him understand that the non-vegetarian diet would not help him, and he should remain on the vegetarian diet. After a few months he wrote that he could not fight any more, that he had become helpless and could not breathe, and that the doctors were insisting on a meat diet. I replied, "All right, do whatever you feel like." When I visited America and reached Santa Barbara, the doctors had then given up hope for him, and he was at the door of death. Violet Gilbert, one of the hospital nurses, was a Satsangi; and she met me and told me about Walter Kirel who was dying in the hospital: "He cries a lot and goes on saying that he has disobeyed his Guru who is now in America but will not want to see his face. Do you think you could visit him, Master?" I said, "Of course I will." When I arrived in his room, Nurse Gilbert told him, "The Master has come." He opened his eyes and saw me, and the tears started flowing down his cheeks. I put my hand on his forehead, and said, "Do not worry—whatever has happened has happened, and it is finished. Do you hear the Sound?" He said, "No." "Do you see the Light?" Again he said, "No." I put my hand on his head and told him to close his eyes and forget all outer things. When he did so, not only the Light came, but the Radiant Form of the Master too. His ears were closed for him and he heard the Sound clearly. I told him, "Now go, with rejoicing." His wife was there, and she was a non-initiate. She said, "Master, I know that he has been forgiven and saved, but I wish he would speak to me before he goes." I again put my hand on his head and said, "Your wife wants you to say something to her before you go." He opened his eyes, and said, "All right," and turning to his wife, he smiled and said, "I am going now." This is what is called protection; it is not a story but a true incident.

I feel sorry for those who get this valuable gift and do not live up to it. Nanak says, *He who has met the Satguru—whatever is written in his destiny is finished.* It is true that the Master winds up the karmas, but not just like that; he adjusts them to further the man-making of the disciples. He takes the children in his charge, but he will make them into something worthwhile before taking them home. It is his duty to clean them first; nobody packs dirty clothes away in storage. When people are initiated, they rejoice and say, "We have got a Master; we have got salvation." When meeting the Satguru, you will get salvation if you obey his words.

> *Satguru cuts the bonds of the disciple,*
> *If the disciple withdraws from wrong deeds.*

Obey the Master. As I have said before, dirty clothes cannot be packed away in storage; and no one wants to wear dirty clothes. The Father wants to embrace you—if you have got clean clothes on. But this kind of cleanliness means having no other thought but of Him.

> *Clean the core of your heart for He who is*
> *    coming;*
> *Take the thoughts of others away, so that He can*
> *    sit there.*

This is what is meant by cleanliness. At times we try to do business with the Master and say, "If our wishes are fulfilled, only then we consider him a Guru, otherwise not. If the Master shows love and affection then it's all right; but if not, he is no Master." This is the sad condition we are in. A Guru is a Guru and will never leave you—even if you leave him. It is a wonderful protection and a great great blessing. The volumes of praises for the Guru which are written in the

Ved Shastras* have not been written idly. They also state that the Guru is greater than God. In the Guru, God Himself is working and there is no difference between the two. For example, here is my watch. That which is holding the watch is my hand; and if the watch could see and think, it would consider that it is just a hand; but who is in the hand? I. God is working through the human pole, and the pole says, "I am not the doer, but He who is in me." God is working from within the Guru, and they are one and the same.

First, the Guru works like a teacher. He shows sympathy, and even allows tears to flow from his eyes for you—sometimes he rebukes, and sometimes he shows love. In fact, he does everything. Then he says, "I am not the body, and neither are you; come, let us go up." He does everything to teach the disciple to break his outer attachments and concentrate within; he has no other motive. He has no desire for people's love. His own love is connected with God and his Guru; there is no place for anyone else. So become receptive to him, and through receptivity, become the image of him. A child grows on milk, and to love the Guru and be receptive to him is the food of life to the soul.

One Master said that though there be thirty or more teeth in the mouth, yet the tongue is not harmed by them. Similarly, the Master is protecting the disciple from all the perils of the world around him.

> *When difficult times come, no one helps—*
> *Both enemies and friends forsake;*
> *All hopes fade away—life becomes hopeless,*
> *But if God is in the heart, the flames of misery will*
>     *not be felt.*

---

*Ancient Hindu Scriptures.

When a man gets disheartened and there seems to be no chance of hope from any direction, then the Satguru comes and takes him across all his tribulations. He first waits patiently until we remove all intellect, worries, attachments and ego from our path; and then when we have fully reposed ourselves in him, then we come under his complete protection. If the disciple falls, the Guru will lift him up, for in this world who is free from difficulties? One cannot find even one man without problems in his life. But if a man has a perfect Master, he is fearless even when confronted by enemies. Kabir Sahib says, *He who lives in constant remembrance of his Master and keeps his Master's words, will be fearless in all three worlds.* Why should he be afraid of anything? After all, his Master is not merely a man. Understand this also: it often happens that the disciple is due for heavy suffering due to the karmic reactions from the past, but through the Guru's protection it can be reduced to perhaps a slight prick from a thorn.

All the ups and downs of life are like passing phases, and should have no pinching effect on the disciple. The worldly life is full of perplexities, and existence here is impossible without them. My Master used to say that if one thinks one can remove all the thorns from the worldly life, well, it is an impossibility; however, if one wears strong boots, one will not feel them. To wear strong boots means to live within the protection of the Master's radiation—not physically, but through thought and attention—be so much in his radiation, and never step out of it. Nothing should change this.

One can be so much within the Guru's radiation that even the powerful Lord of Death cannot come near. For example, I will tell you of one incident when I was living in Lahore. There was a lady who hailed from my village, but she was not a disciple. She became seriously ill, and her family endured constant sleepless nights in looking after her.

I heard that she was sick, and went to see her, accompanied by Dalip Singh (later treasurer in Sawan Ashram). I told them, "You have spent so many nights awake, and must be tired, so you all sleep tonight and I will watch beside the bed." Dalip Singh and I sat together for some time. She was not initiated, but that did not matter, and I asked her, "Do you repeat any holy name?" She affirmed that she did. I told Dalip Singh to go and rest and return about 4 a.m., and I continued to sit beside the dying woman. She went on repeating the holy names, as I had suggested, but suddenly she said to me, "There is an old man here." I looked up and saw the old man, and he explained to me that she was his granddaughter, and that he had come to take her away; but I told him that he could not do so as long as I was sitting there. He tried his best to take the soul out of the body, but did not succeed; so after some moments he went away. I asked the woman if she had recognized the old man and she said, "Yes, it was my grandfather; he was a very pious man."

After some time, Yama, the Angel of Death, appeared in the doorway. I looked straight at him, and he ran away — he could not even enter the room. He returned several times, but could not enter. Then Dharam Raj, the Lord of Death himself, appeared, but he also could not come into the room. He said, "This soul belongs to me." I said, "Yes, that is true, for she has not been initiated, and I know also that you cannot come near her because I am sitting here; so you had better go to my Guru and ask him what is to be done now. If he gives you permission to take this soul, then I will leave." My friends, just see — how great is the Naam! Dharam Raj left, and in a matter of moments returned and said, "I have got the permission to take the soul." I said, "All right, take it." He replied, "How can I when you are still sitting there?" Whatever is written regarding the protection power of the Holy Naam is all true, for I am telling you what actually happened. Dharam Raj said, "Unless you leave, I cannot take this soul." I asked him, "What benefit will she get from my spending the whole night beside her?" He said, "She will receive the fruit of that before any other rewards or debts are accounted." Just then, Dalip Singh entered the room, and I said to him, "Come brother, let us go away from this room, for while I am here she cannot die." As we were leaving, I asked her husband to give away in her name some money which was still due from her to some needy people—that her give and take may be squared up and she may leave the body. Dalip Singh and I stepped out of the room, and in one moment she was gone. Dalip Singh is here, you can ask him about it.

If a person who has got the Naam is sitting somewhere (not necessarily the Master, but anyone who meditates) then Yama or Dharam Raj cannot come near that place. What do you people imagine the Naam to be? I am sorry to say, that you hold it to be of little value.

> *Whenever Masters come, the world speaks ill of*
> *them;*
> *But God takes care of them.*

The world has always insulted the Masters. For their own gain, self-centered people will say many things against them; but there is not one who can harm a single hair of a Master's head if he does not wish it himself, for God's protection is impenetrable. Is it not natural that the Lord will protect him who belongs to Him? A good wife gives herself up completely to her husband, who takes care of her needs and protects her. But worldly examples are poor caricatures compared to the Master's protection. Even the mother, who has deep love for her child, has a selfish thought that when he grows up he will look after her, etc. A true Guru wants nothing from his children; he only feels grateful that another soul has become free and is returning to its own home. He has true love for the soul.

> *Brother, do not think that all is in your hands;*
> *Everything is already ordained.*

Never think for a moment that man has anything in his control. The Controlling Power is doing everything. Fear, death, heat, cold, etc., would never come near him, but for the reaction of the karmas; and it is not in man's control, for they come without him being able to stop them. A person may suddenly be bitten by a snake, and die from it; another will die after reaching old age. These things occur in life according to man's past karmas. When God's pen runs according to one's past karmas, man has nothing to say in it.

> *Such Name of God should be daily repeated within,*
> *O Nanak, that would free one from all bondage.*
> *Be tied to Life's Precious Thing,*
> *Which will be with you here and in the Beyond.*

Who can connect you with the Naam? *In the Guru, He Himself manifests and distributes the Shabd.* St. John tells us that *The Word was made flesh, and dwelt among us.* True Masters have always exhorted all mankind: O man, you have got this physical form, so connect yourself with the Naam, or with the manifestation of it in the human pole, which will protect you now and after death. Whosoever *claims* knowledge in this world is praised by the people who strive with all their might to believe in him, while the Masters are proclaiming the very Truth itself. *Guru and God are both before me; at whose feet shall I fall? I am full of gratitude to my Guru, through whom I discovered who the Satguru is.* God Himself is working in the Guru, and these words are expressing the gratitude that one should have toward one's Master. We cannot truly know and praise God and neither can we know or praise the Guru. He is in the world for the sole purpose of joining the souls back to God, and it is a great privilege to meet such a personality. When you meet him, obey his commands. Make your life as he wants it to be; in this will be your own triumph. He says, "Do your bhajan and make your life chaste and pure." His protection will always be over your head; keep your attention constantly on him, and you will become a true disciple of the Master.

*Sant Kirpal Singh Ji*
*(1894-1974)*

*Sant Kirpal Singh Ji*
*(1894-1974)*

# 14

# The Night is a Jungle

WHAT IS THE DIFFERENCE between God and man? Man has mind, without which he would be the same as God. Kabir tells us that, *All this* (creation) *is a part of God*. The soul is the same essence as that of God; it is a drop of the Ocean of All Consciousness. However, through being joined to the mind, it became *jiva*; but as it is of the same essence as God, when the mind is removed only God is left. So God plus mind is man, and man minus mind is God.

Gold is made into jewelry and other attractive articles, but that which comes direct from the mine is called "ore," although the gold is there. When the mud and other minerals are filtered from it, the pure gold is left. And so, when final analysis is made, and the mind and senses are removed, man is then God.

One can conceive the great possibilities of which to avail oneself, having received the blessing of a human birth, to separate the consciousness from matter and realize who one truly is. When the soul became jiva, by association with the body and the world, it adopted the same identity, for wherever the attention is directed one becomes as that. So now, lost in creation, it cannot find itself and return to its true home or origin until it is free and pure again. He who has found his own Self, has realized himself, has become one with God—he is man-in-God or God-in-man. The same Light which has become effulgent in him is sustaining the whole creation.

What is God? In truth, He is not Light, He is not Sound; but when He expressed Himself these two principles emanated from Him and came into being. Our soul being a drop of the wave of that God-into-Expression Power, a direct connection with It will take us back to the source from which It emanated—which is *Anami* or Absolute God. This is the message extended by all true Masters who have come, in different mode or language, according to the time.

Everything has a natural inclination to return to its original state and source. If you turn a lighted candle upside down, yet its flame will go up; for its source is the sun. If you throw a ball of clay in the air as hard as you like, it will but return to earth again from whence it came. If the soul gets freed from mind and senses it will automatically be drawn toward God.

The first thing we must do is: still the mind. The very foundation of yoga is controlling the intelligence. The word *yog* is derived from *yuj,* which means "to rejoin," and to rejoin the Lord is the ultimate task ahead of man, a task which can be achieved only in human form. Other forms are only for various enjoyments. Some human beings, because of their past karma, also live to enjoy, whereas others are not so heavily burdened and therefore the Truth is more apparent to them; they have better powers of differentiation. The latter type of human being can realize himself and realize God.

Today is the festival of Basakhi,* which is celebrated in different ways according to the various religious customs. Nature itself celebrates by sprouting of new buds and leaves, and the new life begins from this season. We should take a lesson from Nature and sprout forth with a new life. In the Hindu religion there are ten *avatars*, and certain Hindus

---

*The first day of the Indian month of Basakh, corresponding approximately to April 15.

celebrate this day as a double event: the birth of Parshuram, and the overcoming of evil by Narsing Avatar. Parshuram was a great yogi. Narsing was the avatar who saved Prince Prahlad and killed the Prince's father, the tyrant King Hirnaikashya, who while ruling the people with a rod of iron had declared himself God and had made them worship him. By performing severe austerities he had obtained a great boon from the gods: that he would never die by any hand born out of life, nor during the day or night, nor within or without any building, not on earth, nor in the sky, etc. His son Prahlad became a true devotee of the Lord and solemnly declared that God was God and not his father. The King tried to kill the Prince by various methods or torture, but the pure devotion of the child repeatedly drew on the grace of God for salvation, until finally his father ordered that Prahlad should embrace a red-hot iron column. Confronted with such a formidable test, the child at first hesitated, but on seeing an ant crawling up the column he stepped forward with joy and placed his arms around the column. At once the column split asunder and out stepped Narsing Avatar in a form born out of the fiery structure, terrifying to gaze upon. He took the King in his powerful hands, and as the sun went down he stepped into a doorway, neither inside nor outside, and tore the King apart.

I congratulate the Buddhists on this day, for the Lord Buddha was born on Basakhi; on Basakhi he received enlightenment, and on Basakhi he left his body finally—Nirvana. So both religions have good reason for celebration. For us also it can be a great day, for we are constantly lamenting that we should start life anew; so we should start this new day as the beginning of a new life in which the flowers should blossom and the fruit should come forth. There should be so much fruit on each branch that the weight may bow the fruit to the earth.

This is a great day for Sikhs also. In truth, Sikhism is not a cult; this is what I feel. One poet says that the world changes, and a true man is he who changes the world. On this day, some three centuries ago, Guru Gobind Singh, the tenth Sikh Guru, started the Khalsa. In those days the people were killing each other in the name of religion, and he started to erase the controversy by forming the Khalsa. A khalsa is a true disciple, and on this day the Guru found five true disciples among his followers and made them leaders of the people.

There was religious enmity during the life of Guru Nanak, who was once asked who he was and replied, *I am not Hindu, neither Muslim; The breath of this body is Allah and Ram.* He meant that Allah and Ram are one; but they still insisted on further explanation, so he said, *If I say I am Hindu you will kill me, Muslim I am not; Nanak is that invisible Power playing in this puppet of five elements.* They were concerned only with outer labels, and he had no desire to claim the outer form which signifies a Hindu or Muslim. His answer served to show them that man is greater than his outer appearance, for he is truly the power which resides in the physical form. We all stick on labels, sooner or later, entangling ourselves in conformity, but in truth we are just men—just human beings.

On this subject, Guru Gobind Singh Ji says, *The caste of all humanity is one.* We are all born the same way and have been given the same faculties. During the life of Kabir, as an open challenge the Brahmins declared that they had come to the world by direct orders from the mouth of Brahma; but Kabir replied, *O Brahmin, if you came direct from God, why were you not born differently than other men?* Even the outer and inner physical structure of all men is the same: no one has four arms, etc. All have the same privileges, whether born high or low according to their karma. As for these karmas of the past, Tulsi Sahib says, *The great Law of Karma has created the world's conditions; Each will take the fruit of his actions.* Valmiki was a low-caste untouchable who became Maharishi Valmiki! Because according to karma from his past, the change was bound to take place. But these days the children of brahmins are called brahmins indiscriminately, and so on in other castes, for as time passes, chains upon chains are added in the name of religion, and the basic oneness of all men is forgotten.

So on this day, five specially selected disciples were chosen, and they were called *panch piara* or the beloved five. The prevailing conditions of India at that time called for such action, but that is past and is not our concern. In those days, whether friends or enemies, men had no respect for each other, and the Guru sought to awaken the life and meaning of true teaching. He made a public announcement, and asked, "Who will offer his head for sacrifice?" Now, it is a simple matter to find hundreds of people who will agree with everything you say, and still more who will willingly bow down in obeisance. There are many also who will give their wealth for a cause. But how many can you find who will give up their lives? After a moment's pause, one man arose and came forward to the Guru, and then four others, one by one. He did not kill them, but made them his beloved disciples, above all religion—true human beings with the fact accepted. Then he gave them his Light, for from one Light others are kindled. He made the Khalsas—and what is said of the Khalsa?

*The Khalsa is my true form;*
*The Khalsa is my abode;*
*The Khalsa is my full intoxication,*
*The Khalsa is my complete Satguru.*

He is one who will never leave me. *He takes responsibility for the soul until the end; In that Lord does my mind rejoice.* And as further indication: *Think of Him as the Pure One, in whom the effulgent Light is glowing.*

He infused them with the Water of Life. *Religion is no consideration; He who takes God's Name becomes His own.* Masters never make people the prisoners of religion. Religions are our schools of thought, of which we have to make the best use. *I am Thine; O Lord. May Thy victory be everywhere.* The Khalsa has been described as a Living Light. Guru Gobind Singh gave them the Inner Light, and even outwardly bound them unto himself by vows with charged sweetened water given by his own hands. And then he made them offer the same water to himself, showing that the Guru is the disciple, and the true disciple is the Guru — which is an outer pointer to his greatness.

All Masters made disciples of course, including Lord Buddha, Hazrat Mohammed Sahib, Jesus Christ and others. They made disciples that they should become Buddhas and Christs. They regularly took food with their disciples, though the disciples never actually realized them to be as great as they were. I am speaking very frankly. The tenth Guru Sahib said, *I am a Khalsa,* and saying this, he took the *amrit* from their hands; and to combat the conditions of the time he formed a volunteer corps. He changed nothing in their religion; they remained Hindus, but willingly sacrificed their lives for the cause of truth and honor. One is reminded of Vali Khan and Nabi Khan Ali Khan who were Muslims, and who also sacrificed their lives for Guru Gobind Singh's cause. When Nabi Khan Ali Khan was killed, a man went to inform his wife; her first words were not concerning the death of her husband but, "Is my Guru all right?" What sacrifice that was!

## THE NIGHT IS A JUNGLE

When Bhai Nandlal Ji wrote a book of prayer called *Bandgi Nama,* Guru Gobind Singh gave the book the title of *Zindgi Nama,* meaning "The Giver of Life." If you have the opportunity to read it, you will become thoroughly awakened to the true teachings. The tenth Guru said, *We are the worshippers of the same Living Light.* All Masters pointed out that outer practices are of our own making, meant for the preparation of the ground. Maulana Rumi also said that theists and atheists have the same right to realize the Truth, for the soul is the same in both. All rituals are results of superstition.

First the unity of consciousness in creation was set. There is only one Brahm—there is nothing else—which was later qualified by others according to their own approach. *Through God's Light were all His children created into His play; With the same Light was the whole world created— who is good and who is bad?* It is a subject for deep thought. How can you make a Khalsa by merely sticking a label on someone? The greatness of the tenth Guru lies in this: that he himself infused the Light, and then made them as great as himself. *Wherever these five beloveds will be, there will I be also.* If you sit near an awakened soul, you also will awaken.

The system was excellent, but it was difficult to get constituents. He made one Guru-home in which all were equal. No one need worry what he was going to eat, where his clothing was coming from, how his children were going to be fed. He told everyone to do *nishkam seva* (selfless service) and to keep the Living Light within alive always. He gave an example: *Like sparks jumping from a fire, they fall back to become part of it again.* We are the sparks of that Living Light. The soul has an innate desire to return to its own home; but estranged in this foreign land, it has become entangled with the mind and senses, and is superficially reluctant to leave.

Guru Gobind Singh Ji broke down the religious narrow-mindedness; it was a great work. It not an easy task to break old rituals, even though the basic teachings are the same given by Guru Nanak, Kabir, and other Masters. Ravidas Ji says, *He cannot be bought, but is attained through true devotion.* It is also said, *Count the executioner as the purest, if God resides in his mind.* Anyone in whom God is manifested is the purest of all. If the system that Guru Gobind Ji Maharaj introduced could be implemented today, all life's uncertainties would be removed. From the very beginning I have thought that there should be a common kitchen and everyone should eat there. Everyone is subject to the attitude, "this is mine, this is mine," but it is an obstacle. All are not at the same stage of development, but there is great hope for those who are sincere and willing.

So today we celebrate Basakhi, because the Khalsa Panth was started on that date. Many people have the wrong understanding of the word *Khalsa*—he is the one in whom the Light is manifested. It has even been said that, *The Khalsa will reign over all; all those who will sit at his feet will be saved.* You will note that those who come to his feet will be saved, not the rest. The Khalsa is not formed from outer appearances, and in the end only the spiritual men will rule. The spiritual person in whom God has manifested Himself is the Khalsa, and those who come to his feet will be saved; others will have to remain in their humiliation. That which man accepts as law through generations of customary habit is viewed by the Masters from a detached and therefore more accurate angle of vision. They see no value in religious highs and lows. They light the Light within all and reveal that all are one and the same. The so-called gurus remain as gurus and their disciples remain disciples; but the true Masters say no, we are one and the same. Our Hazur used to say, "No emperor wants his son to remain an official." A true Saint desires that his followers also become Saints. All men, from both human and spiritual levels, are one and the same. He who is the Controlling Power is the Giver and the Doer. Even the meaning behind the *puja* or *namaz* (Hindu and Muslim devotional practices respectively) is the same. With puja, a lamp is lit and then the puja performed, while the Muslims place their hands on their ears and utter the sound called *baang*! On the Path of the Masters the initiate is taught how to place the hands on the ears and hear the inner Sound. One should listen to this inner *baang* (Music of the Spheres), which is spiritually efficacious.

Guru Nanak once went to Shiraz (in Persia), and there he met a Muslim priest named Rooknudin, who asked the Guru, "Have you ever seen the house of the Lord?" Guru Nanak replied, "Yes," and proceeded to describe the physical form: *It has twelve minarets, six at each extremity* (joints of the arms and legs); *fifty-two spires* (thirty-two teeth and twenty nails); *and two windows* (eyes). It is also said, *In a lofty special palace, Khuda* (God) *is giving the baang.* So one should be able to understand clearly that the true mosque, church or temple is the human form. Mosques are forehead-shaped, church steeples are nose-shaped, temples and guru-dwaras are dome- or head-shaped, all model imitations of the true temple of God. *This body is the temple of God in which the true Light is seen.*

Maulana Rumi tells us that for those whose eyes are not open, mosques are made with clay and water. For the awak-ened people — the complete Masters — the mosque is this true heart, at the seat of the soul. During my Western tour I told the people many times that God does not reside in temples made with stone, but He Himself made the house in which He resides. But we have forgotten the true temple and respect the man-made outer images of the true house. *What tragedy that we go to the imitation temple, leaving the natural mosque to bear the labor.* The man-made model was intended to teach us that there is such a thing as inner Light and Sound, and we should have learned to withdraw to experience it; but instead we are worshipping any image, indiscriminately. In sacred solemnity we are clutching the outer skin, oblivious to the fruit that lies within.

In the Upanishads it is written, *What is that, the knowledge of which makes everything else known?* The soul is a conscious entity; as long as it does not merge into the All Consciousness, it will never be at peace. Furthermore, the mind can never be controlled while it remains without contact with the Naam or God Power. *When you get the Naam, the mind becomes controlled.* In the life of Lord Krishna it is mentioned that deep in the River Jumna he encountered a thousand-headed serpent, which he overpowered by playing his flute. This serpent represents the mind, which has a thousand ways of poisoning us. *With victory over the mind, you have victory over the world.* There is no other obstacle between us and the Lord but the mind. If your heart holds a strong desire to realize God, then put one foot on your mind—to still it—and the next step will take you to the home of the Lord.

In the Koran it is written that if a man can recognize his true self, then he will recognize God. The same teachings are brought by all Masters for all people. A Light appears in the human form, and all religions are enlightened by It, for those who meet him receive the enlightenment. When each enlightened soul leaves, a new religion starts to keep his teachings alive; but without the practical guidance, a decline sets in. Everyone is over-zealous in upholding his own beliefs, and no one is willing to sit on common ground on equal footing to discuss spiritual matters. The true teaching remains the same, age after age—Truth is One, for everyone. God is not different for Hindus, Muslims, Christians and so on; He is the God of the whole world and is not a Hindu, Muslim, Christian, Buddhist, etc.

Even now a small amusing incident remains in my memory, which happened when I was in Peshawar, studying in the ninth grade. I used to take my books and study in a garden named Shahi Bagh, and one day a man whose name I still remember—Darbari Lal—asked me, "Where is Shahi Bagh?" I told him that he was standing beside that very garden, and he said, "I have come to settle judgment on a dispute, for I have been told that the Hindu God is crying because the Muslim God has beaten him up and broken his leg." (People gathered in Shahi Bagh specially for discussing different controversies.) Even at that young age I was shocked to discover that people thought each religion had a different God.

Poor understanding is widespread because men do not rise above the worldly level to see the facts from a more accurate angle of vision. Up to the time of the tenth Guru, no Master had revealed the circumstances of his past births so openly as he did. In the latter part of his life he talked of many strange things, including the "seven-pointed splendor" of Hemkunt, a place of seven hills where he had performed many austerities in a past life, through which he lost individuality and became one with the Lord. He was there seated in great bliss, but the Lord gave him orders, "Child, go into the world and work." Guru Gobind Singh Ji recounts that he had no desire to return to the world, but was persuaded, so he said, "What are your orders, my Lord?" The Lord said, "Those who are there and most of those who have been there have encouraged the praise of their own names. Go and tell of My Name—show that there *is* God."

When Guru Gobind Singh was asked who he was, he

said, *I am the servant of the Most High who has come to see the play in the world; Know me as His servant, there is no difference between Him and me.* He has also said, *They who think of me as God will all go to Hell.* God is sending His Water of Life through a vessel, but the vessel should not think of himself as the Doer. No true Master will say, "I am the Guru," for the ray is of the sun, but through being connected with that ray one can reach the Sun itself. With one single ray of the Lord, the whole world was created. *From one source, millions of rivers emerged.* What and who exactly is God, no one can know, for man has exhausted himself in attempting to sing His praises. In the Jap Ji, Guru Nanak says:

> *Some sing of His greatness, but only according to*
> *        the power bestowed upon them;*
> *Some sing of His bounties, taking them as His*
> *        signs;*
> *Some sing of Him as incomprehensible;*
> *Some sing of Him as transmitting dust into life, and*
> *        life into dust again: Creator and Destroyer, the*
> *        Giver of Life and its Withdrawer.*
> *Some sing of Him as at once the nearest; and the*
> *        most remote.*
> *There is no end to His description.*

Nothing has been mentioned of God Himself—only the things He created. *You cannot know Him by talking; though you may talk for millions of years.* Even the Masters have failed in the attempt. Finally, they resort to observing *Neti, neti*—He is not this, He is not that. A Muslim prophet says, *Through philosophy, generations have passed in descriptive attempts, but God's character remains unsaid.*

Today is Basakhi and our new life should start. All differences in our hearts should be removed. A man once asked me why it was that no Master has said, "Put your attention on me," but rather they say, "Put your attention on Him." I told him that the instructions must be properly understood.

Lord Krishna said, *Put your attention on that true form of mine.* The method remains the same regardless of where the Power is manifesting. Electricity will sometimes heat and sometimes chill. Avatars and Saints are manifestations or phases of the same Lord. Misunderstanding and narrow-mindedness create separation of brother from brother, but God's intoxication is one and the same. We are all worshipers of the Living Light, regardless of which religion we belong to.

Some Christians came to the Prophet Mohammed and requested him to give them a place where they could build a church, and what did he do? He gave them half the mosque for their church! Would anyone do such a wonderful thing today? Think carefully over his action and what it means. Are we prepared to follow in the footsteps of our elders?

Guru Har Gobind, the sixth Sikh Guru, built mosques and temples as well as gurudwaras side by side whenever necessary. In Amritsar, the foundation stone of the famous Sikh Golden Temple was laid by Hazrat Mian Mir, a Muslim Saint, at the special request of Guru Arjan. To rise above body consciousness means to rise above illusion; then one realizes in truth that there exist no differences—religious, sectarian or other. This is truly the ultimate goal; outer things are merely helping factors leading toward it, and man as a social being must live in some social group; otherwise, corruption starts its corroding process.

Once in Lahore, an atheist called people from various religions together to discuss the question, "Is religion necessary?" Each religious leader spoke at length, proving the necessity of the different forms and rituals, etc. I was present, sitting in the front row. Then the atheist stood up to give his proof as to why religion is not necessary, giving various examples. Among these, he stated that when a marriage is to take place it is merely a matter of the priest, pundit or mulla placing his hands on the couple in blessing before a group of witnesses, to join them together, so as to prevent corruption. It does not make any difference if it is performed in one religious way or another.

I stood up and said, "Brother, is it not true that if ten or twenty thousand people were of your thought, then a new society or sect would have to be formed? In that society, some rules and regulations would have to be made. You desire to save yourself from organizations, but you are inadvertently creating another. If each man stayed in his own sect and learned how to know his true self or soul and that Power which controls all things, would that not be better?" He was an atheist, but he replied, "What you have said is correct." For as long as I lived in Lahore we used to meet on very loving terms.

There is a great deal of misunderstanding existing regarding this subject. In holy places only Truth should be discussed—and realized—for Truth is Truth. Keep the company of someone who has realized the Truth and get right understanding. We say "God is One" and even this is not true, but we are finite beings and must therefore use finite terms. Let us now take a hymn of Guru Gobind Singh on this celebrated day:

*Oh mind, take such a sanyas:**

---

*Sanyas means renunciation or ascetic discipline. The Master has inserted a comment here, after the first line of the hymn. This line refers to the following lines which explain it.

This is a lesson for the mind, that it should adopt such renunciation that will still all desires. To leave one's hearth and home is not the true sanyas; one must become desireless; and then the very silence sprouts forth into Light and that same silence becomes vocal.

> *Regard every place as a lonely forest;*
> *In the mind alone will complete silence come.*

You can make your home a lonely forest. Is not the night a lonely forest? Just consider for a moment. Those who have made the best use of their nights, by knowing oneself and the Overself, have themselves been made. Those who have wasted their nights in frivolous pursuits have wasted themselves. Even a student of worldly knowledge becomes intellectually strong if he makes full use of the night as well as the day. Those men who exercise the physical body through the cold nights become giants in muscle and strength; it is obvious how strong they are. And the disciples who spend their nights in sweet remembrance of the Lord become God themselves. If man can control the dim hours from sunset to sunrise, he becomes a true human being. But instead we eat, drink, enjoy the worldly pleasures until midnight, and then snore the rest of the night away.

One Master has said that in the night, the Lord's fragrance is given out—he who remains awake receives this precious gift. Do the worldly duties in the daytime, and at night consider that you are all alone, deep in the country. One's duties and social obligations with family and friends should be performed with pleasure, because God has joined you together for the sake of give and take. But in the night you can feel free from all this and repose in His lap. It is not at all necessary to leave your home and family for meditation when you have the long lonely nights. When you are wholly absorbed in some object, it is a true sanyas, cutting off from

all other things; and if we start from today, most definitely
our lives will change.

This invaluable guidance is written in the sacred books,
but sadly it remains there, or it penetrates only to the
intellectual level. We have to take the knowledge and live
up to it; only then does it become a part of life. The night
is a jungle—do your work in the daytime and then benefit
from the night.

The true purpose of having a human form is to make
daily progress toward the great goal, so sit down each day
and see where you are. The meaning of keeping a diary
is of utmost importance, but very few fully understand it.
Remove those things which are obstructing your progress—
weed out the imperfections, one by one. A strong man revels
in his strength and the weaker man wonders how he got
it. When a wrestler walks abroad, people turn to stare and
remark on his strength. He has not achieved that overnight,
but through many nights of hard exercising. As the renunciate leaves everything and goes to the woods, you can sit
down nightly in your own home, forgetting the world and
freeing yourself from all entanglements.

> *Make the jatta of chastity and purity, and take a*
> *bath of Yog;*
> *Grow the nails of regularity.**

One should make one's *jatta* out of the purity of life—guard
carefully one's *brahmcharya* (chastity). Chastity is life and
sexuality is death. Our whole house has to stand on this
foundation; do not make it out of sand. You will then be able
to live properly; your mind and intellect will be wholesome.
This in itself is a most valuable thing, for even if you have

---

*Renunciates let their hair grow, cover it with ashes and coil it on their heads; this
is called *jatta*. They also stop cutting their nails.

only dry bread to eat, yet you will have full strength. You won't need any tonics.

In regard to the householder's life: marriage is not a bar to Spirituality, if one lives according to the scriptures. There may be one duty of begetting children, but that is not the be-all and end-all of married life; there is grossly wrong understanding on this subject. Do not make the human form a mere machine for vice. Instead, make your life pure and controlled.

If you wish to have one or two children, well and good; but look after them properly and help them to become something good. Set a worthy example for them, and remain aware of the responsibilities of parenthood. Furthermore, the whole family should sit together and sing the praises of the Lord.

The Guru Sahib tells us to take a bath in the Yog. If you want to become one with God you must throw away all worldly thoughts. To take a bath in Yog means a daily bath in His contact—become one with Him. If you cannot wash your hands of worldly affairs, you should not sit in God's remembrance. The Muslims do *vazu* (washing of the hands, face and feet) before they sit for the namaz, for they believe that unless this is done, the prayer will not be accepted. So we should wash the worldly environments out of our thoughts before we sit in meditation. The Hindus say that puja should not be done unless one first takes a bath. The most effective bath is to withdraw your attention from outer things.

Grow the nails of regularity. An army without a commander will end up in chaos, so we must command our lives with regularity. If you are employed somewhere, you go there daily at the proper time, without any trouble; and for meditation we should adopt the same attitude and sit daily at the regular time. Sadly, we are adrift; sometimes we sit, sometimes we don't. If we were truly regular, we would find that if we should happen to have a day without meditation, we would feel ill at ease, as though we had missed something. If possible, there should be a room in the home set aside for God's remembrance alone—you would find that the very atmosphere of that room would remind you of Him.

In the last stanza of the Jap Ji, you will find, *Make chastity your furnace and patience your smithy.* To fashion gold into something beautiful, a goldsmith must first melt the metal by the aid of a furnace. Take these two things, patience and chastity, and go on working toward your goal. With patience one will continue to persevere, even when the progress seems slow. *Blessed are the pure in heart, for they shall see God.* It is a promise Christ gave. So take these things into your lives: patience, perseverance, chaste and pure living, and regularity. Then? Make the nights your jungle, and see what a beautiful program will result.

In the past, a true *brahmcharya* would spend his first twenty-five years in a jungle ashram, learning the Vedic and Shastric scriptures. Then he would enter the *grehastha ashram* (take up the duties of a householder). After conscientiously bringing up his one or two children to the stage of adulthood, he would then return to the forests in the *vanprasth ashram* wherein he would study for self-realization. Having realized the Truth, he would leave that stage and journey around in the world, helping the people to awaken. Today's preaching is done for the stomach only. Some people earn their livelihood by their own hard labor in one way or another, and some take their living from religion or religious books.

So make your home a jungle. He who lives in his own home, remaining aloof from worldly taints, yearning within for the Lord, will receive far more benefit than from taking a bath in the limpid waters of the holy River Ganges. Become so closely connected with the Lord that either He or you remains—not two.

*Get connected to the pure Naam, through the Guru's knowledge of the soul.* This Guru's knowledge is a practical experience; there is nothing academic about it. *This knowledge is of Attention (Surat) and Sound (Shabd); It cannot be brought into words.* The word "knowledge" here refers to the Music of the Spheres which is vibrating within our very being. It can only be experienced. *The one who makes audible the Sound coming from the gaggan* (astral heaven) *is my Gurudev.* Who gives that experience? *Through the Guru's knowledge I got the true eye, through which the veil of ignorance was pierced and the Light revealed within.* So what is the value of Gurubhakti (devotion to the Guru)? *All living souls should do Gurubhakti, and become one with the Light within.* Become connected to that Light and develop your devotion—which should increase so much so that each pore vibrates with the Guru's Naam. When a little love awakens in a person, does it not bubble up and overflow? It should be developed steadily up to full realization, through which all peace and serenity will reign in your being.

> *Eat less, sleep less; have mercy, forgiveness*
> *and love.*

The Prophet Mohammed said that one should eat one mouthful less at each meal. Sheikh Saadi said that half of the stomach should be filled with food, one-fourth with water, and one-fourth left empty. Swami Ji Maharaj said that those who desire to taste the Nectar of Shabd should eat one meal per day only. We eat too much—naturally sleep will come to our house. If your food is regularized you will rise up punctually in the morning. The awakened man's body may sleep, but he does not. Remember, the soul is a conscious entity and usually when a person sleeps, the soul withdraws to the throat and the man experiences dreams. If it withdraws to the navel, deep sleep ensues. The Masters remain awake. Unlike others, they are awake while sleeping. This is a very noble aim to aspire to. These three things will help you: to eat less, sleep less and have mercy, forgiveness and love.

> *Mercy is the interest gained from righteous living,*
> *pride's interest is sin;*
> *O Tulsi, leave not mercy while this body breathes.*

A person has more pity for his family and friends than for strangers. Is this compassion? If one's neighbors are dying of starvation while one is eating one's fill, what kind of mercy is this? Should your own child be sick, yet you hear of another's that needs help; if you have true mercy you will give more attention to the strange child. When Guru Gobind Singh's children were killed in battle, his wife came crying to him—"Where are my four sons?" His words are noteworthy: "For the heads of all these sons (the followers) have I sacrificed the four." This is what you can call compassion. He sacrificed all that was his for the sons of others. Did he win any empire or property for himself? True Masters have real compassion for people. When Jesus Christ was sitting with some people, he was told that his mother and relatives were outside, desiring to speak to him. What was his reply? He said, *Who is my mother? Who are my brothers?* and indicating his disciples and followers, he said, *Behold; my mother and my brothers!*

If someone makes a mistake, forgive him. But people prefer justice to forgiveness. Remember this, that with justice, the heart is never cleansed. I will give an example from my own experience. My wife was once traveling home by train, and I went to meet her at the railway station. As soon as she stepped off the train, and before I had even approached her, a pickpocket stole her purse and ran off. As it happened, a wide-awake police constable had witnessed the incident, quickly caught the man and returned the purse to my wife. With a firm grip on the thief, the policeman turned to me and said, "You must also come along to the police station." I pointed out to him that as we had recovered the purse, we were quite satisfied; but he protested and said, "This sort of thing is happening frequently, you must come and make a charge."

I went along to the police station and sat there for more than an hour without anything being done. I told the inspector, "I am not concerned with this, you can also keep the purse—I am going." He took my statement at once, and eventually I had to go to court. It was the first time I had ever stepped into a courtroom. While waiting for the proceedings to start, the inspector remarked to me, "Justice must be done." I told him, "Brother, along with justice, there should also be compassion; both should go side by side. With justice the heart remains affected, but compassion washes away all impurities." When the judge had heard the case, I said, "Your honor, if you can find a way of releasing this man, I have no objection." The judge was surprised, but he asked the police about the man's previous record, and was told that no charges were recorded against him. The judge agreed to let him go with a good warning and he was released. That man returned to his family with a happy heart; he went around telling people, "If he had not saved me, I would now be in prison."

Outwardly a person may be emphatic that he forgives; but in his heart he wants to strike out at the offender and cut the very roots of him. If you have no compassion in the mind, how can you honestly say you forgive? God is love, and as a part of Him, the soul's innate nature is also love. Guru Gobind Singh Ji has said, *Hear ye all, I tell you in Truth; God is realized by one who loves.* Kabir says, *Love the Lord, oh mind, love the Lord.* And in the Bible, *He that loveth not, knoweth not God; for God is love.* We pray and perform rites that the love of God may be born in us—what other purpose is there? But what results will come from the prayers that are mingled with gossip? What will it avail us to leave the place of worship without a trace of love in our hearts for our fellow beings?

> *Chastity, contentment, and remain stabilized;*
> *Then you will go beyond the three gunas.**

Adopt a righteous way of life and be content. You may have certain desires, but stop there; don't increase them. Then reconsider the desires and where they will take you. What lies ahead, and what will you take with you? We are hurrying, scurrying through life; we are not even conscious of what we are doing most of the time. So the Guru advises us to handle all our affairs with tranquil serenity; then you have a chance of reaching *Trigun-atit* (beyond the three attributes), and then going beyond. Lord Krishna, in the famous Bhagavad Gita, told Arjuna, *Oh Arjuna, go beyond the three gunas.* Unless you go beyond, you will continue coming and going round and round in Pind, And and Brahmand.

> *Desire, lust, anger, pride, greed, perversity,*
> *attachment;*
> *Do not allow these in your mind.*

---

*Attributes of the mind: *satva* (pure aspect), *rajas* (active aspect) and *tamas* (inert aspect).

To go more deeply into the matter, what constitutes desire? *All conceptions in the mind are desires.* So, be desireless. You will have noticed that when an obstacle blocks the achievement of one's desire, anger arises. Then there is pride—"I must have this (or do this), otherwise I will be belittled in the eyes of others." One can accept pride as being the basis of all sins, for it turns into I-hood. He recommends us to leave off perversity, or stop being obstinate. Always be sure and listen to the other person's point of view—you may find that what he is saying is correct. Perversity just binds a person more; there is no room for expansion. Dogmatic knowledge of books, for instance, which might be right or wrong, should be discarded. It goes without saying that all attachments should be broken away—you must finish up the give and take—you must leave the body and all its environments. If an obstacle comes between you and your desire, it grows even stronger. Just put a large rock in the middle of a fast-flowing stream and you will create two things, froth and noise. When a man is angry he cannot speak softly, and finally he froths at the mouth. If you do get the thing you desire, it turns into attachment. There is only one cure for all this: *Only after seeing your true self can you realize the Lord.* And now, we will take something for Basakh:*

> *How can Basakh bring contentment*
> *For him who is parted from his love?*

The soul's natural inclination is to return to God. If it could only withdraw from outer attractions, its automatic course would be straight toward God. Is it possible to withdraw? *The Guru has put your house under control and made you the mistress.* Furthermore, *Ten servants did my Lord give me.* Five gross and five subtle senses to come under control, through the grace of the Guru. Until now the soul has been

---

*The Master is now taking up another hymn, this time one by Guru Arjan.

under the control of mind and senses, and has never seen its Beloved—how can it rejoice and be content? A loved one's greatest desire is to be with his Beloved; how can one go through life separate from Him? How did we forget Him?

> *When the separation from God came, the illusion*
> *engulfed everything.*

It seems as if the illusion left all other work to cling to us. Illusion's other name is forgetfulness. *The whole world is sleeping in attachment and forgetfulness; tell me, when will this illusion go?* If the One whom we have forgotten comes before us, would not the innate love within us awaken? It is a heart-rending story, for all the harvest is ready; you have got the physical form, after great struggle—but you are cut away from the Beloved and cannot enjoy the fruits of the harvest.

> *Sons, family, wealth, none are with you;*
> *Only the Immortal God.*

We have been joined to our family and relatives through God's will and the prarabdh karmas, and we should accept the conditions joyfully. Only he who truly knows, willingly pays his way through life. Who knows how many difficulties are due to our unpaid debts? *How can I say who is my friend in this world? All love is a lie, and all seek their own happiness—enemies and friends.* Only God will remain with you in the end—He who is the true companion of our soul. Whoever has turned his face toward Him will return to His lap. He who is in love with the world will return to the world. It might be love for this world or the hereafter, but he will go on circling around the physical, astral and causal planes.

> *All this illusory meaningless work takes my*
> *whole time.*

It is good to work, and one should work whole-heartedly; and then forget it. To continue concerning oneself with countless petty matters will fritter away the attention. This only causes further enmeshing attachments, and wherever your thoughts are, there will you reside. Get connected to the Immortal Lord; all else is changeable and impermanent. If we have not yet been connected to Him, and are a true seeker, we should pray: "O Lord, my attention is attached to this perishable matter, how can I find contact with You who are immortal?"

*Without the Naam of the Lord, the future is lost.*

Without a connection with the All Sustainer, our life is wasted; nothing remains but preparation for the return to the field of action. *What shall it profit a man if he gain the whole world and lose his own soul?* A wise man is he who works with foresight, but unfortunately most people never give a thought to permanent things; that which is momentary becomes their god and their life.

*By forgetting God, you have wasted your life;*
*Without Him, you have no one.*

Protect this wealth you have been given with your very life. *By meeting the Saint, take and preserve the true Naam.* It is a gift that will remain in both worlds—here and hereafter.

*Those who sit at the Beloved's feet,*
*Even their company is pure.*

Those who live in the world, but have made their home a jungle—have become one with the Lord—even to overhear some word about them will bring happiness. Go and search until you find such a personality. Only through his guidance can we realize God; it is a natural fact.

*Nanak entreats Thee, O Lord, may we also
    meet Thee.*

True prayers are accepted, for whatever comes deep
from the heart is granted by the Lord. In Gurbani, it says,
*The Father Kirpal (Merciful) has given this order: What-
ever the child asks for will be given.* In the Koran it says,
*Whatever man wants, I will give him.*

*Basakh will be wondrous, if only we can meet the
    Saint.*

The month of Basakh, the start of new life, can only be fulfilled if we meet the one who has realized the Lord. But there
are two kinds of meeting: one is outward, and one is through
the heart becoming receptive. *Through a true darshan, all
sins are forgiven.* All one's work can be accomplished by
meeting the Saint.

*Those who meditate on the Naam, their work
    will be successful,
Those who have the Perfect Master will be
    glorified in God's house;
Those at His feet will find permanent happiness,
    and will cross the ocean of life.
No poisons can affect those who develop love
    and devotion;
All perishables vanished, all duality
    disappeared, when the Truth was received.
Those who worship Him beyond Brahm become
    one in His bliss.
That month is blessed in which the Lord showers
    his mercy,
Nanak desires only one boon: that through Thy
    mercy I will get Thy darshan.*

After getting the human form, we should ask for but one thing: that we might have a glimpse of Him. This should be our ideal and our aim in life. Today is Basakhi, but do you understand what you are doing? Be the worshipper of the Living Light—become a slave to it. Do not attach yourself to anything else, for everything is changeable. He in whom that Light is manifested gives the Light to the whole world. Truth is One, and although Truth is above all, yet true living is above Truth. Guru Arjan has laid out a wonderful program for us, and in conclusion he says that the month in which we realize the Lord will be truly blessed.

*Sant Kirpal Singh Ji*
*(1894-1974)*

# About the Author

Considered by many people who met him in the East and in the West to have been a living example of a true Saint of Spirituality, Kirpal Singh was born in a rural setting in Sayyad Kasran in the Punjab (then in India, now in Pakistan) on February 6, 1894. He followed the career of a civil servant in the government of India, and retired on his own pension in 1947. Following instructions from his Master (Sawan Singh Ji Maharaj, 1858-1948), he founded and directed RUHANI SATSANG. He was Commissioned by God and authorized by his Master to carry forward the spiritual work of contacting sincere seekers after God with the WORD (or NAAM). He continued in that capacity until he left the earth plane on August 21,1974. Elected four times, consecutively, as President of the World Fellowship of Religions, he upheld the truth that, though the various religions are different schools of thought, the Aim of all religions is One and the Same. Kirpal Singh visited the major cities in the United States on the occasions of each of his three world tours: in 1955, in 1963-64, and again in 1972, staying in this country for three months or more each time. From his intense study at the feet of Sawan Singh Ji Maharaj and from his own personal inner experiences of a spiritual nature, Kirpal Singh was eminently qualified to convey to sincere people everywhere the importance of self knowledge and God realization.

*Sant Kirpal Singh Ji*
*(1894-1974)*

# Source of Talks

The talks (each chapter) in this book were originally published in the monthly magazine *Sat Sandesh*. The talks of the years 1968 and 1969 were published in India in the English edition of the magazine. After 1970 the English edition was published in New Hampshire (USA).

# BOOKS by Kirpal Singh

**CROWN OF LIFE**

A comparison of the various yogas and their scope; including Surat Shabd Yoga—the disciplined approach to Spirituality. Religious parallels and various modern movements cited. Paperback; 256 pages; index.

ISBN 978-0-942735-77-2

**GODMAN**

If there is always at least one authorized spiritual guide on earth at any time, what are the characteristics which will enable the honest seeker to distinguish him from those who are not competent? A complete study of the supreme mystics and their hallmarks. Paperback; 185 pages.

ISBN 978-0-942735-64-2

**A GREAT SAINT: BABA JAIMAL SINGH**
*His Life and Teachings*
A unique biography, tracing the development of one of the most outstanding Saints of modern times. Should be read by every seeker after God for the encouragement it offers. Also included, **A BRIEF LIFE SKETCH OF THE GREAT SAINT, BABA SAWAN SINGH,** the successor of Baba Jaimal Singh. He carried on Baba Ji's work, greatly expanding the Satsang and carrying it across the seas. Paperback; 230 pages; glossary; index.

ISBN 978-0-942735-27-7

**THE JAP JI: The Message of Guru Nanak**
An extensive explanation of the basic principles taught by Guru Nanak (1469-1539 A.D.) with comparative scriptures cited. Stanzas of the Hymns in English, as well as the original text in phonetic wording. Paperback; 189 pages; glossary.

ISBN 978-0-942735-81-9

**HIS GRACE LIVES ON**

During 17 days in the month of August 1974, preceding His physical departure on August 21st, Kirpal Singh gave 15 darshan talks, mostly in the form of questions and answers, to a small group of His disciples at His ashram in India. These talks have been bound together with the unabridged text from Master Kirpal's address to the Parliament of India and His 1971 afternoon darshan talk, True Meditation. Hard cover and paperback; 17 photos; 203 pages.

Hard cover ISBN 978-0-942735-93-2
Soft cover ISBN 978-0-9764548-3-0

**THE LIGHT OF KIRPAL**
A collection of 87 talks given from September 1969 to December 1971, containing extensive questions and answers between the Master and western disciples visiting at that time. *A different version of this book was published under the title Heart to Heart Talks.* Paperback; 446 pages; 15 photos.                                   ISBN 978-0-89142-033-0

**MORNING TALKS**
A transcription of a sequence of talks given by Sant Kirpal Singh between October 1967 and January 1969. "To give further help and encouragement on the Way, my new book *Morning Talks* will soon be available for general distribution. This book, which covers most aspects of Spirituality, is a God-given textbook to which all initiates should constantly refer to see how they are measuring up to the standards required for success in their man-making. I cannot stress sufficiently the importance of reading this book, digesting its contents, and then living up to what it contains." —Master Kirpal Singh Paperback; 258 pages.                          ISBN 978-0-942735-16-1

**NAAM or WORD**
"In the beginning was the WORD... and the WORD was God." Quotations from Hindu, Buddhist, Islamic, and Christian sacred writings confirm the universality of this spiritual manifestation of God in religious tradition and mystical practices. Paperback; 335 pages.     ISBN 978-0-942735-94-9

**THE NIGHT IS A JUNGLE**
A compendium of 14 talks delivered by the author prior to 1972, the first four of which were given in Philadelphia in 1955. The remaining ten talks were delivered in India. All of these talks were checked for their accuracy by Kirpal Singh prior to their compilation in this book. Paperback; 368 pages; with an introduction.                   ISBN 978-0-942735-18-5

**PRAYER: Its Nature and Technique**
Discusses all forms and aspects of prayer, from the most elementary to the ultimate state of "praying without ceasing." Also contains collected prayers from all religious traditions. Paperback; 147 pages; including appendix; index of references.                          ISBN 978-0-942735-50-5

**SPIRITUALITY: What It Is**
Explores the Science of Spirituality. Man has unravelled the mysteries of the starry welkin, sounded the depths of the seas, delved deep into the bowels of the earth, braved the blinding blizzards of snowy Mount Everest, and is now out exploring space so as to establish interplanetary relations, but sad to say, has not found out the mystery of the human soul within him. Paperback; 103 pages plus introductory.       ISBN 978-0-942735-78-9

**SPIRITUAL ELIXIR**
Collected questions addressed to Kirpal Singh in private correspondence,
together with respective answers. Also contains various messages given on
special occasions. Paperback; 382 pages; glossary.

ISBN 978-0-942735-02-4

**SURAT SHABD YOGA** (*Chapter 5 of Crown of Life*)
The Yoga of the Celestial Sound Current. A perfect science, it is free from
the drawbacks of other yogic forms. Emphasis is placed on the need for a
competent living Master. Paperback, 74 pages.

ISBN 978-0-942735-95-1


**THE TEACHINGS OF KIRPAL  SINGH**
Volume I: The Holy Path; 98 pages.          ISBN 978-0-9764548-0-9
Volume II: Self Introspection/Meditation; 180 pages.

ISBN 978-0-9764548-1-6
 Volume III: The New Life; 186 pages          ISBN 978-0-9764548-2-3
Definitive statements from various talks and books by the author, reorganized
by topic to illuminate the aspects of self-discipline pertinent to Spirituality.
Relevant questions are answered. This collection allows the reader to
research by topic. Three volumes sold as one book; 464 pages

ISBN 978-0-9764548-4-7


**THE WAY OF THE SAINTS**
An encyclopedia of Sant Mat from every point of view. This is a collection
of the late Master's short writings from 1949 to 1974. Included is a brief
biography of Baba Sawan Singh, the author's Master, plus many pictures.
Paperback; 418 pages.          ISBN 978-0-89142-026-2


**THE WHEEL OF LIFE & THE MYSTERY OF DEATH**
Two books in one volume. The meaning of one's life on earth and the Law of
Karma (the law of action and reaction) are examined in the first text; in the
following text, the reader is presented with the whys and wherefores of "the
great final change called death." Paperback; 293 pages; plus index for the
first text; and introduction.          ISBN 978-0-942735-80-2
**THE WHEEL OF LIFE**
Available in hard cover; 98 pages plus glossary and index

ISBN 978-0-9764548-5-4

**THE MYSTERY OF DEATH**
Available in hard cover; 125 pages          ISBN 978-0-9764548-6-1


**THE THIRD WORLD TOUR OF KIRPAL SINGH**
This book was printed directly from the pages of *Sat Sandesh* magazine,
the issues from October 1972 through February 1973, which were primarily
devoted to Master Kirpal Singh's Third World Tour. 160 pages, 80 black
and white pictures.

# BOOKLETS BY KIRPAL SINGH

**GOD POWER / CHRIST POWER / MASTER POWER**
Discusses the ongoing manifestation of the Christ-Power and the temporal nature of the human bodies through which that Power addresses humanity. "Christ existed long before Jesus." Paperback; 17 pages.

ISBN 978-0-942735-04-8

**HOW TO DEVELOP RECEPTIVITY**
Three Circular Letters (of June 13, 1969; November 5, 1969; and January 27, 1970) concerning the attitudes which must be developed in order to become more spiritually receptive. Paperback; 20 pages.

ISBN 978-0-942735-05-5

**MAN! KNOW THYSELF**
A talk especially addressed to seekers after Truth. Gives a brief coverage of the essentials of Spirituality and the need for open-minded cautiousness on the part of the careful seeker. Paperback; 30 pages.

ISBN 978-0-942735-06-2

**RUHANI SATSANG: Science of Spirituality**
Briefly discusses "The Science of the Soul"; "The Practice of Spiritual Discipline"; "Death in life"; "The Quest for a True Master"; and "Surat Shabd Yoga." Paperback; 44 pages.     ISBN 978-0-942735-03-1

**SEVEN PATHS TO PERFECTION**
Describes the seven basic requisites enumerated in the prescribed self-introspective diary which aid immeasurably in covering the entire field of ethics, and help to invoke the Divine Mercy. Paperback; 20 pages.

ISBN 978-0-942735-07-9

**SIMRAN:  The Sweet Remembrance of God**
Discusses the process of centering the attention within by repeating the "Original or Basic Names of God" given by a true Master. Paperback; 34 pages.     ISBN 978-0-942735-08-6

**THE SPIRITUAL AND KARMIC ASPECTS
OF THE VEGETARIAN DIET**
An overview of the vegetarian diet containing a letter from Kirpal Singh on the Spiritual aspects, a letter from Sawan Singh on the karmic aspects, and excerpts from various books by Kirpal Singh. Paperback; 36 pages.

ISBN 978-0-942735-47-5

*Books, Booklets and Audio-Visual Material of Master Kirpal Singh
can be ordered from this address or directly online.*

**RUHANI SATSANG®**
250 "H" St. #50, Blaine, WA 98230-4018 USA
1 (888) 530-1555     Fax (604) 530-9595 (Canada)
E-mail: MediaSales@RuhaniSatsangUSA.org
www.RuhaniSatsangUSA.org